AIR-DRY MASTERPIECES

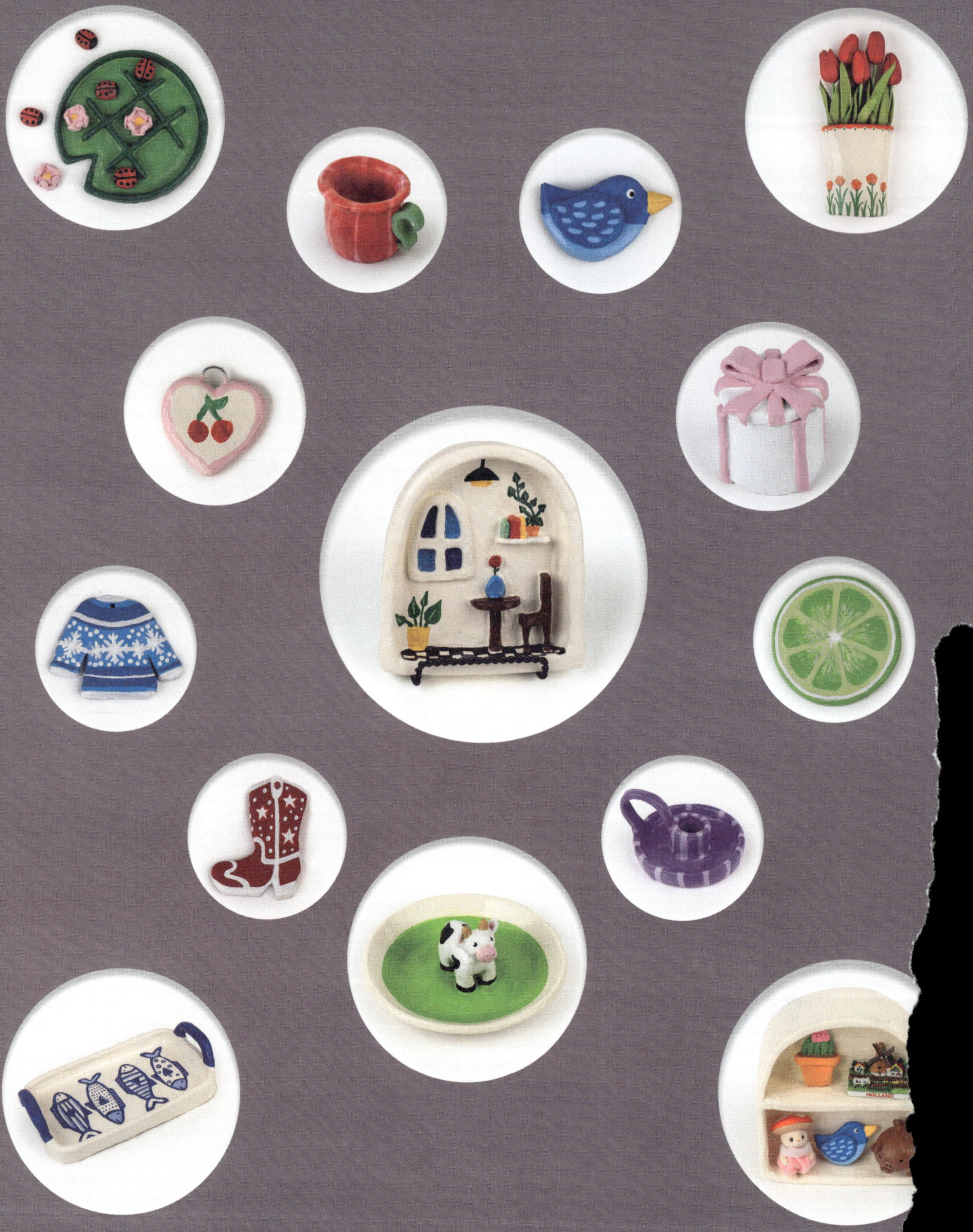

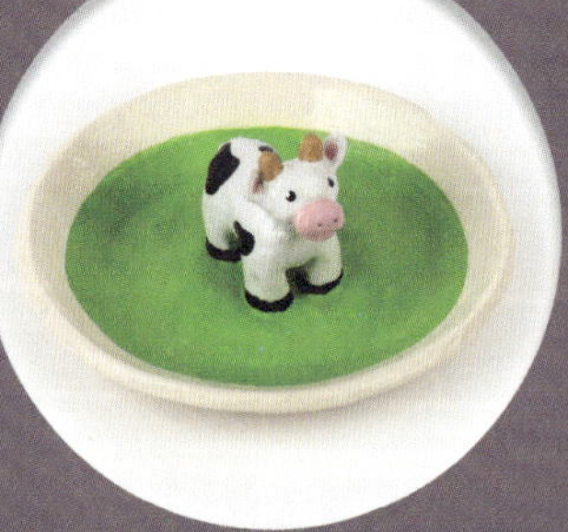

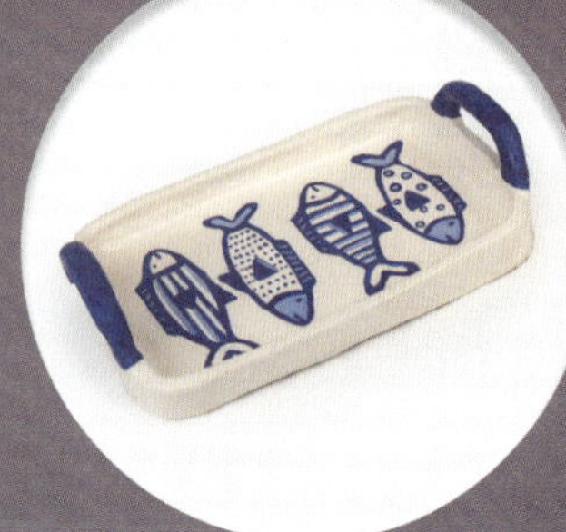

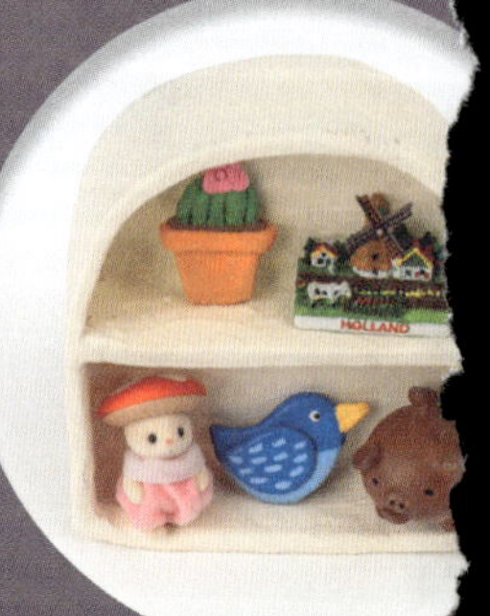
HOLLAND

AIR-DRY MASTERPIECES

OVER 50 CREATIVE PROJECTS FOR EVERYDAY SPACES

HAZEL BRADY

Owner of Hazelbean Ceramics

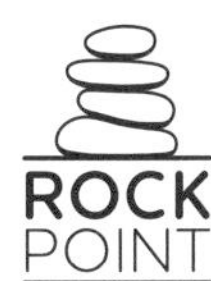

CONTENTS

INTRODUCTION

Hello! My name is Hazel Brady, and in March 2021 I started Hazelbean Ceramics. Back then, months into my move back home to Santa Barbara, California, I posted a mushroom vase to a new Instagram account with about 100 followers that consisted of my friends and family.

Ceramics had been a part of my life for long before that launch. I love working with my hands—it's what has always come easiest to me. Even after a long night of crying to my dad about how my fifth-grade math homework didn't make sense and how I would never get it, I'd get to school early that Friday for "The Splash Zone," which opened for students on Friday mornings to work on ceramic projects. If you were to ask my parents, they would tell you that me getting up early for school was *notable*.

Because of a conflicting interest in theatre, I only took one more ceramics course before I graduated high school. I loved this class! It was my favorite type of creative environment—one with loose guidelines and a teacher who didn't think there was a "right" way to make art. Maybe it was the lack of seating arrangements or the messy work, but this was also the place where my friends and I were suddenly the funniest people alive.

Hazel Bean is the nickname my mom has always called me. She is an artist, and ever since her days making ceramics in college—and my Friday morning ceramics sessions—we have both always wanted to have our own kiln. However, they're very large and expensive! If I had known about air-dry clay back then, I like to think I would've happily sat down for hours with a tub of clay and this book.

We finally decided to get a kiln when I moved home due to the COVID-19 pandemic. I hadn't done ceramics in years, but I immediately got the bug back. (I'm sure the lack of purpose I was feeling as a 21-year-old stuck inside all day helped get the ball rolling.) Once I started my Instagram account—at the time, featuring mostly small pots and dishes with pretty silly-looking animals on them—I made contactless deliveries to friends around town who had commented on posts wanting to buy my pieces. This interest surprised me and motivated me to expand!

Today, I work at a shared studio in Los Angeles and sell and post my pieces online. I work with white clay, which I glaze and fire in a kiln. I love the process and the satisfying feeling of finally seeing your finished piece out of the kiln after weeks of work. The goal of this book is to share that feeling by inspiring people and creating a launching point for their creativity. However, to create the projects for this book, I leaned into a more accessible medium: air-dry clay. I wanted to make functional objects, and with some added structural integrity and a coat of Mod Podge, the pieces turned out solid like traditional pottery, and something I love having in my home. The techniques you'll learn can take you far beyond the projects you'll see here.

From tiny charms to a shelf for your trinkets, you can fill your space with one-of-a-kind pieces and have more holiday and birthday gifts than you'll know what to do with. I love art that makes people smile and want to look closer. Something small with lots of personality is always my favorite. Learn the basics and put *your* personality into these projects—make your cow pink, sculpt the world's tiniest vase—there are no wrong moves. Art is for everyone, and with a trip to the craft store, the world of ceramics is quite literally at your fingertips. No kiln? No problem!

MATERIALS

AIR-DRY CLAY

Most types and brands of air-dry clay will work for the projects in this book, but there are pros and cons to consider when purchasing your clay. For the most part, higher quality clay will give you more professional results. You'll experience less cracking, and it'll likely not dry up as fast when you store it for future use. Air-dry clay generally takes 24 hours to dry to the touch and 72 hours to dry completely, regardless of type or brand.

DAS Air Hardening Clay

This is a more expensive clay made of water and natural fibers. It's easy to sculpt—the clay is malleable and soft. It even feels rubbery, which can make the process feel easier for the sculptor. It does have some drawbacks. The clay tends to crease when manipulated during the building process. During the drying process, be wary of rubbing or scratching the clay because it can tear and come apart. However, kneading is helpful to keep it workable. For this reason, make sure to wait until the clay is bone dry to easily remove imperfections by scraping or sanding them off and smoothing creases. If you are willing to wait longer for a finished product, DAS Air Hardening Clay will work for you.

Crayola Air Dry Clay

This clay is the most affordable option. It's malleable (maybe less so than DAS), but it dries rather quickly. Because of this, the clay can be brittle and cracks somewhat easily. Crayola Air Dry Clay requires free use of water to keep the project hydrated while working the clay. It is good for larger projects—like bowls, vases, and picture frames—but it can be more difficult with small detail work. This is the best clay for first-timers and parties—it's easy to carry home your masterpiece at the end of the night!

Air Dry Clay by Craftsmart

This clay is well-priced and great for the projects in this book, especially small, detailed pieces. It comes out of the box a bit hard, but that's easily fixed by working it in your hands with a bit of water. It can become brittle when drying but re-moistens well for fixes.

BASIC TOOLS

A pack of sculpting tools (available online or at most craft stores) should provide the following instruments for shaping, detailing, and finishing.

Needle tool: This thin metal pointed tool is used to add detail, cut, score, and carve.

Household substitutes: *Toothpick, corn holder, thin knitting needle*

Rib: This flat-ended wooden or plastic tool is used for smoothing and shaping small surfaces.

Household substitutes: *Spoon, handle of butter knife*

Loop Tool: A rod with a metal loop at the end used for carving and removing clay.

Household substitutes: *Teaspoon, small cup*

Wooden Crescent Tool: A flat, rounded wooden tool used to shape and smooth large surfaces.

Household substitute: *Wooden spoon*

Metal Crescent Tool: This flat, sharp metal tool is used for smoothing large surfaces and very thin slabs.

Household substitute: *Old credit cards*

Pottery Sponge: For smoothing, adding and removing water (moisture control), shaping, and creating a clean surface. Keep your sponge nearby when working.

Household substitutes: *Dish sponge, wet rag*

Wire Tool: This long metal wire with handles is used to cut pieces off large chunks of clay. Rather than struggling with a knife (which is dangerous) or breaking away clay with your hands (which can take a while), this tool is important for working with large slabs of clay.

Household substitutes: *Wire hanger, garden wire*

Rolling Pin: The easiest way to form a slab is by rolling it out with a rolling pin. This will create an even surface that is easy to cut into your desired shape and use for many functional objects. Pounding down clay and smoothing it with your fingers and a sponge can also create a slab, but it will take longer and be harder to get a polished, even surface.

Household substitutes: *Wine bottle, stainless-steel water bottle, thick cardboard tube, dowel, wooden rod, PVC pipe*

Rulers or Spacers (optional): Rulers or other spacers can help you maintain an even thickness when rolling out slabs.

Household substitutes: *Books and magazines*

Water: Use for the sculpting phase of your projects. Fill a medium-sized bowl with room-temperature water that you can easily dip your fingers into to transfer water onto your clay for sculpting and smoothing.

Spray Bottle: Fill a small spray bottle with water to evenly cover your clay in a layer of moisture as you work.

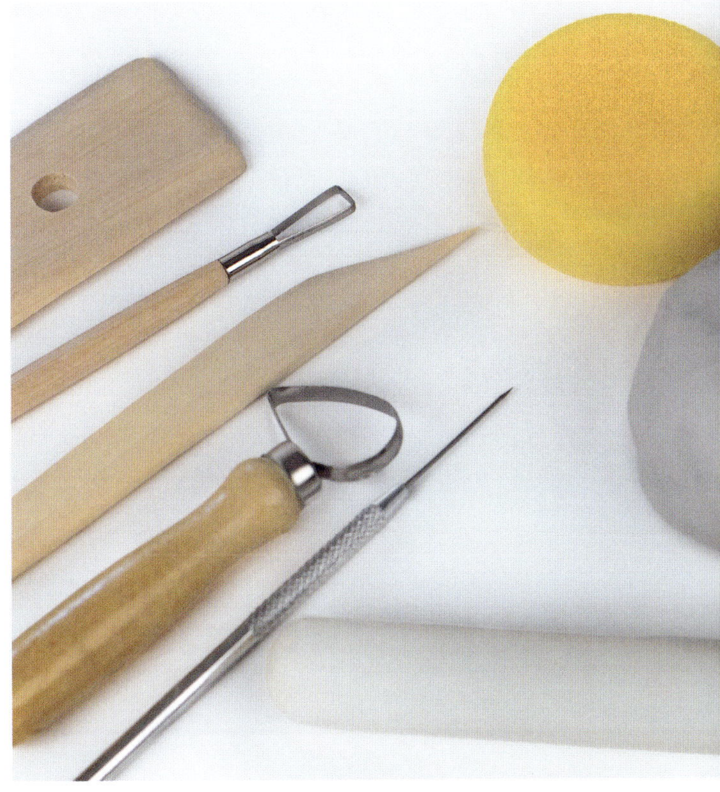

PAINT AND RESIN

Paintbrushes

For finishing and decorating your pieces it's important to have paintbrushes in a variety of sizes and shapes. For the projects in this book, you should have the following:

- At least one pointed detail brush
- A small round brush
- A medium round brush
- A medium flat brush
- A large flat brush

Synthetic acrylic brushes have smooth, thick bristles that are good for detailing and even strokes. Cheaper craft brushes can also be used but make it harder to get a polished finish. Have two brushes designated for Mod Podge/resin and slip (see page 15) to keep your painting brushes from getting quickly worn out.

Acrylic Paints

Acrylic paint is best for air-dry clay. In this book, I am using a Craftmate pack from Michaels. Watercolors, acrylic markers, and tempera paint can also be used but will not provide the same quality as acrylic paint. Make sure your piece is fully dry before you paint it!

Resin and Mod Podge

To seal your pieces and achieve a nice shiny finish, you can use epoxy, resin paint, or Mod Podge (which is used in the finished pieces in this book). Use a flat brush to apply an even coat. Sealing your finished pieces in this way is not necessary but will make them more durable, and they'll look professional and clean!

> **Note:** *Acrylic paint and Mod Podge are not food safe and should not be used on pieces that will come into contact with anything consumable.*

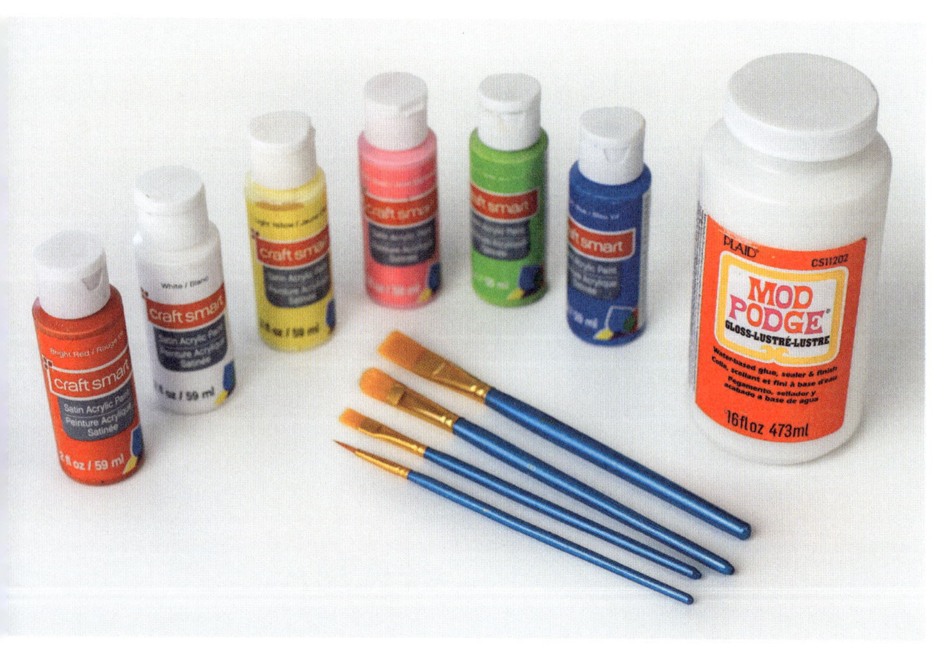

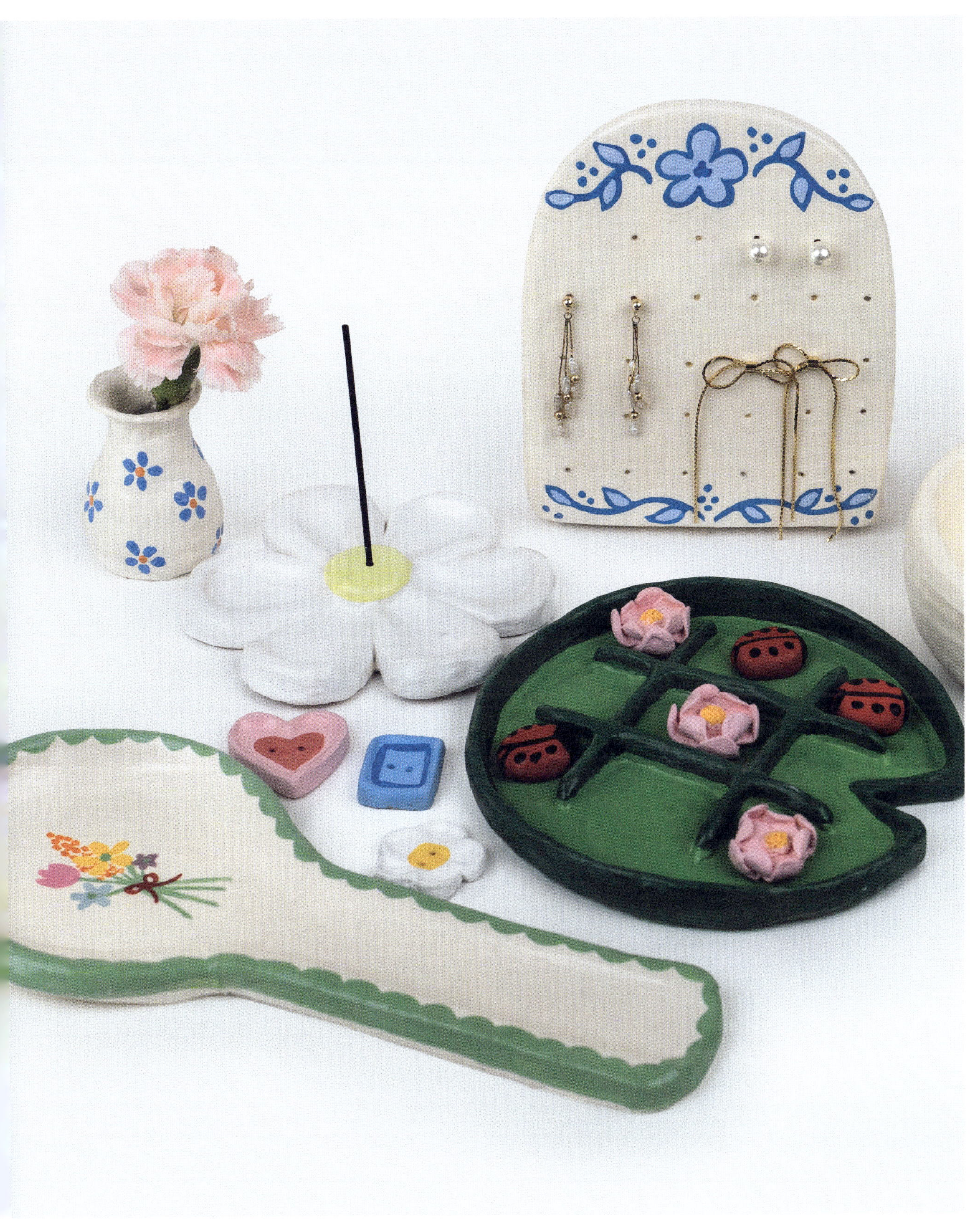

TECHNIQUES

CUTTING CLAY

The first thing you are going to do when you start a new project is cut off a piece of clay from your supply. You can do this with a wire tool, or a needle tool (great for large and small slabs as well as coils), or if you're not worried about precision, just rip it off with your hands.

KNEADING

The goal of kneading your clay is to make it easier to work with and remove air bubbles. To knead, place your ball of clay on a flat, hard surface. Push the clay away from you until it's slightly flattened. Next, fold the clay back toward you, rotate, and repeat. ↓

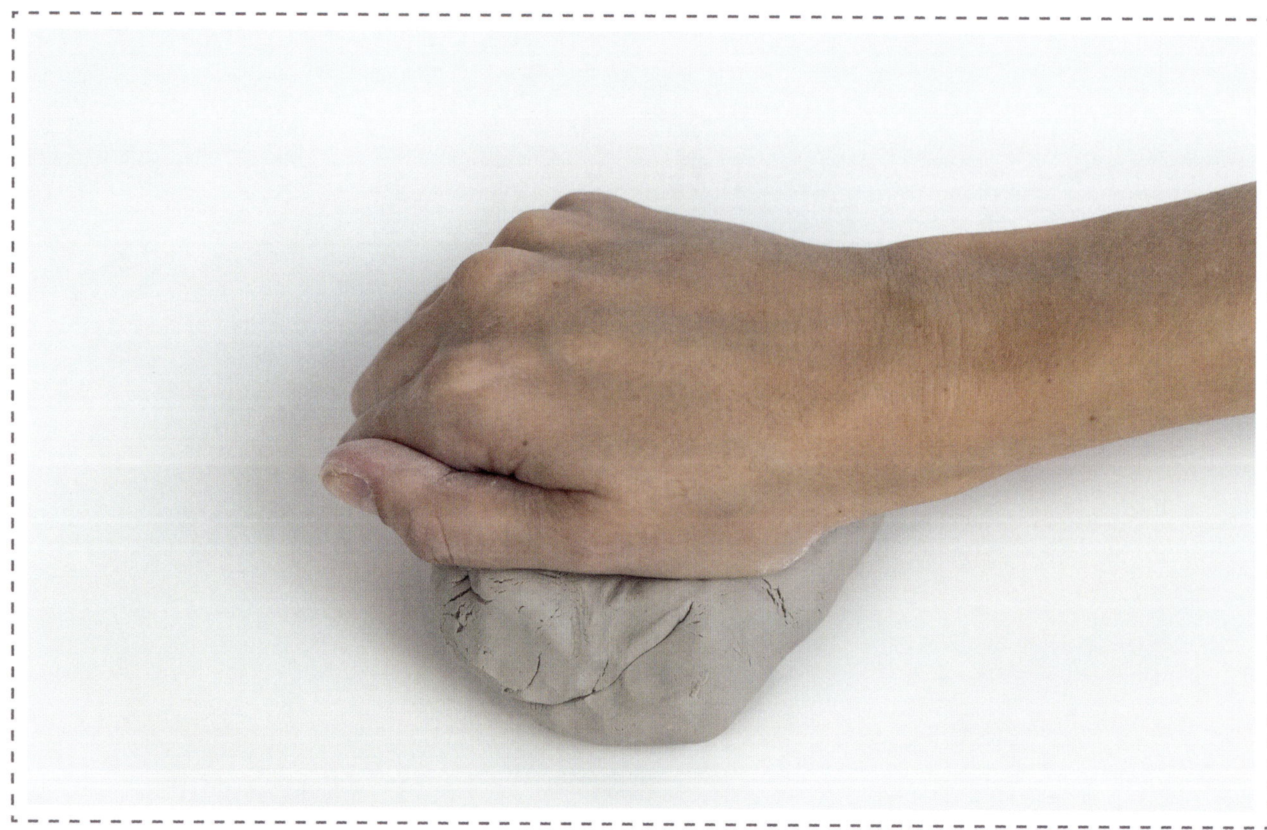

CREATING SLABS

Slabs are used in many hand-built projects and are relatively easy to make. To make a slab:

1. Place your desired amount of clay on a hard, smooth surface. Ideally, add a piece of canvas, a wooden cutting board, or a piece of parchment paper on top of your surface to prevent sticking. No worries if these aren't available; just be wary of sticking, and pick up and put down your slab a few times as you roll it out.
2. Consider placing spacers, like rulers, on either side of your clay, running about the length of your desired slab. These will provide a barrier to keep you from rolling the slab too thin.
3. Press the clay down gently with your hands until it resembles a thick pancake.
4. Roll the clay out with a rolling pin (or rolling pin substitute) back and forth, turning it 90 degrees occasionally, until it's reached your desired thickness. Most projects will require a slab about ¼ inch (6 mm) thick. ↓
5. Smooth the slab by stroking it lightly with a crescent tool until flat. Wet a sponge and use it as needed to finish smoothing.

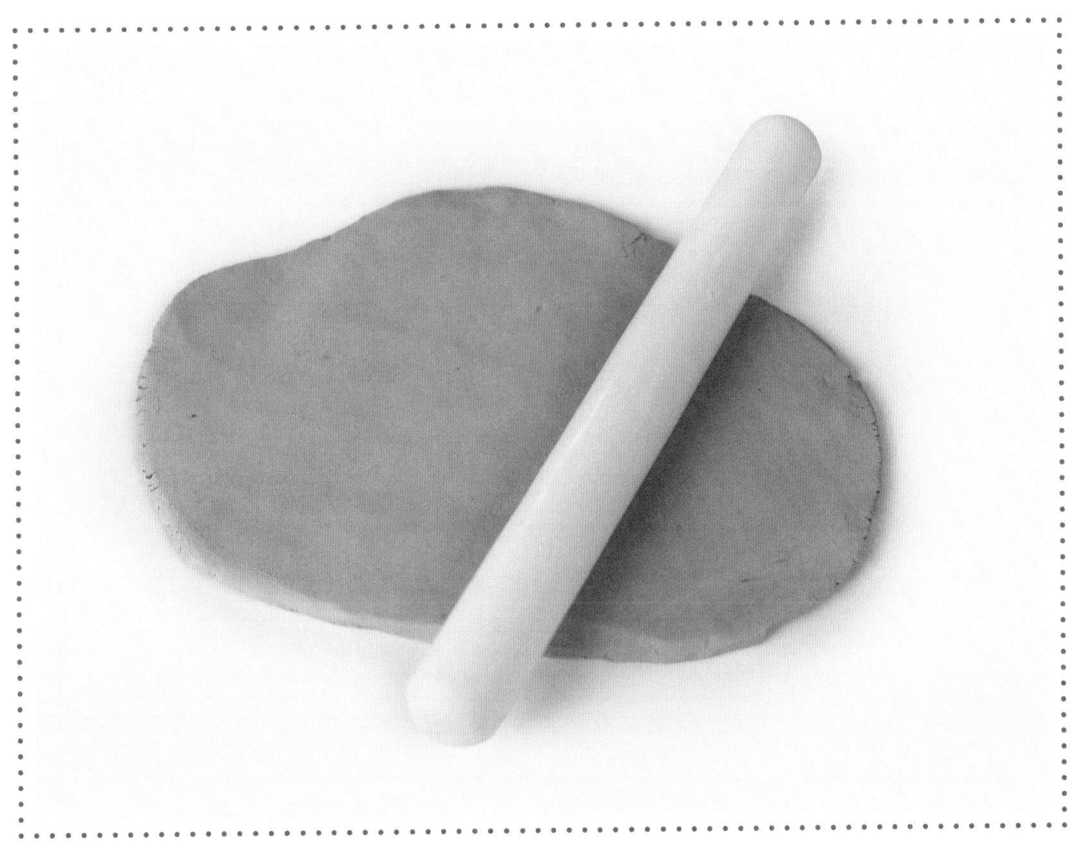

ROLLING COILS

Coils are rope-like lengths of clay. They are used for many aspects of hand building, including adding extra structure, creating coil pots, and sculpting shapes and forms. Coils will be used often for creating animals in this book. To make a coil:

1. Place a chunk of clay on a hard, smooth surface. Roll the clay out with the palms of your hands a few times back and forth until it's formed a thick log.
2. Continue to roll, using two hands to evenly distribute pressure along the length of the coil. Add a bit of water if the clay begins to crack. If the cracking continues, it may be best to re-ball the clay and start again.
3. Once the coil becomes too thin to use your full hand, use the tips of your fingers to roll the clay out instead. ↓

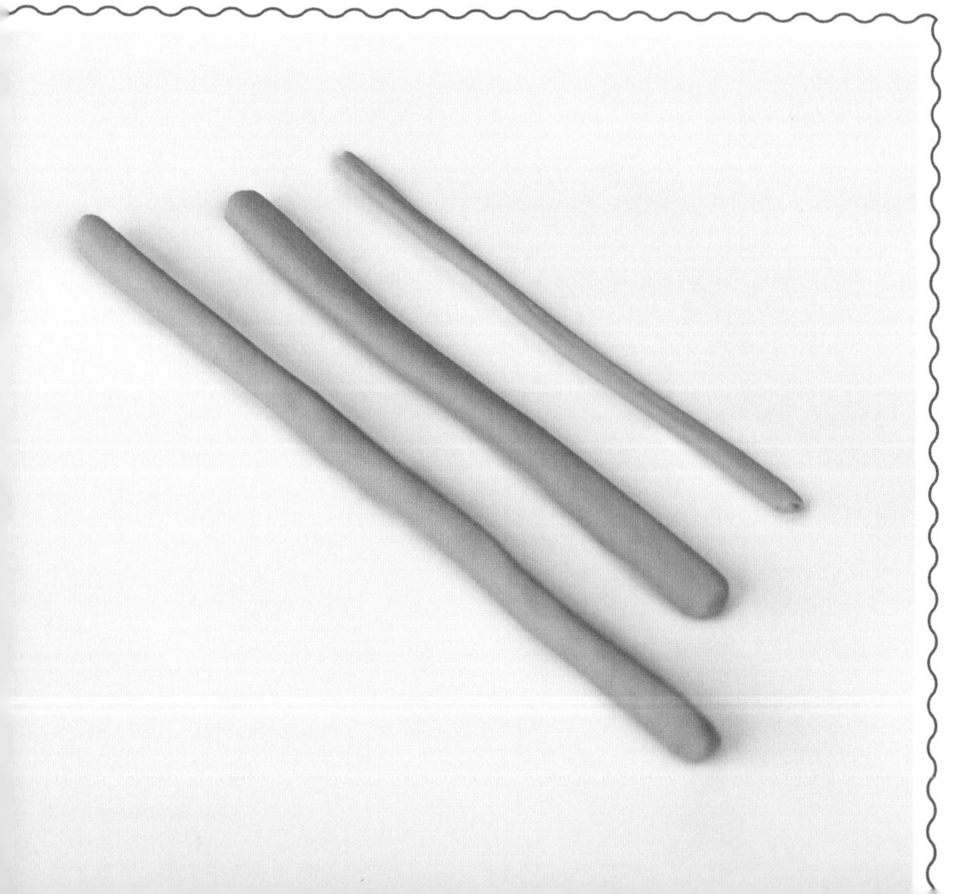

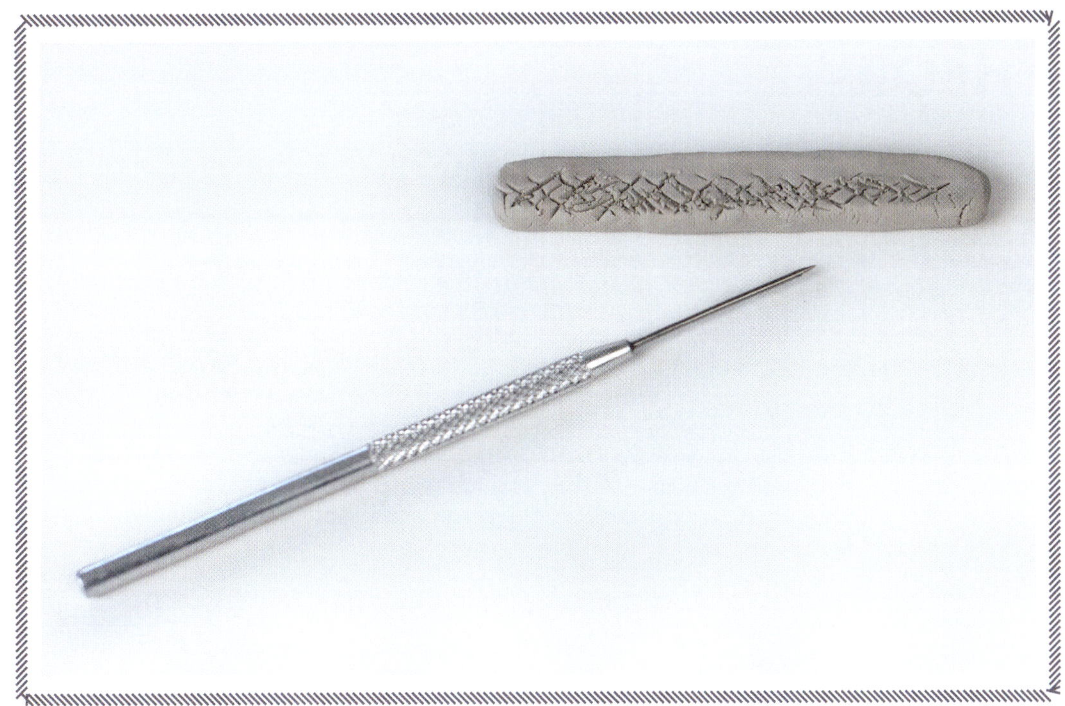

SCORING

Scoring is the process of roughening or scratching the surface of clay before joining two pieces together. Scoring increases the surface area of the pieces where they will be joined, creating better adhesion. Use a needle tool to carve shallow intersecting lines at the connective point. ↑

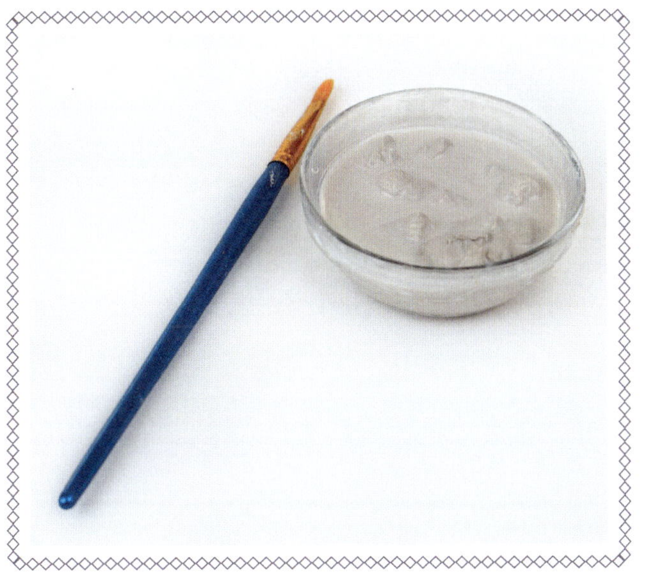

MAKING SLIP

Slip is a liquid mixture of clay and water. It is used as a glue and is applied on scored areas before joining pieces of clay. To create about 1 cup (236 mL) of slip:

1. Break a piece of clay, about palm-sized, into small chunks. Allow to dry fully.
2. Place the chunks into a container and crush up. Add enough water to just cover the crushed clay.
3. Let the mixture soak for 3 hours.
4. Stir the mixture until it becomes a smooth, creamy slurry (add water if too thick).
5. Store slip in an airtight container placed in a cool environment. Slip can last months if stored properly. ←

COLOR THEORY

When creating a piece of art, I always like to consider the colors I'll be working with. Let's say I'm creating a dish with a frog in the center. I might ask myself some questions like: Should the frog be a classic green? Or blue like a tropical tree frog? Should the frog blend in with the water or stand out? Do I want the overall piece to be bright and bold, or soft and muted?

How I answer these questions will help me determine which paints to use. Color choices can completely change the overall look of the piece. For example, a dark-green frog sitting in blue water will look very naturalistic. By contrast, a bright-pink frog sitting in orange water might look funky or otherworldly. Both frogs will look great! It just depends on what kind of piece I'm trying to create.

To decide which colors to choose, it can be helpful to understand how color *works*. Here are some things to consider when you are choosing colors for your artwork.

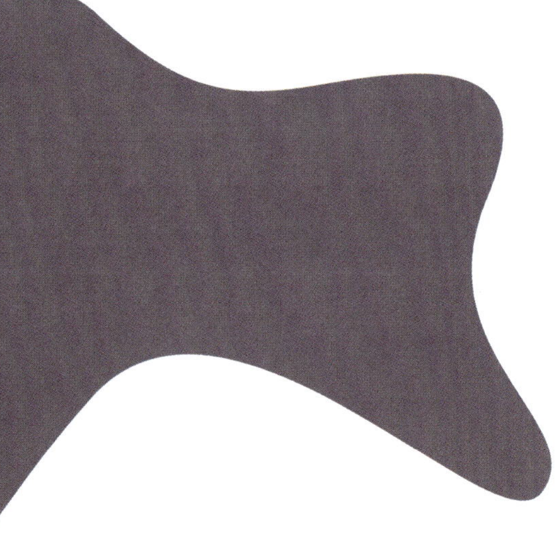

WHAT *IS* COLOR?

Isaac Newton, the English physicist and theorist, began studying the nature of light and color in the seventeenth century. In 1666, he conducted an experiment with glass prisms, through which he discovered that white light was made up of colors. What we perceive as colors are actually different wavelengths of light; our eyes take in the different wavelengths, and our brain then processes them as color.

All of that is pretty abstract, so Newton developed the color wheel to organize the range of colors visible to the human eye.

THE COLOR WHEEL

In the nineteenth century, the German philosopher Johannes Wolfgang von Goethe expanded on the color wheel developed by Newton. He used it not just as a way to understand the different wavelengths of light, but to understand the way colors relate to each other. He theorized that different colors, when placed next to each other, can create different effects and moods.

Goethe's wheel is based on the three primary colors: red, yellow, and blue. You can then make secondary colors—green, orange, and purple—by mixing two of the primary colors together. From there, you can keep mixing to create tertiary colors: yellow-green, blue-purple, orange-red, and any other color you can think of!

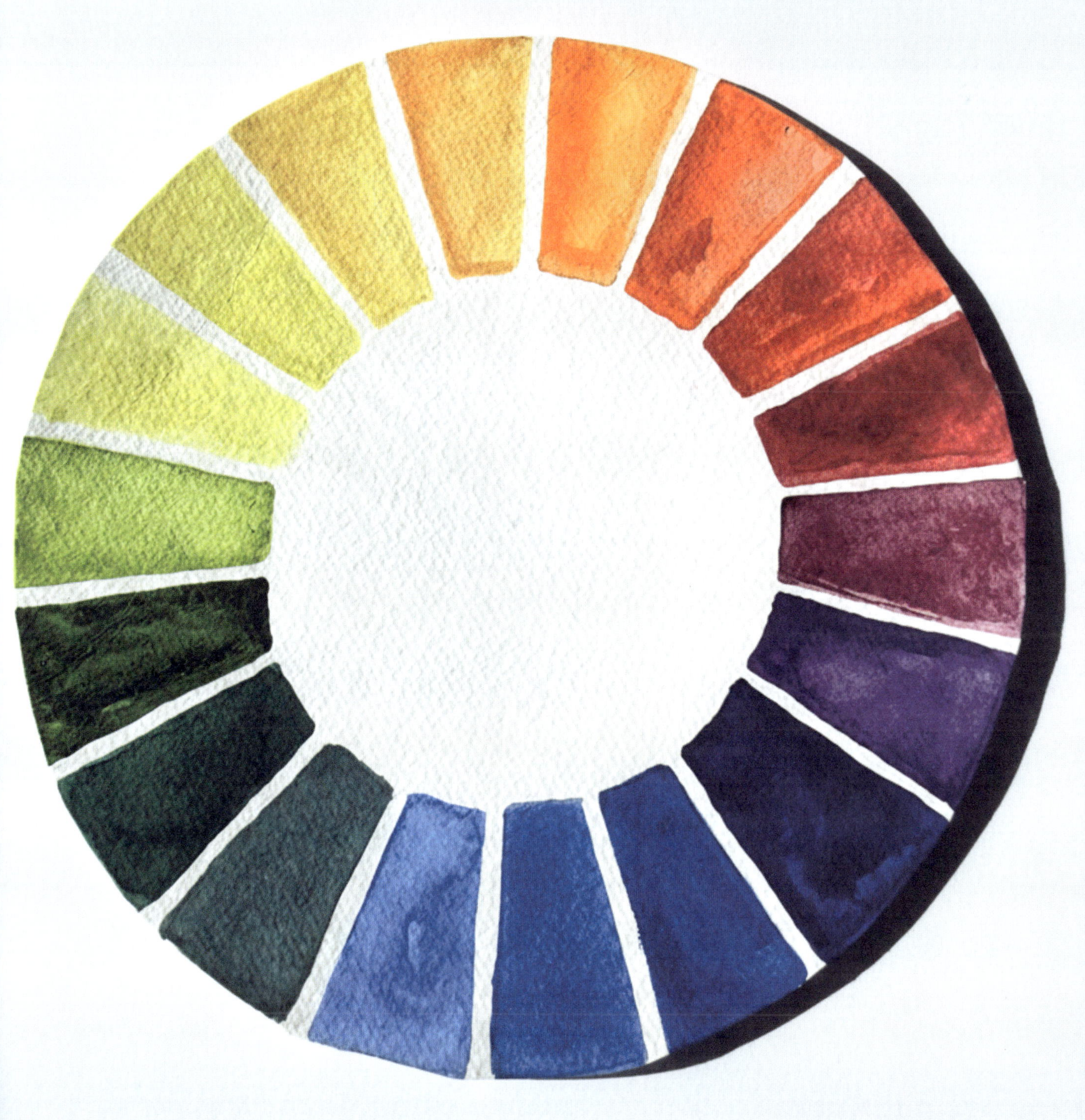

The wheel can also be used as a map for artists to create color combinations. Colors that sit next to each other on the wheel share a primary color, and can be blended to create a gradient. Let's say you want to paint a sunset over the ocean. You might notice that its light appears red closest to the horizon line. You could then find red on the color wheel, and see orange and purple on either side. That would give you a guide for which colors to use in your sunset.

Colors that sit directly opposite each other on the wheel are complementary colors, such as yellow and purple, blue and orange, and green and red. Complementary colors can be really fun to pair together, since they have a high level of contrast. Try placing dabs of blue paint and orange paint next to each other on your palette, and notice how they make each other appear brighter.

COLOR TEMPERATURE

Another thing to consider when choosing paints is color temperature. Johannes Itten, a Swiss artist and cofounder of the Bauhaus school, expanded on the ideas of Newton and Goethe. He created a twelve-part color wheel and used it to identify even more attributes of color, namely temperature, hue, value, and saturation (more on these last three later).

Color temperature refers to a color's warmth or coolness. Warm colors include red, yellow, and orange. Cool colors include blue, green, and purple. You could use a palette of entirely one color temperature to create a harmonious picture, or place warm and cool colors next to each other to create contrast. Try to decide whether you want your piece to be primarily warm or cool before you select your paint colors.

One optical trick to keep in mind is that cool colors tend to recede (appear farther away) while warm colors pop to the front. Choosing cool colors for your background, like a bluish purple for a distant mountain range, and warm colors for elements in the foreground is an easy way to create depth.

HUE, VALUE, AND SATURATION

Finally, you should consider hue, value, and saturation. Hue refers to the basic pigment (i.e. red, green, yellow). A color's value is how light or dark it appears, and saturation is the intensity of the hue.

To play with these concepts, try placing a dab of paint on your palette and identify its hue. Is it green, blue, red, orange, purple, or yellow? Then, try mixing in a little bit of black paint. You've just changed the color's value by making it darker. Now, take a dab of the original paint color and mix in some water or white paint. The color is now less saturated.

You can play with all of these elements to figure out which colors to use on your clay creations. Art projects are wonderful opportunities to experiment with new color combinations, layering colors, and blending. I hope you try something unexpected on at least one of your air-dry projects!

Tips

1. Smooth your slabs with a rib tool and then a wet sponge before cutting into them. This will get some of the smoothing out of the way!
2. When your clay is in an open-air ball or container while you're working, add a bit of water to it and work the moisture in with your hands to keep it from drying out.
3. Don't over-apply water to your pieces! This will make your workspace, project, and hands messy and hard to work with.
4. Take a moment every now and then to tidy your workspace and discard dried-up pieces of clay. These can get stuck in your piece and are hard to get out without damaging your work. This tidying also makes your sculpting experience more enjoyable!
5. The back of your nail is a great tool for smoothing small imperfections.
6. Once they are leather hard (see Glossary, page 22), touch up your pieces before painting them. Use a loop tool and a wet sponge to eliminate and carve away bumps and imperfections.
7. Make sure you let your clay dry FULLY before painting. If there is still moisture in your clay, the paint may create lots of tiny bubbles.
8. Avoid air bubbles! Even though this is air-dry clay and air bubbles won't cause explosions in the kiln, they don't look nice. Poke a hole in them with a needle tool, toothpick, or fingernail and smooth them out. If the bubble is large, you may need to add a bit of clay to the crater the air bubble will leave behind when popped.
9. When applying Mod Podge, spread it in thin, even layers to keep it from drying thick and white.
10. Wash your brushes! If a brush dries with paint, clay, or Mod Podge on its bristles, it can be ruined.
11. When making magnets, make sure the pieces have flat backs and aren't too heavy.

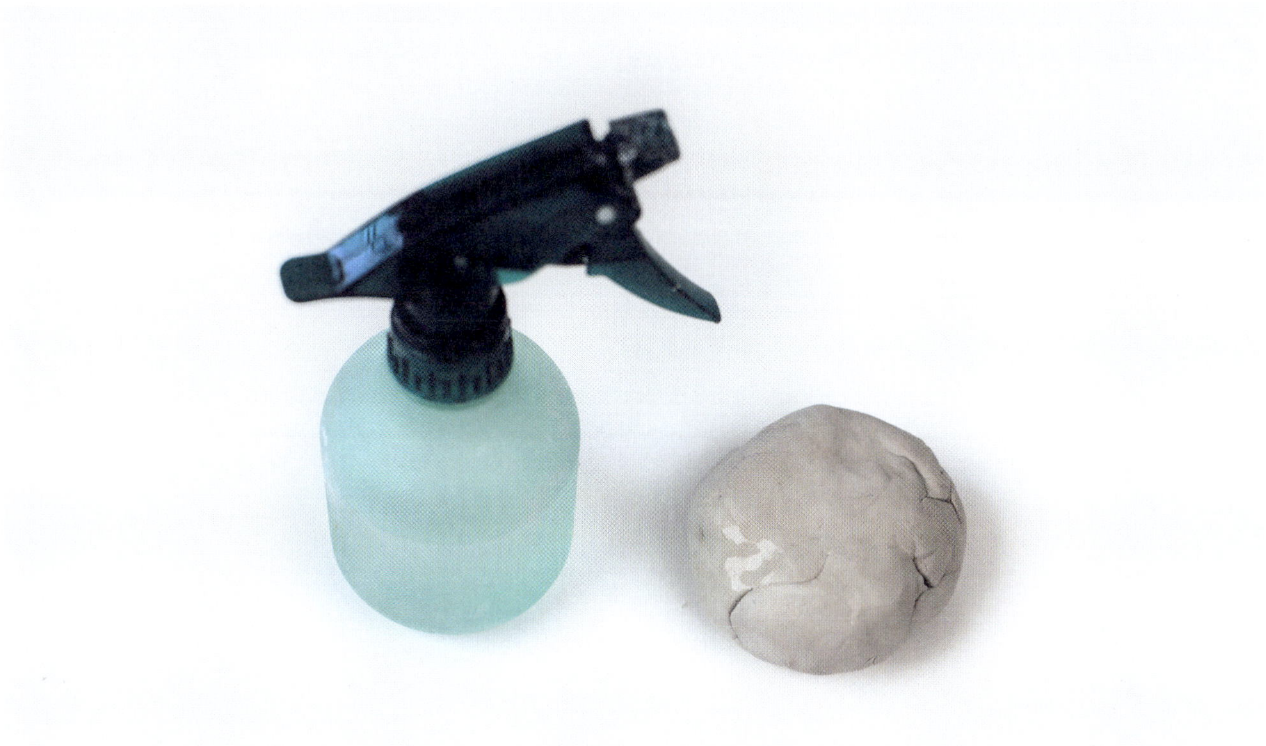

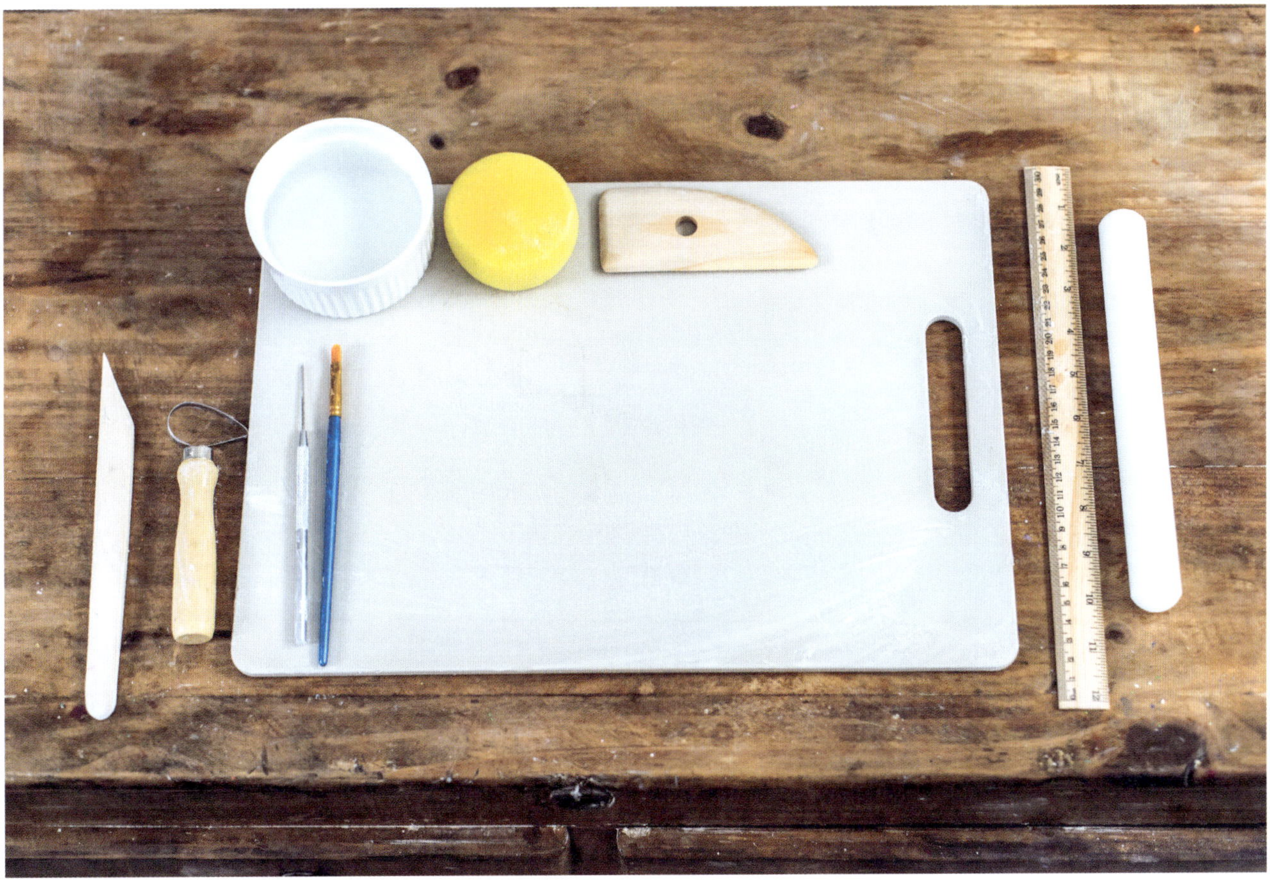

GLOSSARY

Attach: The process of securing one piece of clay to another using the Score and Slip Method (see page 15).

Base: The bottom or floor of a clay masterpiece.

Bone dry: The stage when the clay is completely dry. Get ready to paint and add resin! ↓

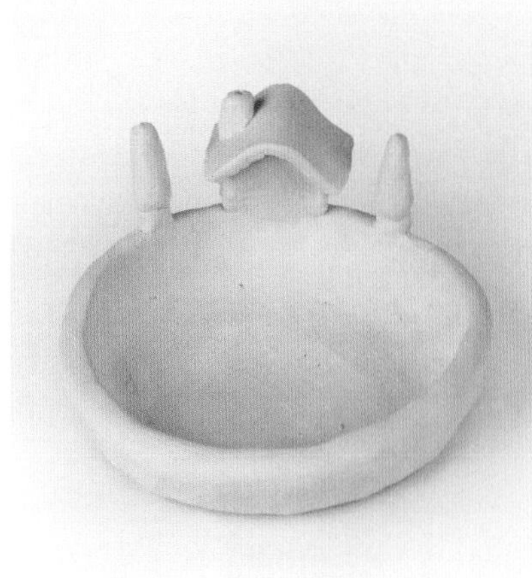

Ceramics: The craft of making objects out of clay. Traditional ceramics require the use of a kiln and firing.

Clay: A natural, inorganic substance extracted from the earth's crust. When mixed with water as a lubricant, the clay particles slide past each other and create a "workable" plastic quality. Often, air-dry clay has added fibers or materials for ease of use.

Coil: A piece of rope-like or snake-like clay. See Techniques (page 14) for more.

Coiling: A hand-building technique involving spiraling a long, rope-shaped piece of clay. This creates a cylinder, used for vases or cups.

Compress: The process of pushing the clay together to adhere the clay and build it up.

Kneading (or Wedging): The process of preparing the clay for use by working the clay with your hands or against your work surface, pushing the clay forward with your palms. See Techniques (page 12) for more.

Leather hard: A stage in the drying process of clay when it has lost most of its moisture but is still slightly damp.

Pinching: A technique that involves inserting a finger into a ball of clay and pinching it outward to form walls, as for a pot. Instead of coiling, using slabs, or throwing the clay like with ceramics, air-dry clay mostly relies on pinching to shape it. →

Plasticity: The quality of hydrated clay (25 percent water) that allows for it to be shaped and manipulated without cracking or breaking.

Slab: A technique wherein the clay is pressed into thin slabs that are cut, assembled, and shaped into the desired form of the masterpiece. See Techniques (page 13) for more.

Slip: A mixture of clay and water used to adhere pieces together for shape building or decoration. The mixture should be 50 percent water and 50 percent clay, and have the consistency of mayonnaise. See Techniques (page 15) for more.

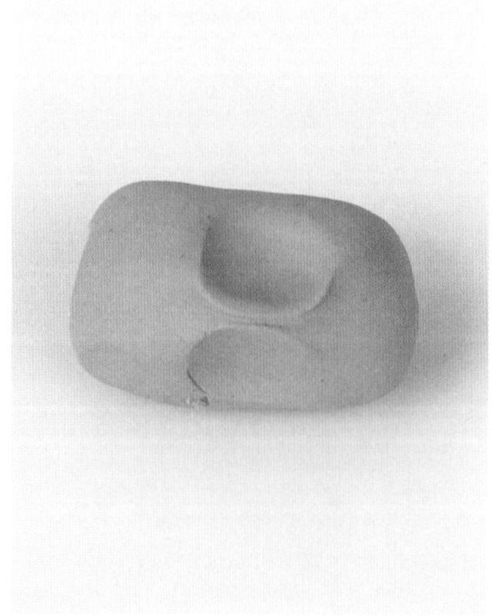

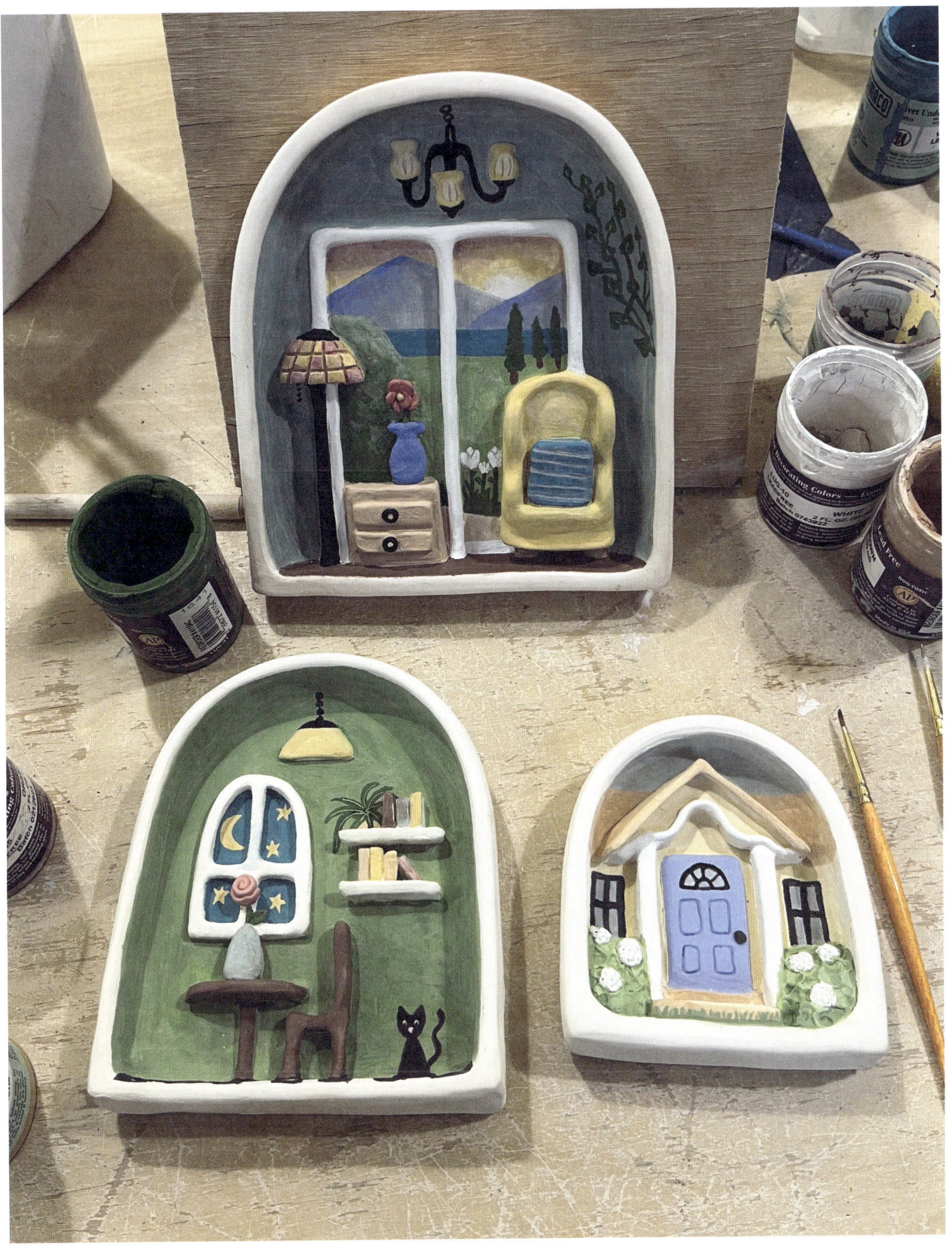
Decorating Colors
WHITE
Lead Free

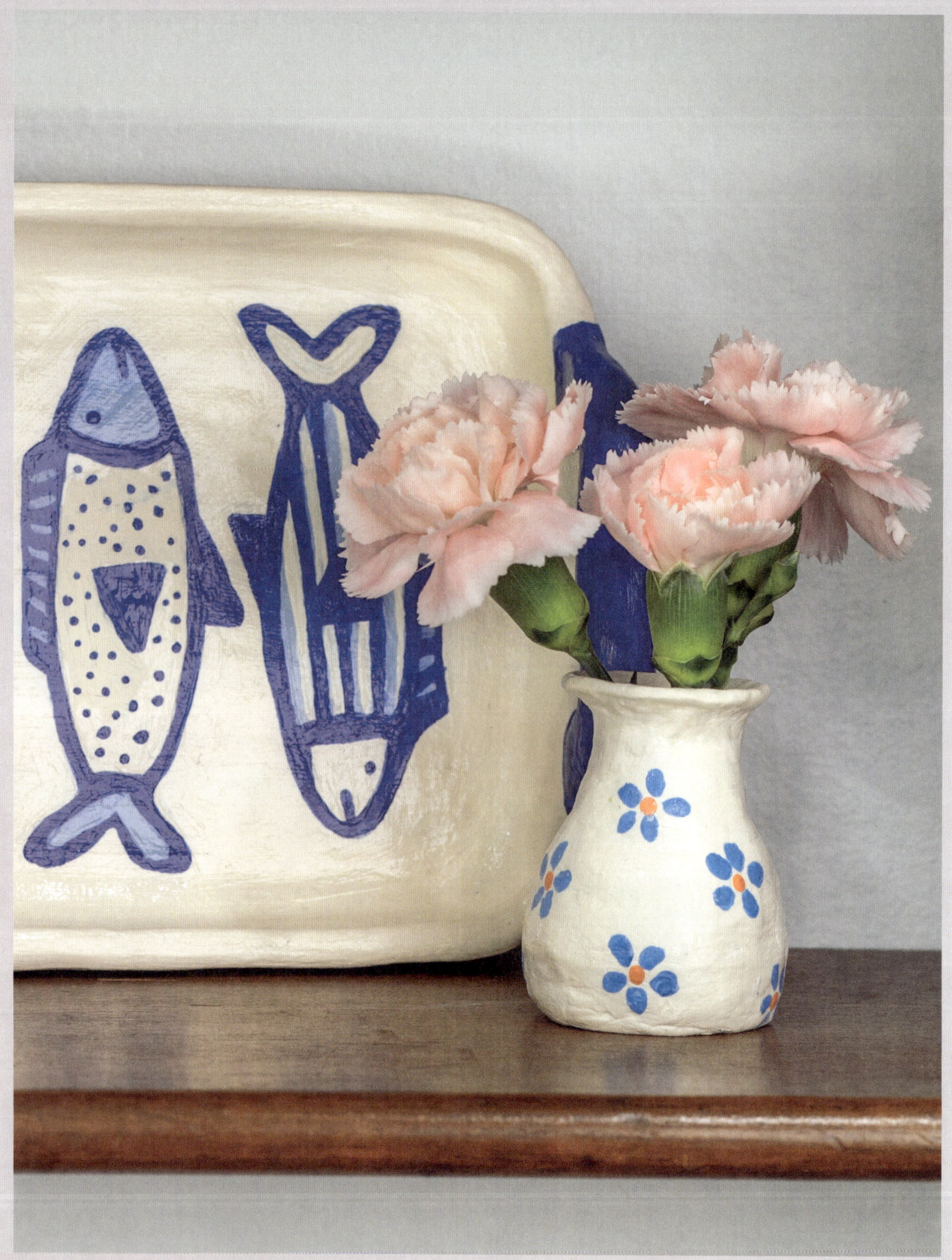

LIFESTYLE & HOME

Pinch Pot Tutorial

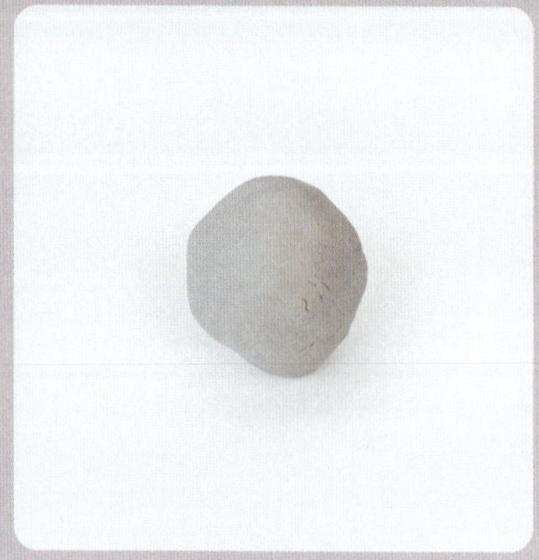

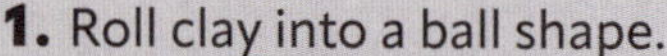

1. Roll clay into a ball shape.

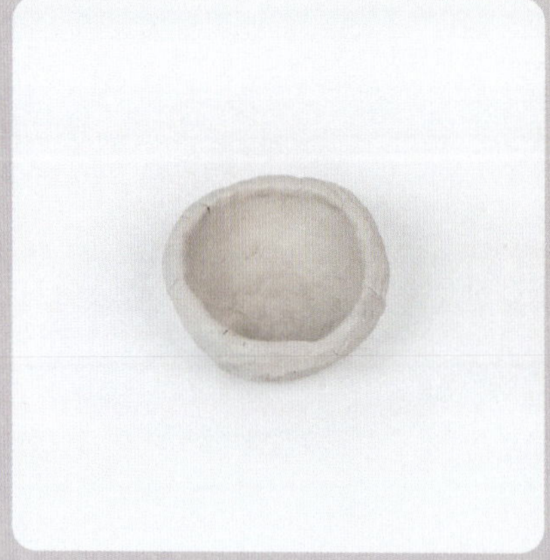

2. Press into the center of the ball with both thumbs to create a small well. With your thumbs on the inside of the well and your pointer and middle fingers on the outside, slowly pinch the clay outward.

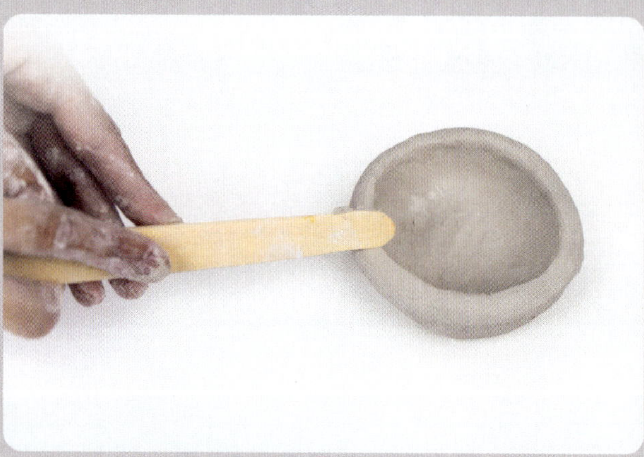

3. Add water and smooth with a sponge and rib tool. Make any final tweaks to imperfections and let dry.

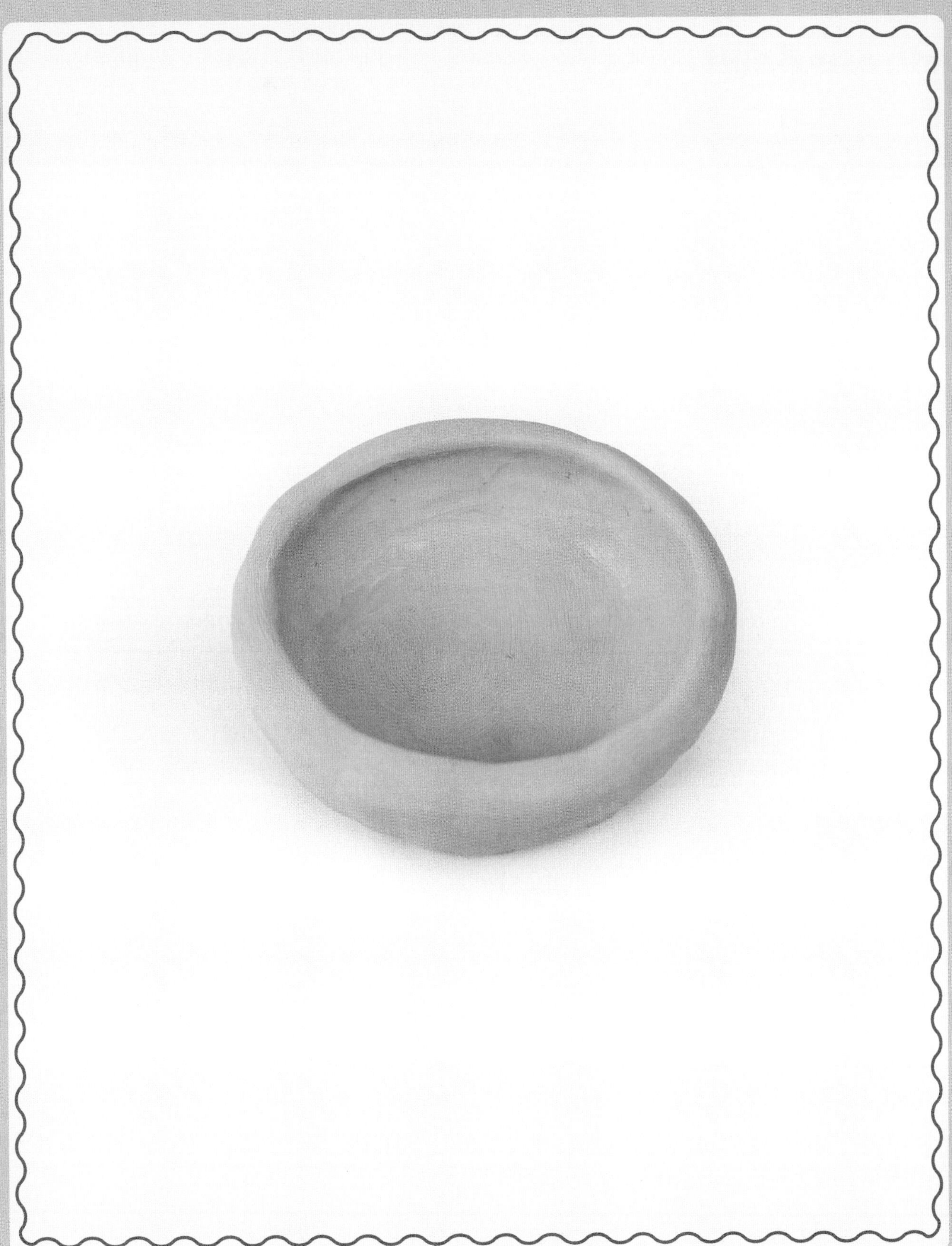

House Bowl

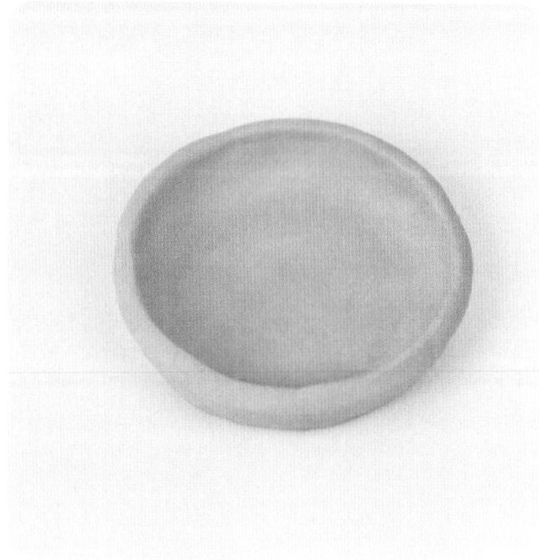

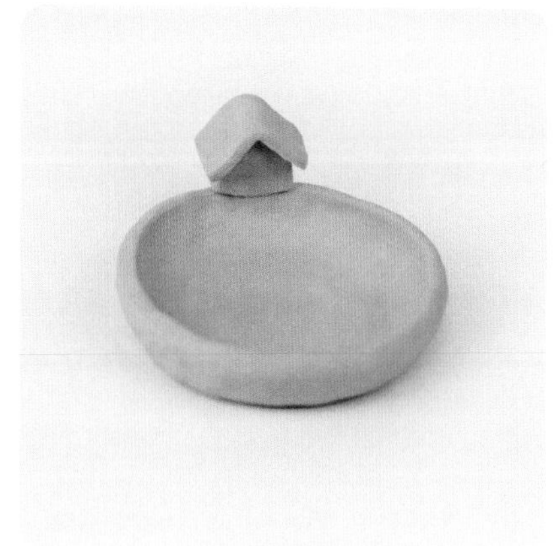

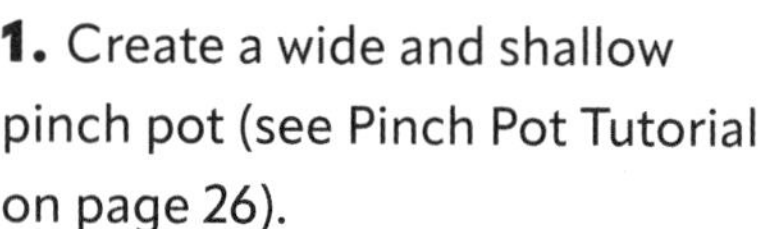

1. Create a wide and shallow pinch pot (see Pinch Pot Tutorial on page 26).

2. To shape the house, sculpt a small cube. Use a sharp, flat cutting tool to create a slanted roof shape on the top sides of the cube.

3. To create the roof of the house, roll out a very small, thin slab of clay, then cut a rectangle long enough to drape over the sides of the cube. Score and slip the top of the cube and the underside of the roof piece (see page 15), then gently fold the roof piece in half, matching the angle of the top of the house, and press it into place. Attach the house to the edge of the bowl.

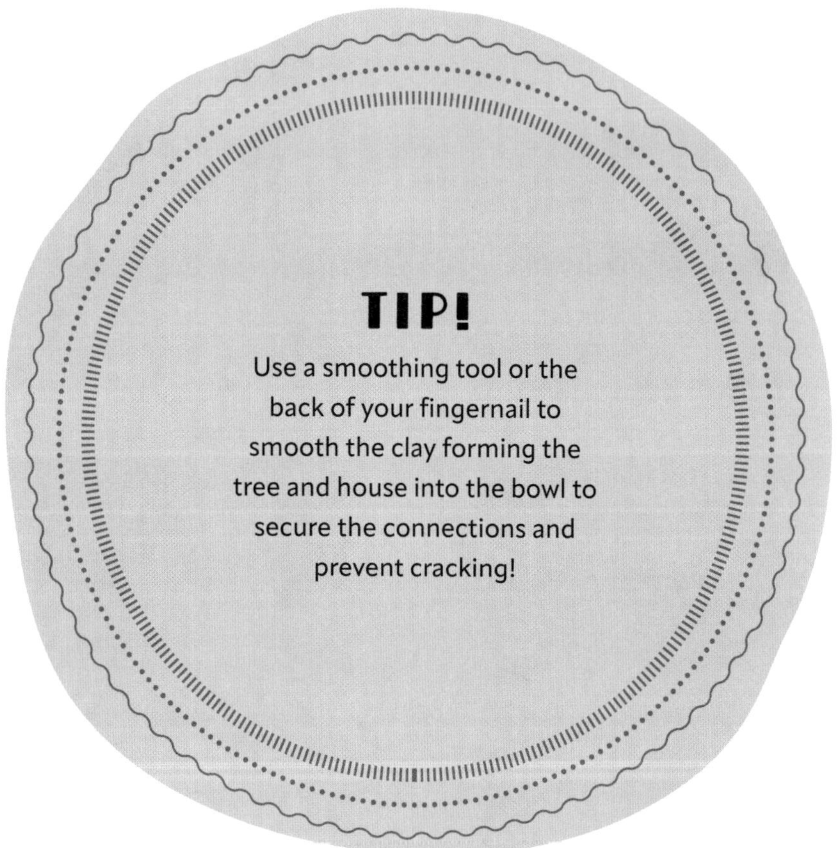

TIP!

Use a smoothing tool or the back of your fingernail to smooth the clay forming the tree and house into the bowl to secure the connections and prevent cracking!

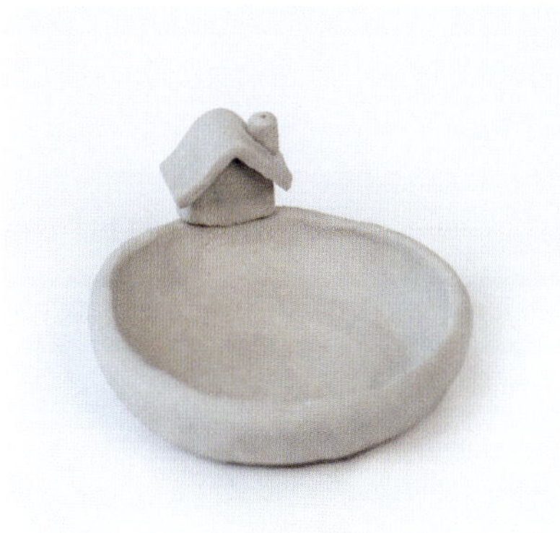

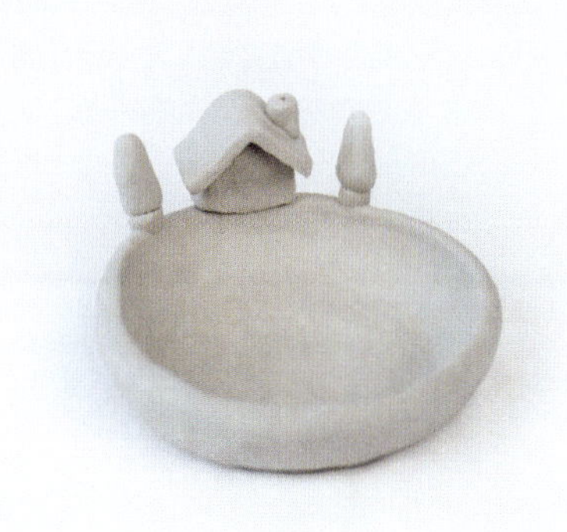

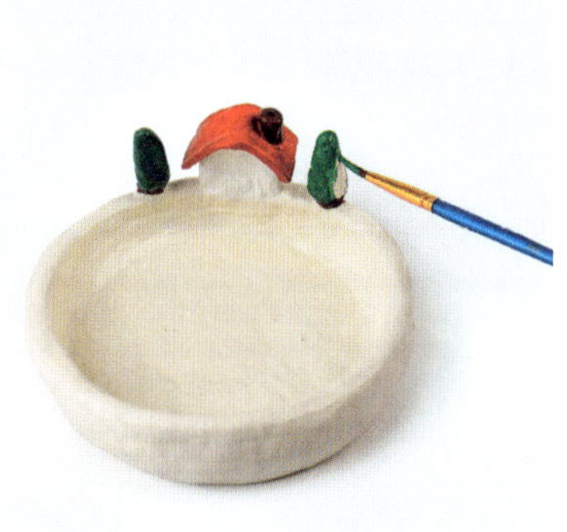

4. To create a chimney, roll out a very small coil and cut it into a log shape. Cut one side at an angle to match the roof's slope. Attach the angled side of the chimney to the side of the roof and poke a small hole in the top with a needle tool.

5. Roll out another slightly thicker coil and cut it into 2 small segments. Attach these as tree trunks to the bowl on either side of the house. Then sculpt 2 small cone shapes—the treetops—and attach them to the 2 trunks.

6. Smooth the bowl, house, and trees as needed and let dry. Paint the house and trees, then add painted details. When the paint is dry, seal the piece with Mod Podge to finish.

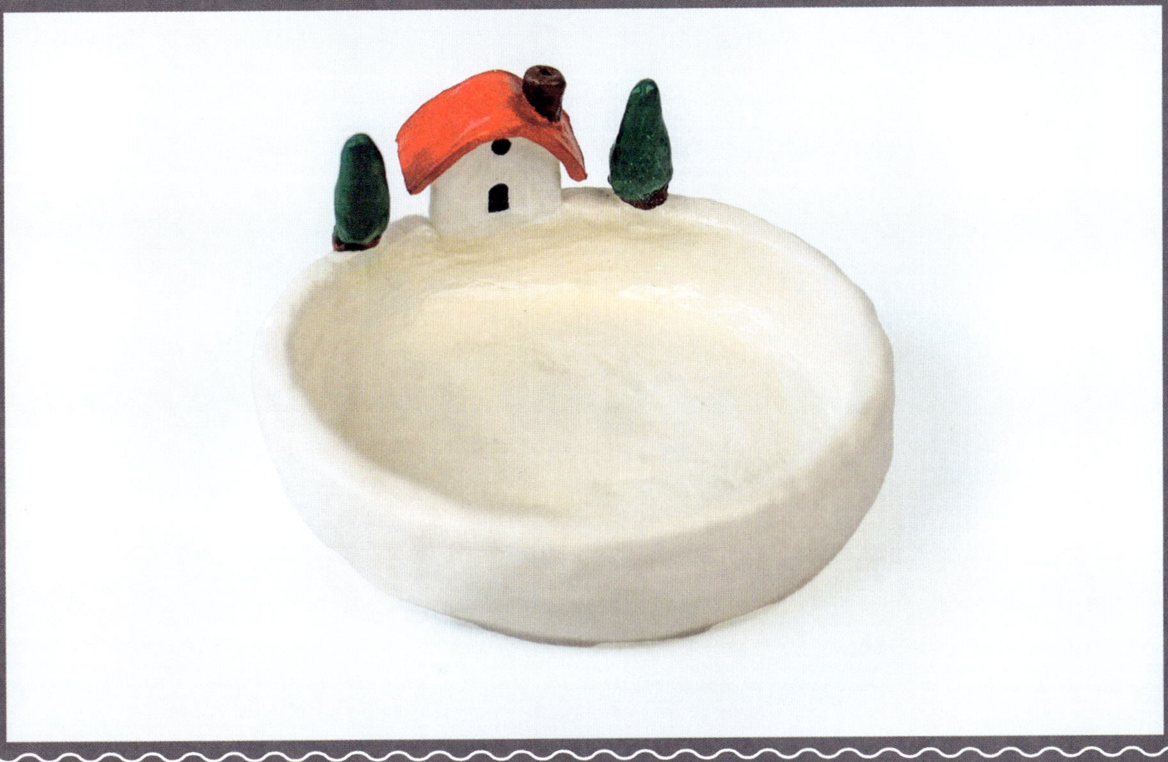

Bunny Bowl

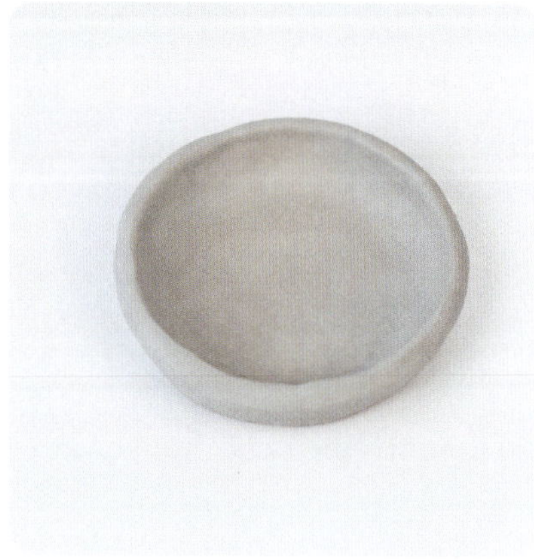

1. Create a wide pinch pot (see Pinch Pot Tutorial on page 26).

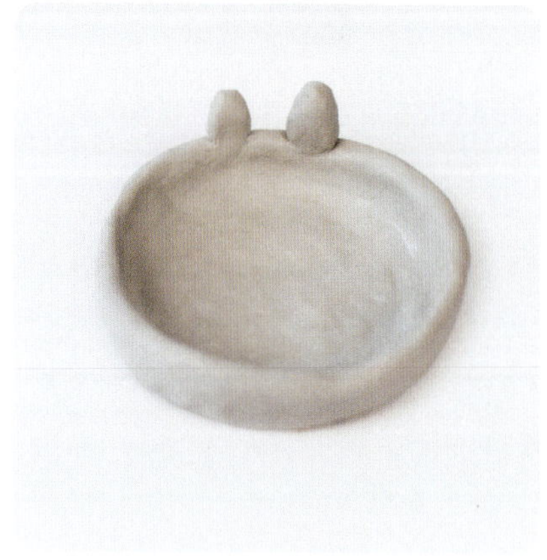

2. Make 2 bean-shaped bodies, one slightly larger than the other. Attach them to the side of the bowl.

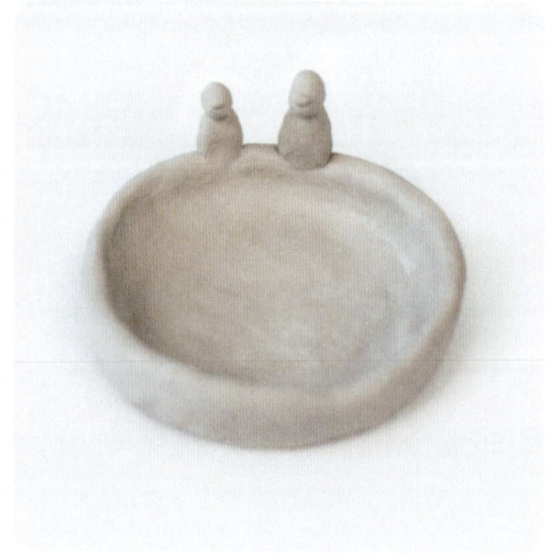

3. Roll out 2 smaller ovals and attach them to the bodies to create heads. Add a flattened ball to the front of each head to create noses.

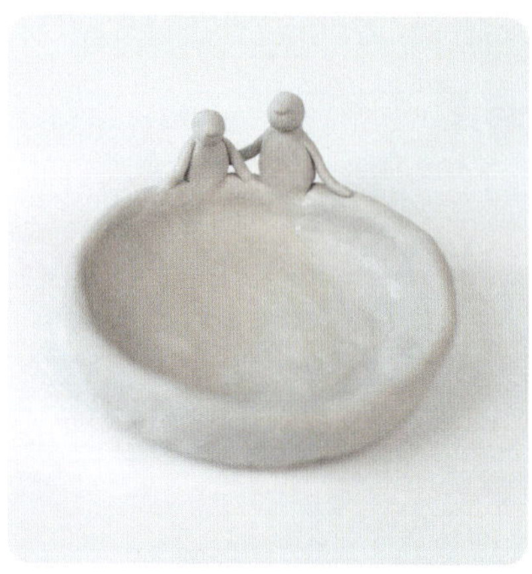

4. Roll out 4 small coils for arms. Attach the smaller bunny's 2 arms on the side of the body right below the head. Attach the hands to the rim of the bowl. Next, attach the larger bunny's 2 arms in the same way, placing one hand onto the smaller bunny's back.

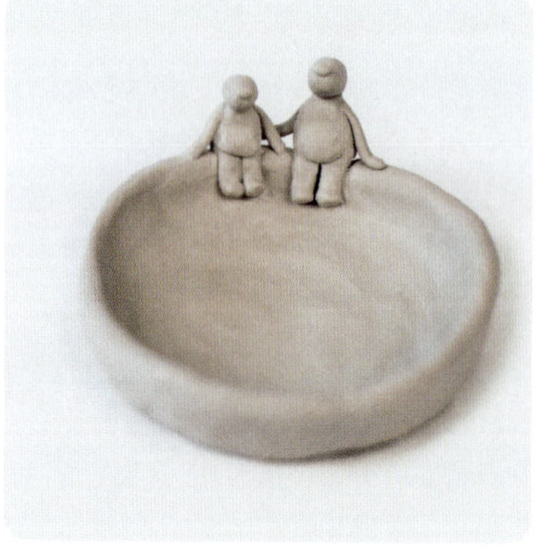

5. Roll out 4 small coils and attach 2 coils to the bottom of each body for the legs. Lift the ends forward to create feet. Add small balls to the bunnies' backs for tails.

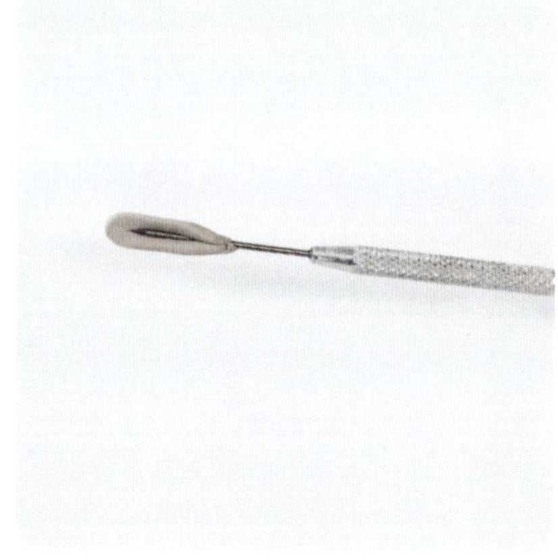

6. Sculpt each ear by wrapping a flattened coil around your needle tool. Attach to the back of the bunnies' heads. Bend one ear slightly downward in the middle, toward the bunny's face.

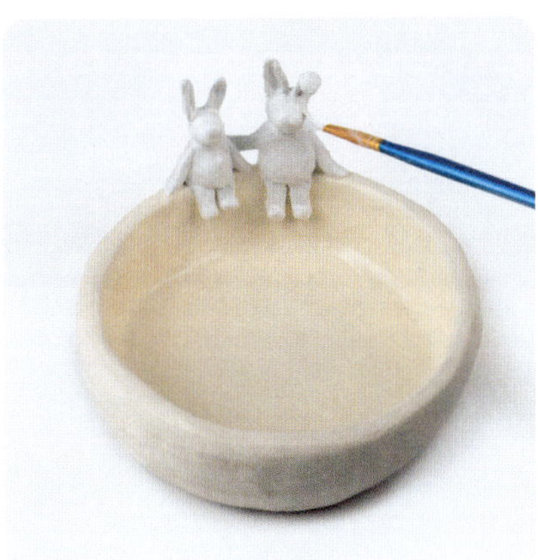

7. Smooth bowl and clean up bunnies. Allow to dry, then paint bowl and bunnies and add details—eyes, noses, and mouths—to bunnies. When the paint is dry, seal the piece with Mod Podge to finish.

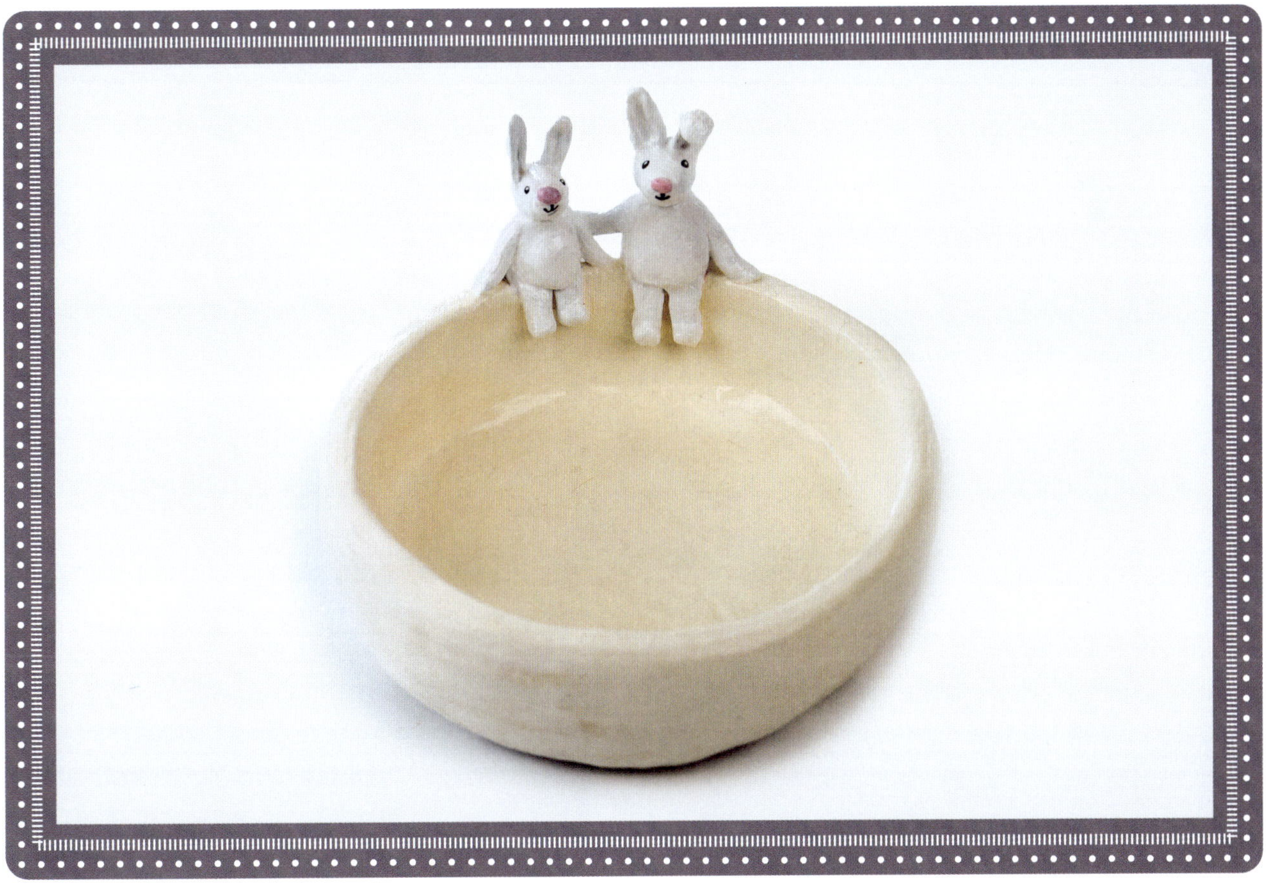

Mother Goose Bowl

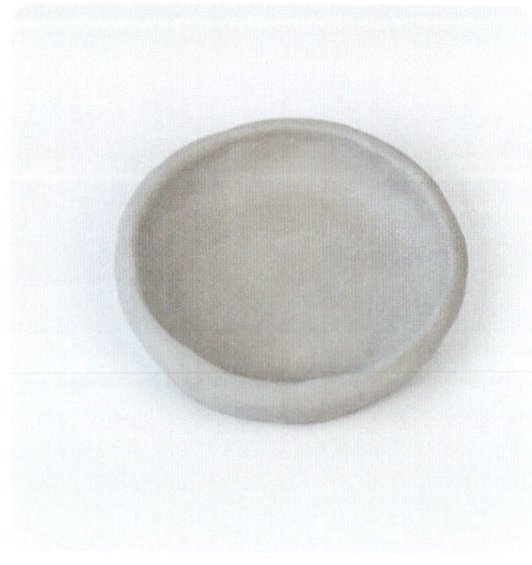

1. Create a wide and shallow pinch pot (see Pinch Pot Tutorial on page 26).

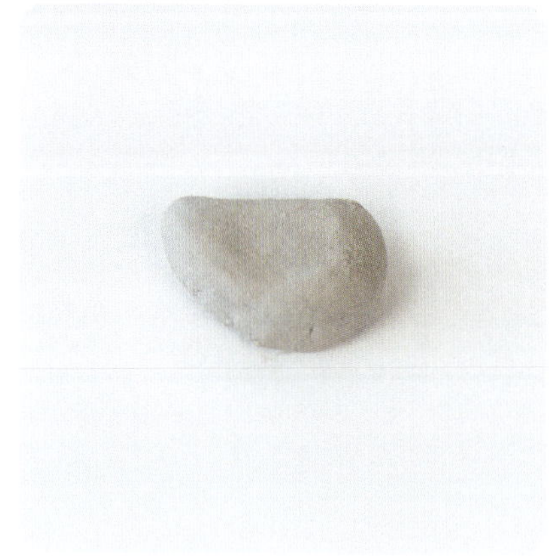

2. Sculpt a flattened teardrop shape. This will be the mother goose's body.

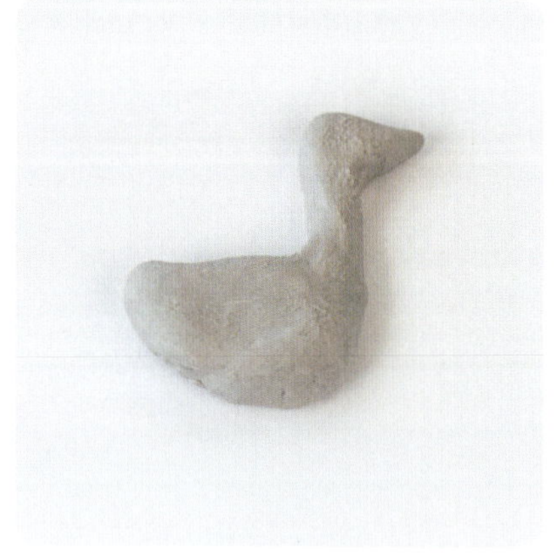

3. Sculpt the neck and head by rolling out a small coil and bending it about one-third of the way to the top. Next pinch the tip of the bent end into a beak shape. Attach the neck/head to the body.

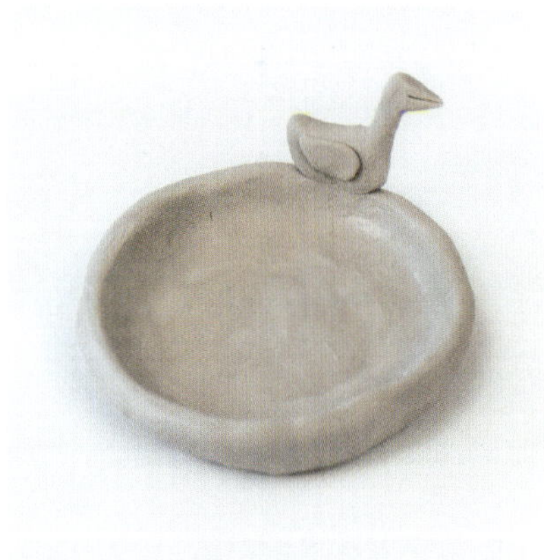

4. Attach the mother goose to the edge of the bowl. Add a flattened teardrop shape to the side of the goose to make a wing.

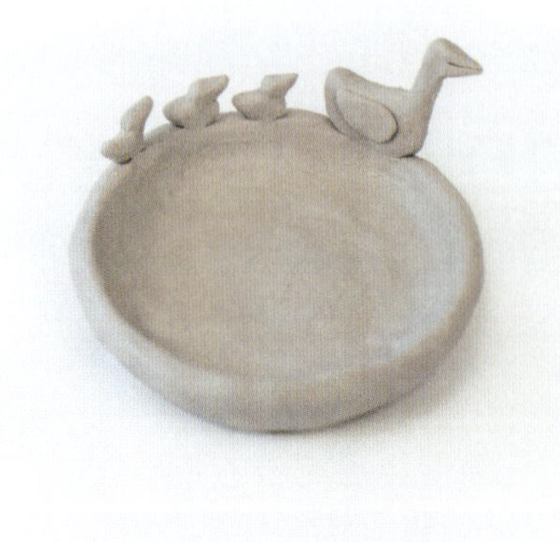

5. Sculpt 3 gosling bodies out of a small ball of clay. Add even smaller balls for the heads and pinch the beaks. Attach the goslings to the edge of the bowl.

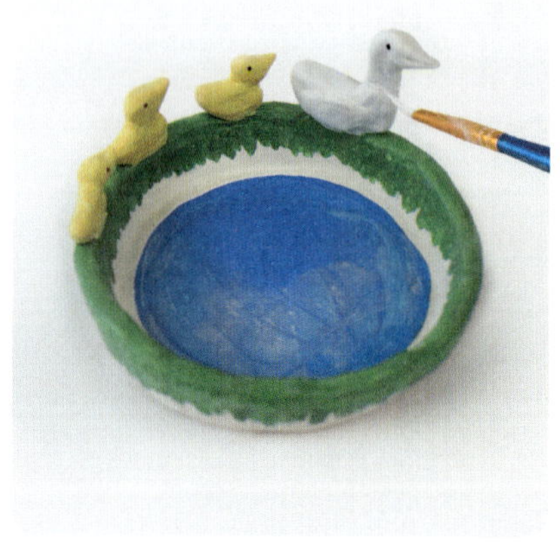

6. Once dried, paint the bowl an off-white color, then decorate with green grass and a blue pond. Paint the geese, adding black pupils to each. When the paint is dry, seal the piece with Mod Podge to finish.

TIP!

Place an object behind the mother goose and the goslings while they dry so that they remain upright.

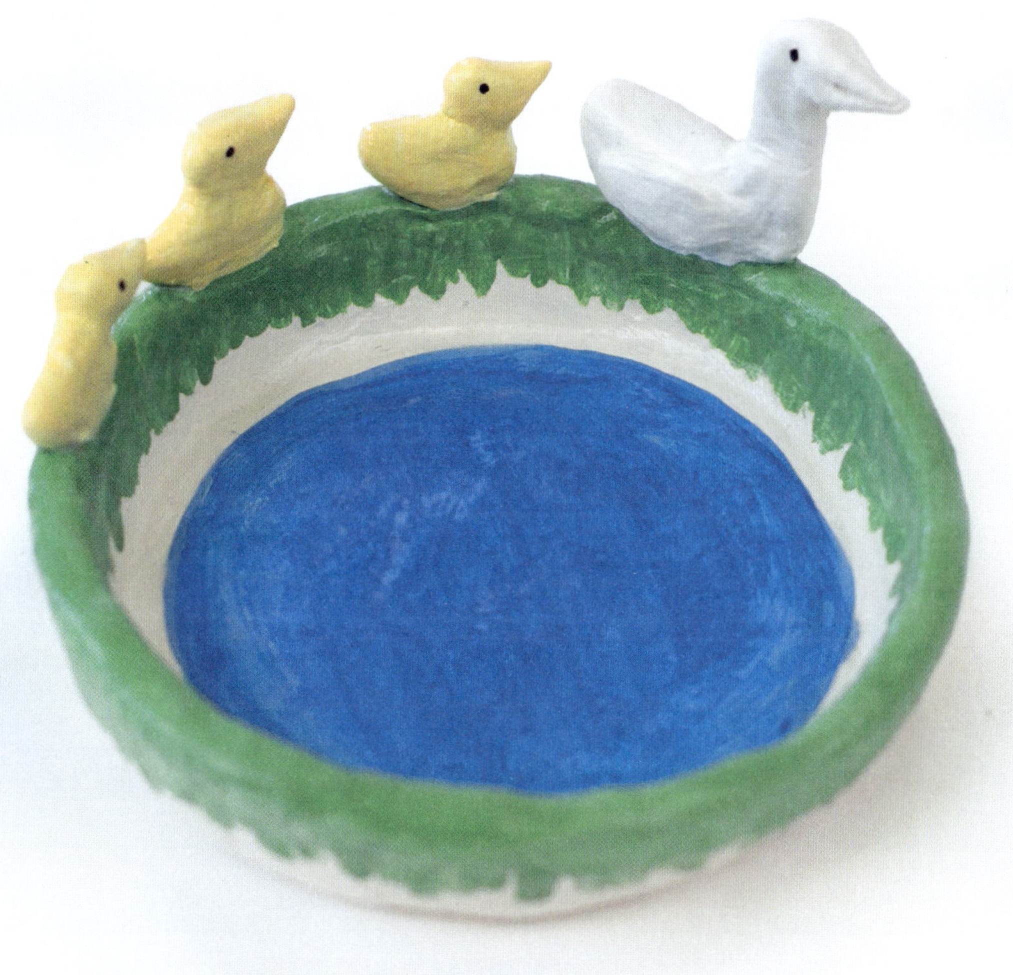

Dachshund Bowl

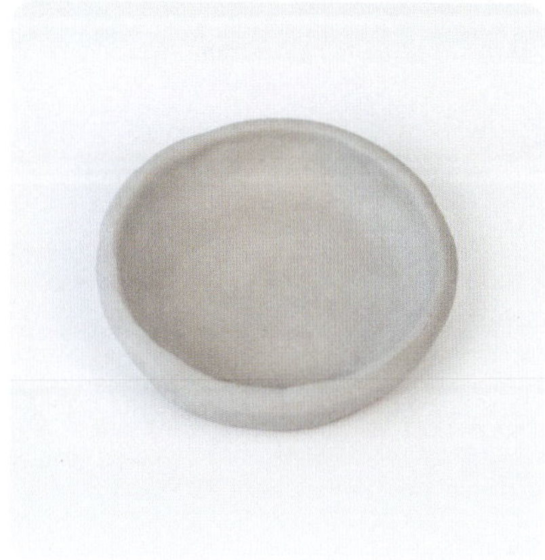

1. Create a large and shallow pinch pot (see Pinch Pot Tutorial on page 26).

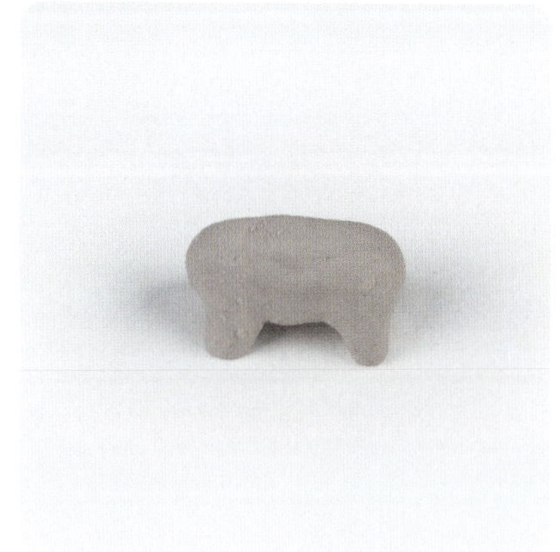

2. To form the dachshund's body, roll out a small coil and cut it into a log shape. Roll out a thinner coil and cut out 4 pieces for the legs. Attach the legs to the sides of the log.

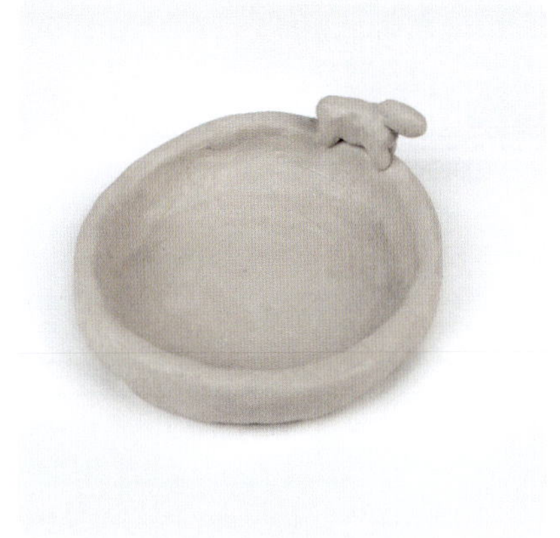

3. Attach the dog's body to the rim of the bowl. Roll out a small bean shape for the head and attach it to one end (now the front) of the body.

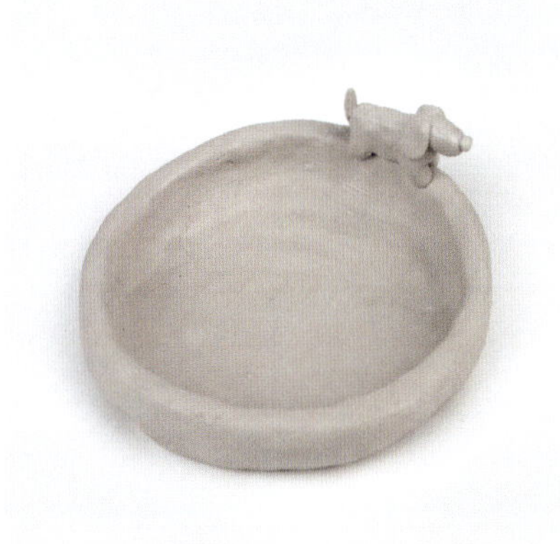

4. Sculpt 2 more small, flat bean shapes into ears and connect them to either side of the head. Add a tiny ball for the nose and small nub for the tail.

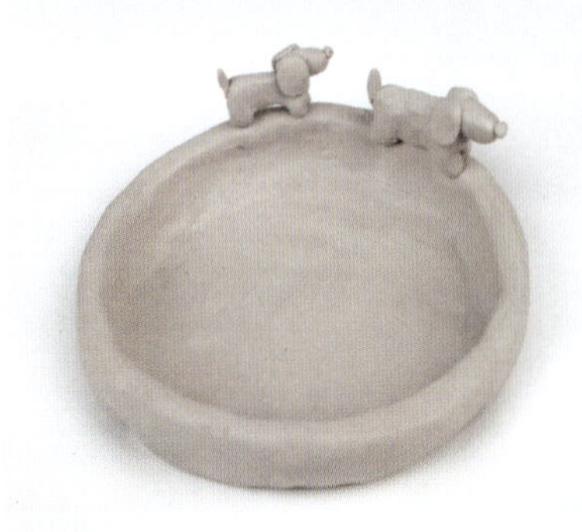

5. Repeat steps 2 to 5, making each piece slightly smaller than in the first dachshund, for the puppy. Attach it to the edge of the bowl behind the first dog.

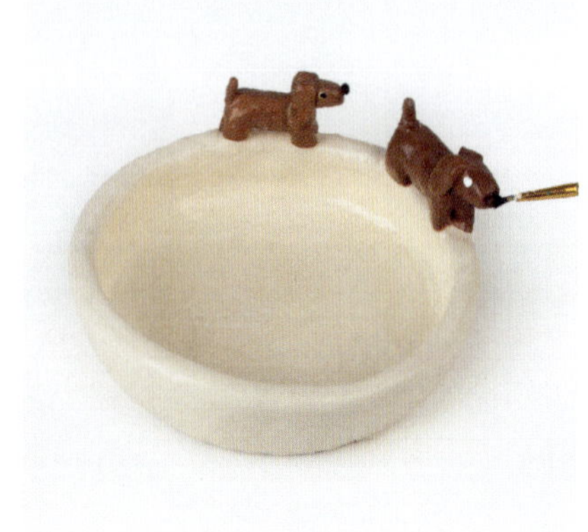

6. Smooth and touch up, then allow the piece to dry. Paint the bowl a base color, such as off-white, and paint the dogs and details on their bodies. When the paint is dry, seal the piece with Mod Podge to finish.

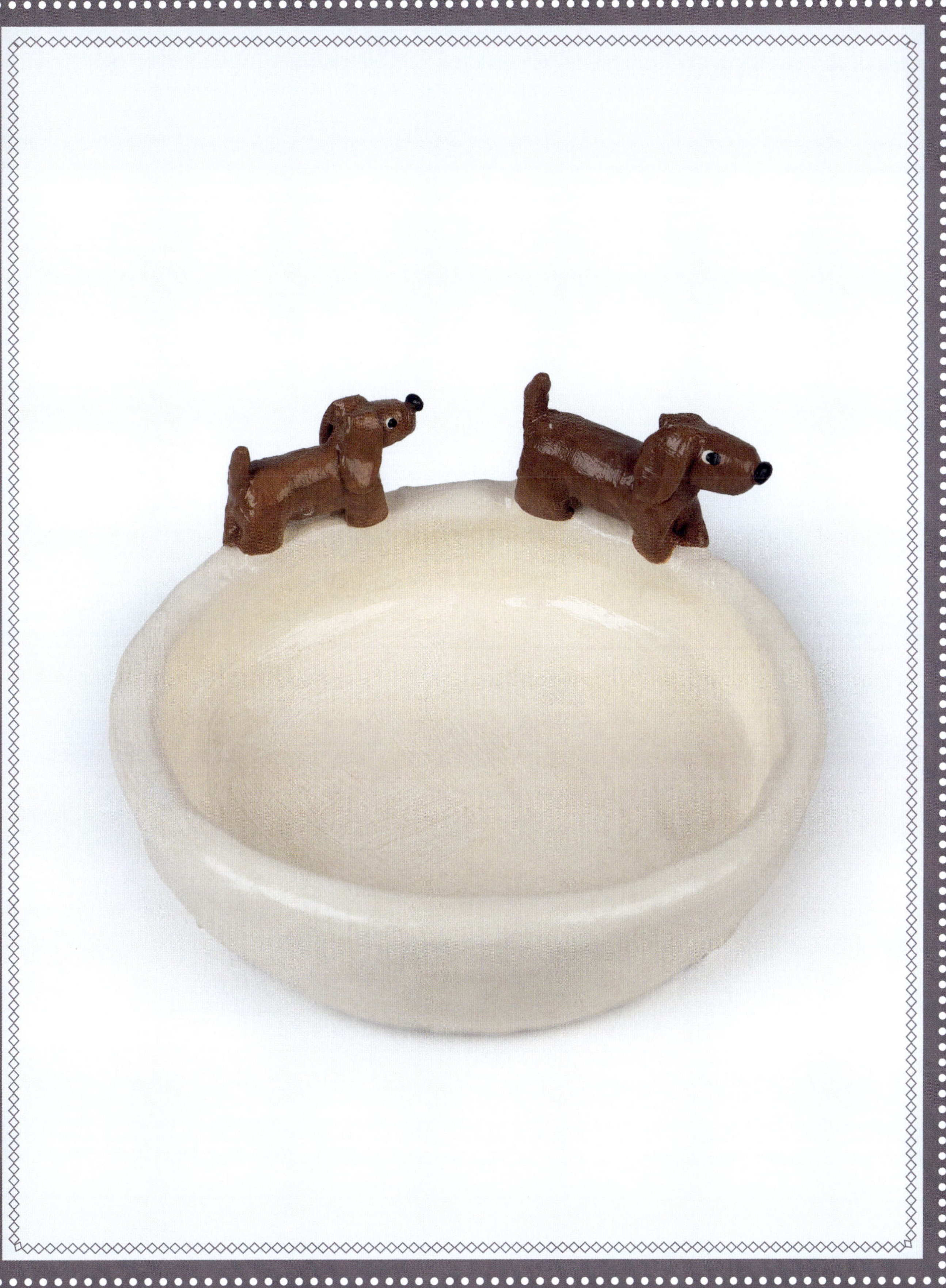

Serving Tray

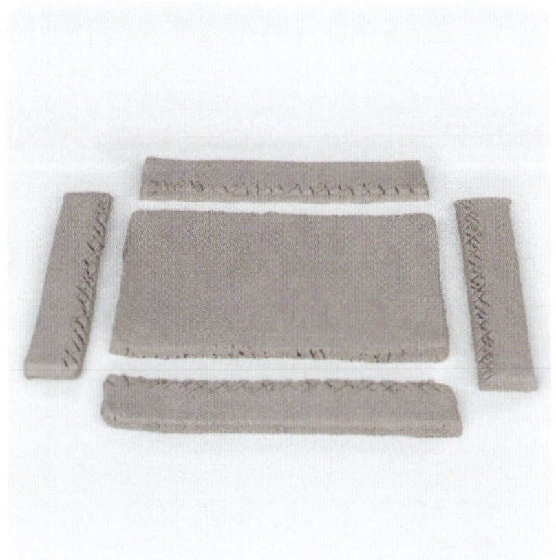

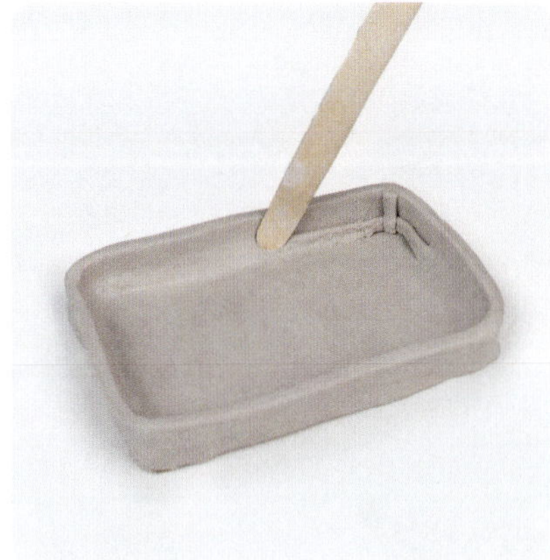

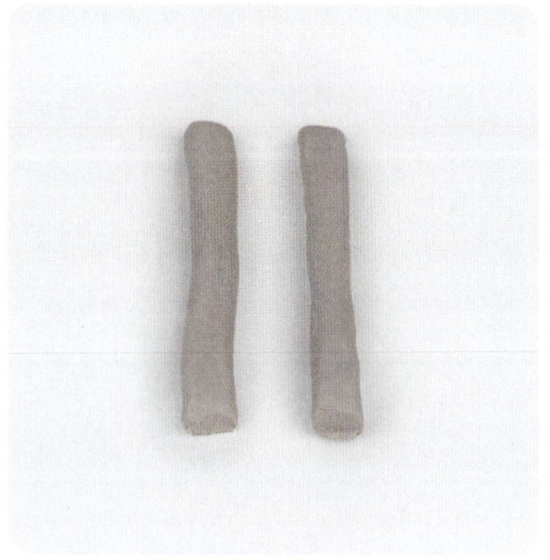

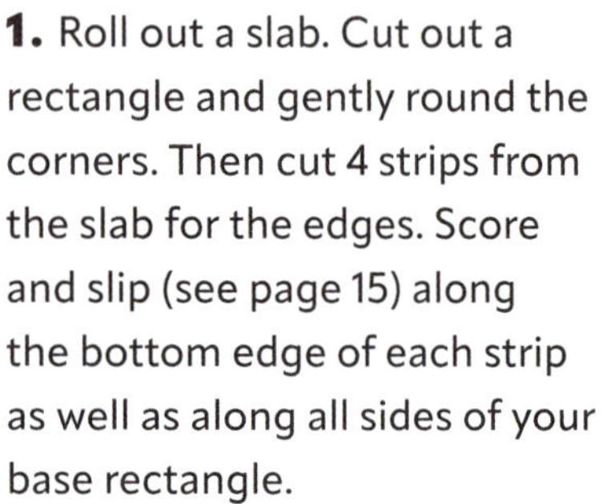

1. Roll out a slab. Cut out a rectangle and gently round the corners. Then cut 4 strips from the slab for the edges. Score and slip (see page 15) along the bottom edge of each strip as well as along all sides of your base rectangle.

2. Attach the strips around the base, keeping the rounded corners. Add a thin coil along the inside seams where the strips meet the base, then smooth it out. Carefully flip the piece over and smooth the bottom.

3. Roll out a coil. Cut it into 2 segments the same length as the short sides of the tray for the handles.

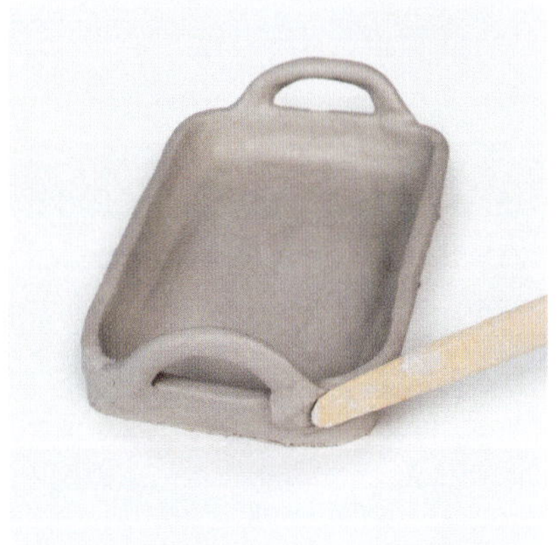

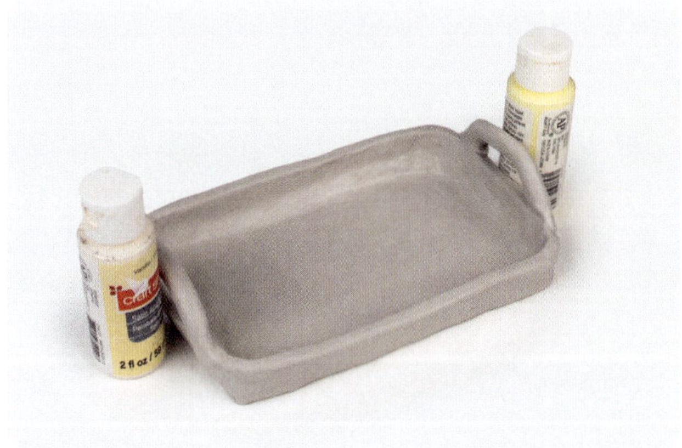

4. Use your fingers to flatten both ends of each coil. Score and slip the flattened areas, then attach them to the short sides of your tray.

5. Smooth the areas around the handles, pulling and blending the extra clay from the flattened part of the coils up and over the tray edges to fully connect it. Place a sturdy object on either side of the handles to keep them in place while drying.

TIP!

If needed, add a bit more clay to the inner connection points of the handles to create strong, smooth transitions.

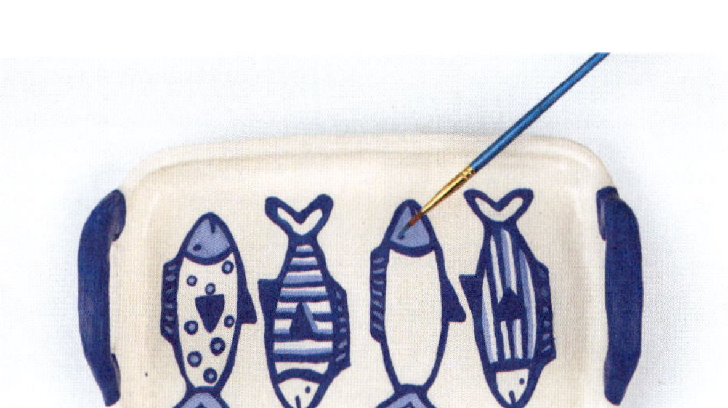

6. Once dry and smoothed of any bumps or imperfections, paint the tray a base color like off-white and add a design of your choice. When the paint is dry, seal the piece with Mod Podge to finish.

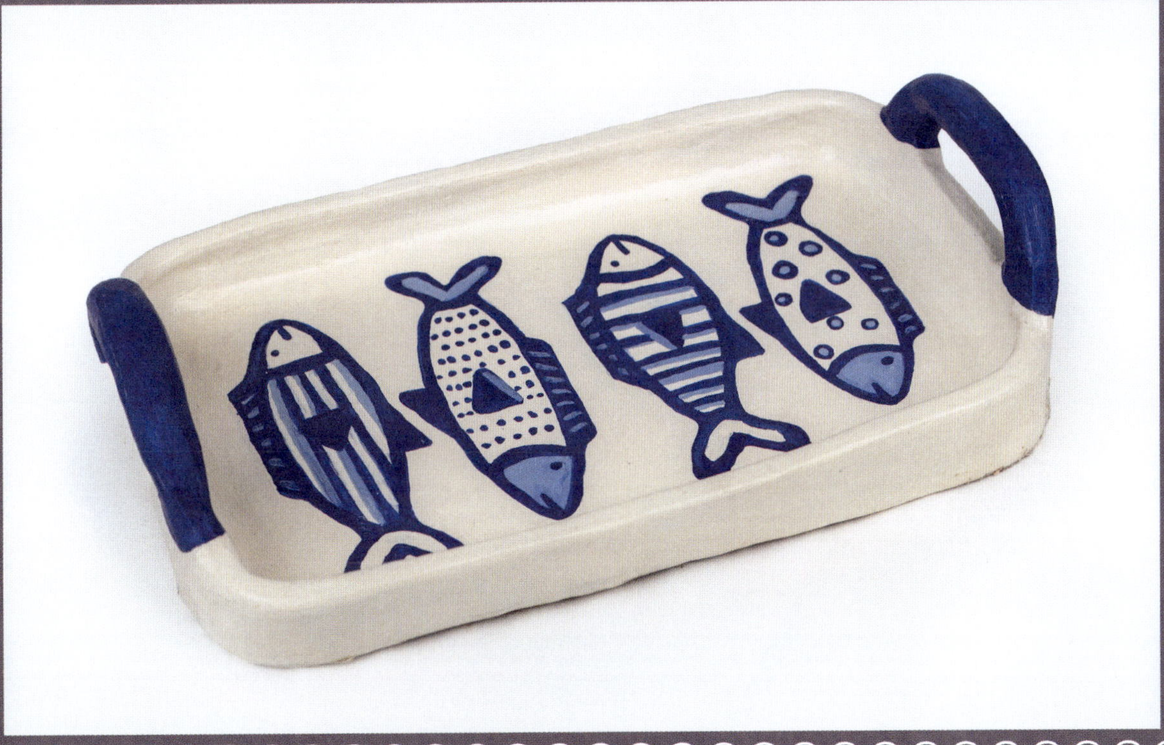

Citrus Coasters

1. Roll out a large slab, then cut out a circle using the rim of a cup. Use a wet sponge to smooth the edges.

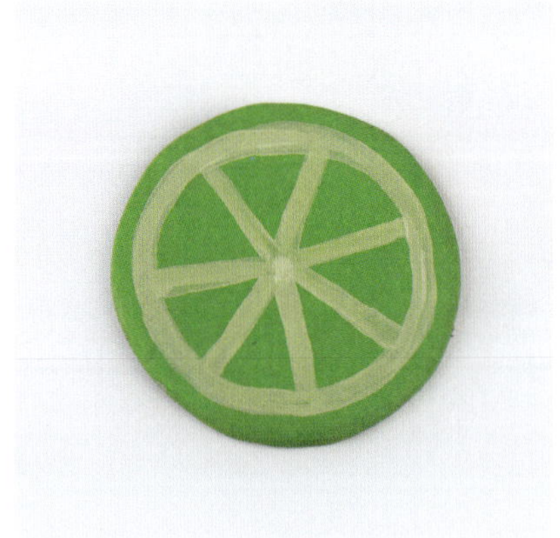

2. Paint the coaster's base a dark color such as lime green. Use a lighter shade of that color to paint a wheel on top: Start by putting a dot in the middle of the coaster to mark the center. From that dot, paint 7 lines going outward like spokes.

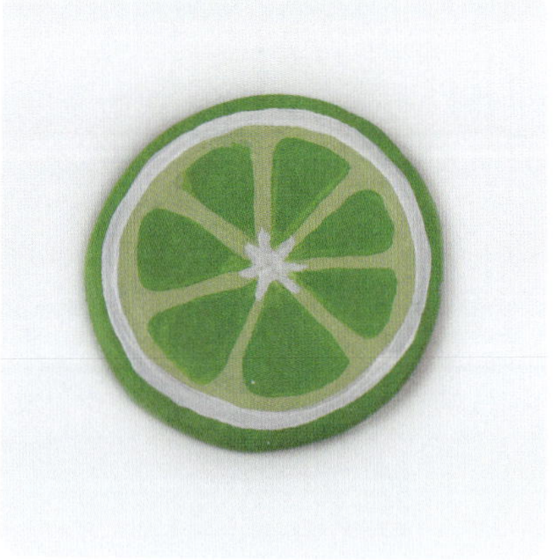

3. Add a white line around the outside of the wheel. In the center of your wheel, paint short white lines like a starburst coming out of the dot toward each spoke.

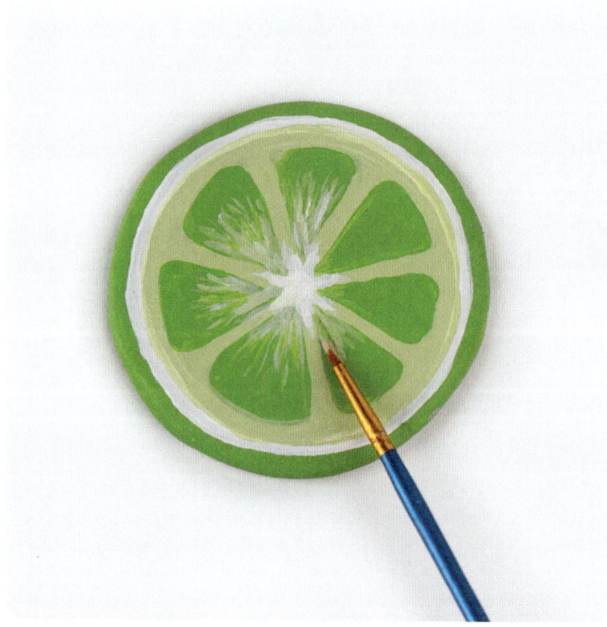

4. Mix a bit of white paint with your light shade and gently brush lines outward from the center, within each wedge of the wheel. Add a few very small white lines or dots for texture.

5. Repeat steps 1 to 4 in different colors and seal all coasters with Mod Podge to finish.

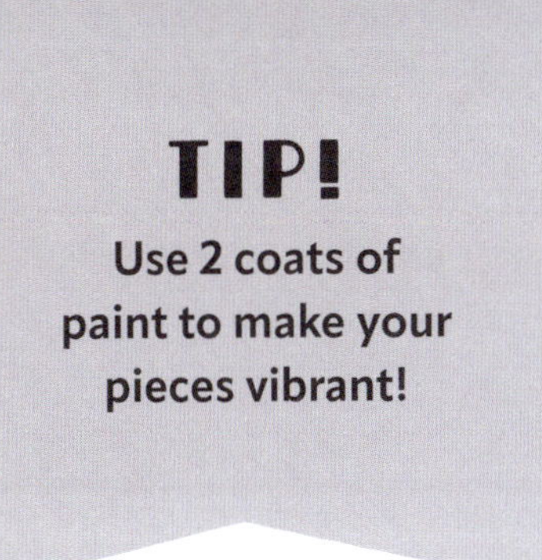

TIP!

Use 2 coats of paint to make your pieces vibrant!

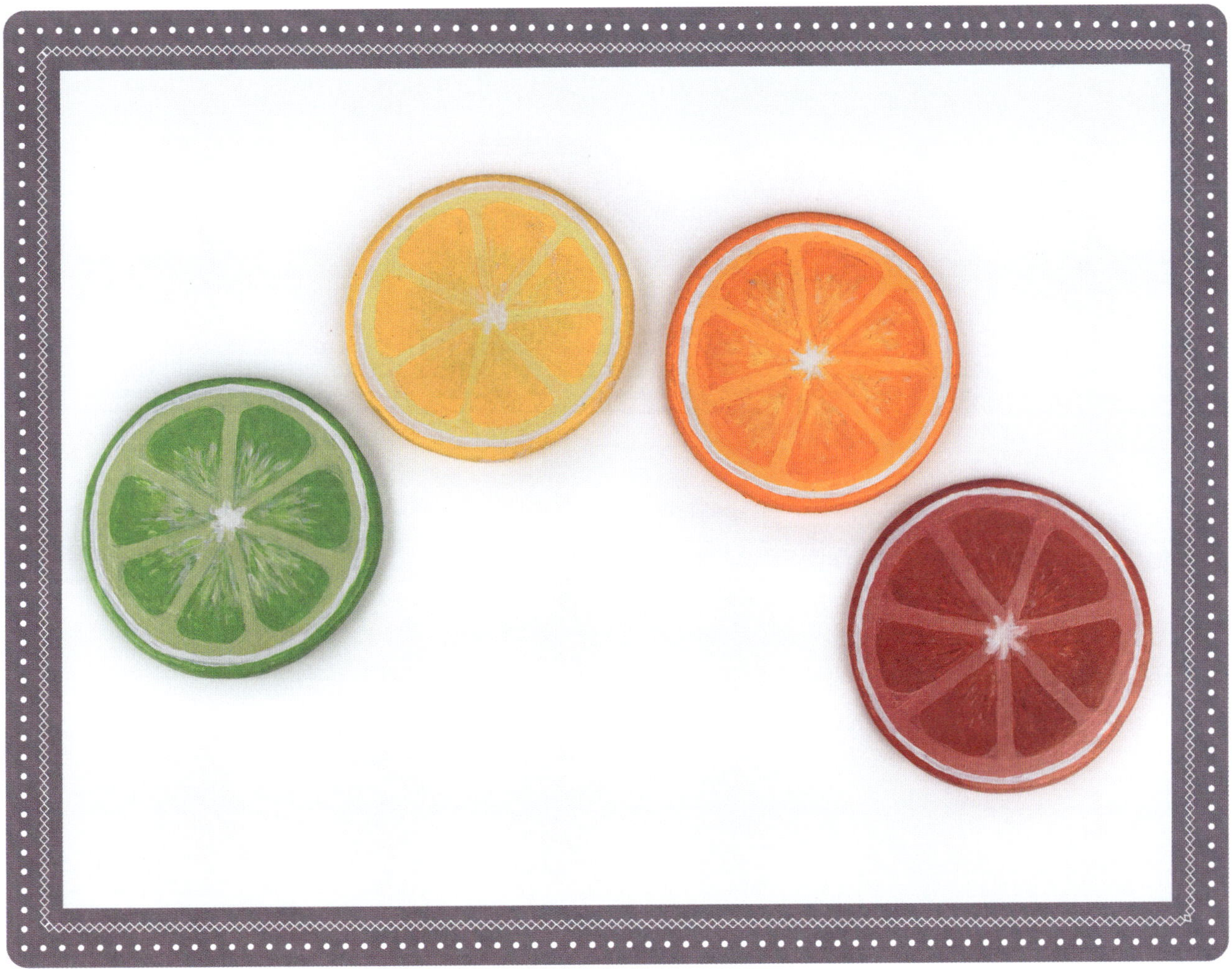

Spoon Rest

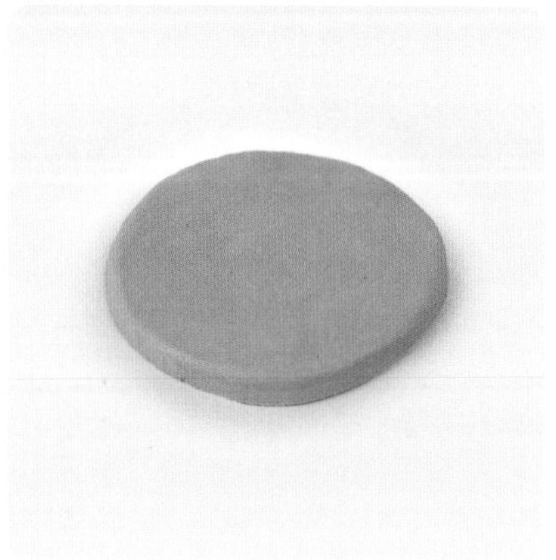

1. Roll out a small slab and use the rim of a cup to cut out a circle.

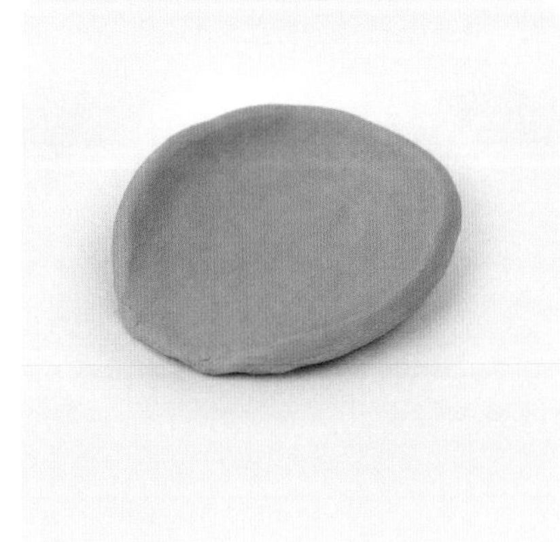

2. Use your pointer finger and thumb to lift the edges of the circle upward while pressing down in the center to create a shallow dip. Leave about 1½ inches (4 cm) of the edge unraised.

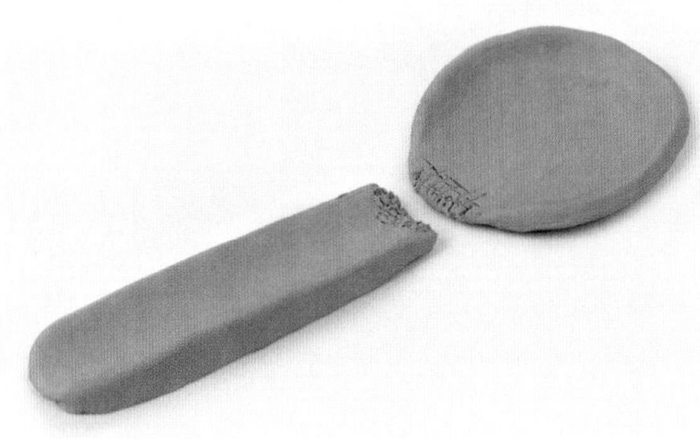

3. Roll out another long slab. Cut one end into a slightly rounded shape. Use your pointer finger to create a dip down the middle. Score and slip connection points (see page 15) between the unraised edge of the circle and the flat end of the slab.

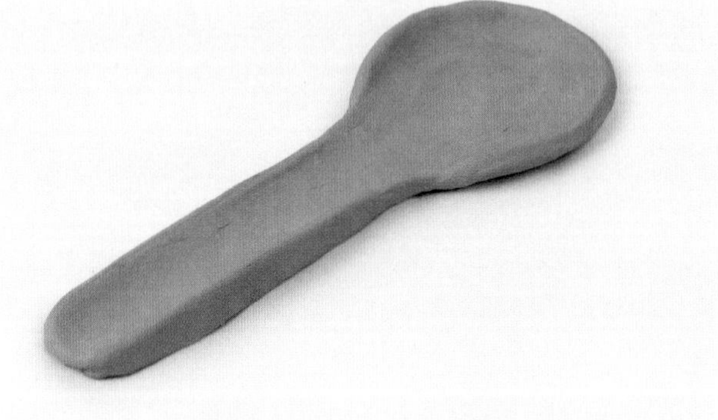

4. Smooth the seam where the pieces were joined (add a bit of clay if needed to maintain shape). Carefully flip over the piece and smooth the back.

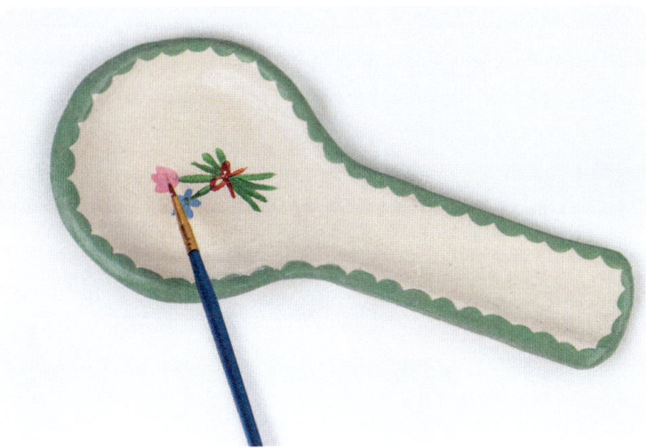

5. Once dry, paint the base a solid color and add decorative touches of your choice, such as scalloped edges in a contrasting color and a central bouquet.

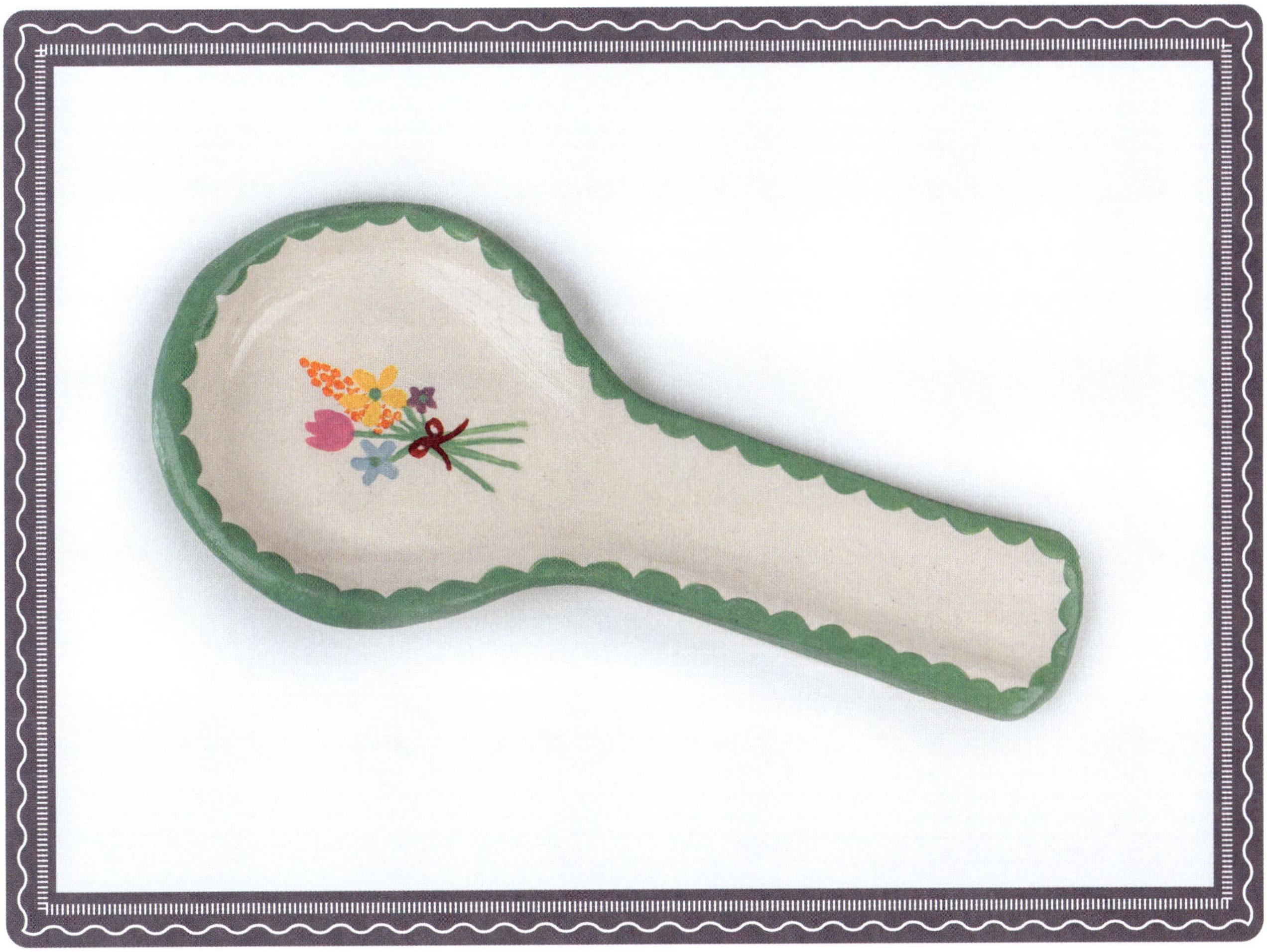

Tulip Mug

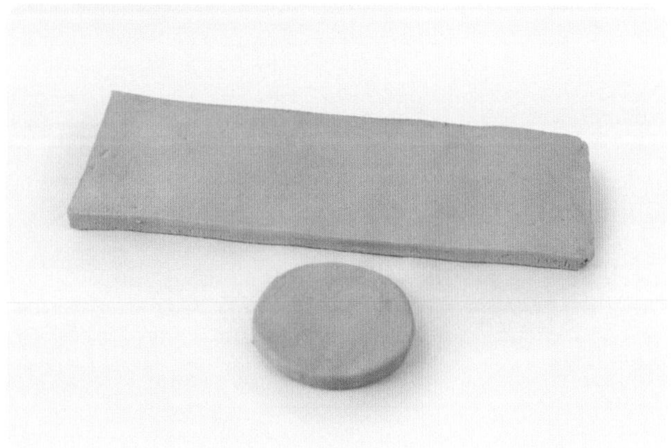

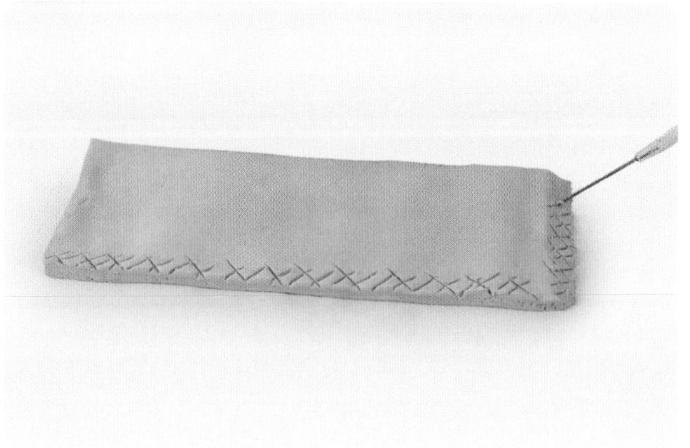

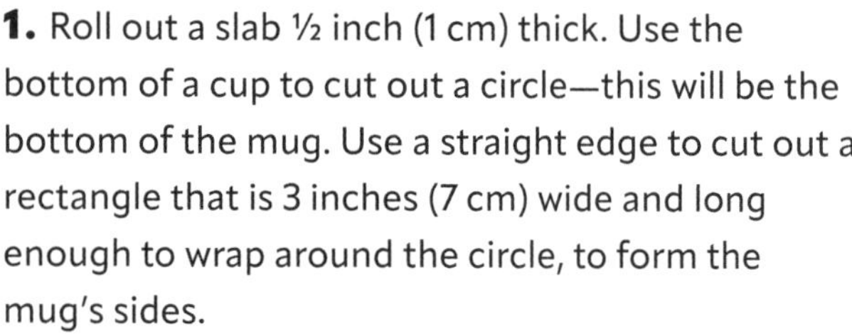

1. Roll out a slab ½ inch (1 cm) thick. Use the bottom of a cup to cut out a circle—this will be the bottom of the mug. Use a straight edge to cut out a rectangle that is 3 inches (7 cm) wide and long enough to wrap around the circle, to form the mug's sides.

2. Score and slip the edges of the rectangle (see page 15).

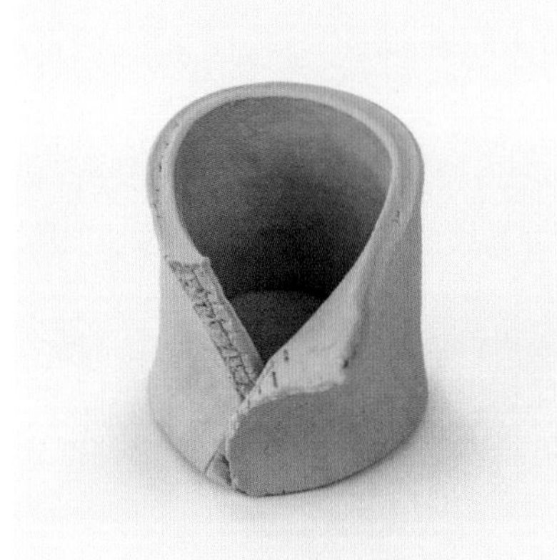

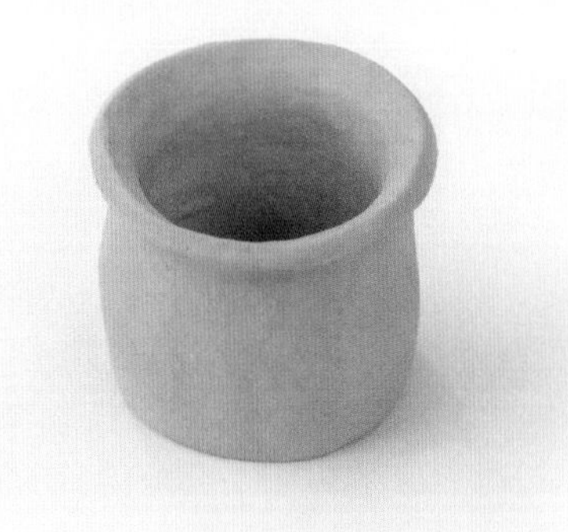

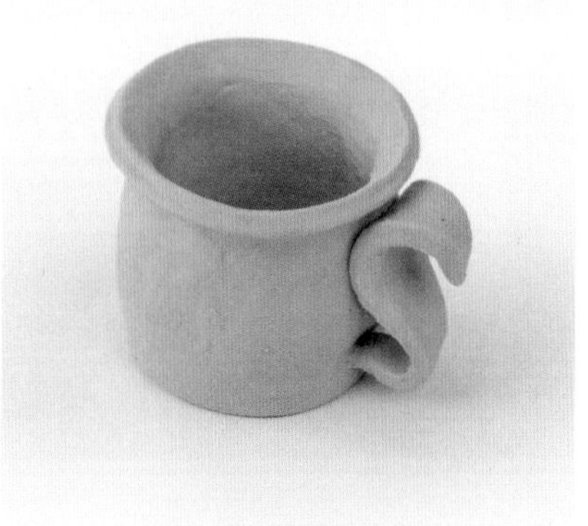

3. Score and slip connection points between the rectangle and circle. Wrap the rectangle around your circle base. Roll out a thin coil and place it along the inside connection point, then carefully smooth it to join. Smooth inside and out.

4. Use your thumb and pointer finger to push the walls outward into a bulbous shape. Pinch the top of the cup and gently pull outward to create a petal-like lip.

5. Use leftover clay from your slab and cut out a long leaf shape for the handle. Bend it into an S shape and attach the end and the middle of the S to the mug.

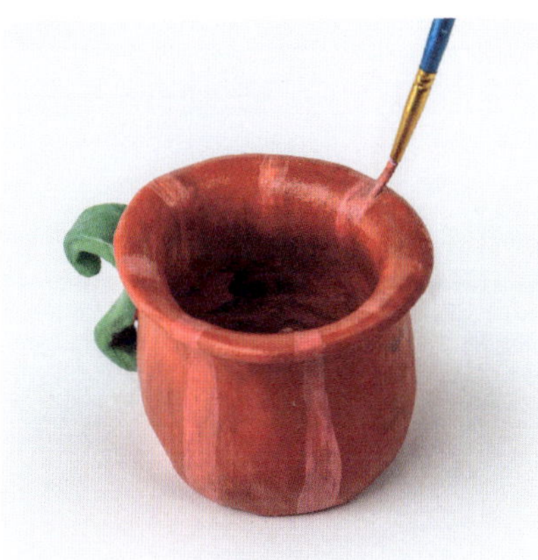

6. Clean up and allow the piece to dry, then paint the handle green, paint the mug a base color, like red, and add a petal design to the mug. When the paint is dry, seal the piece with Mod Podge to finish.

TIP!

Keep this mug on your desk to store pens and pencils. The paint and resin are not food safe!

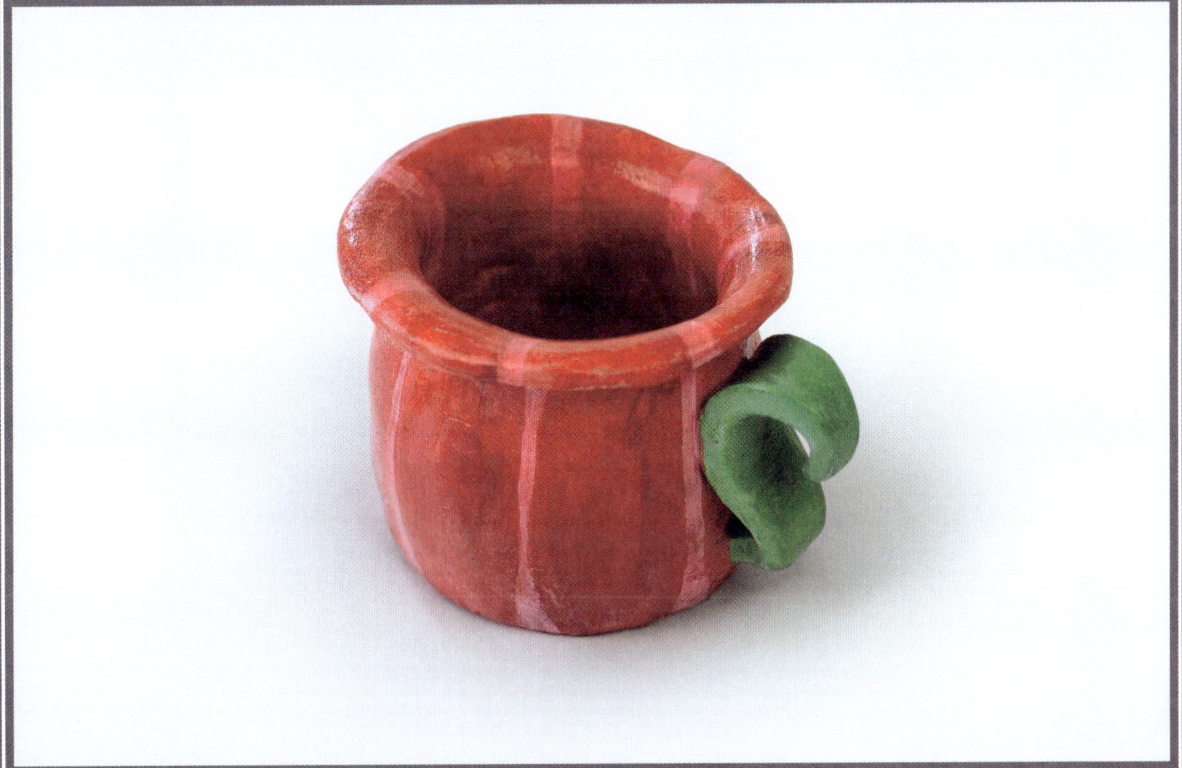

Picture Frame

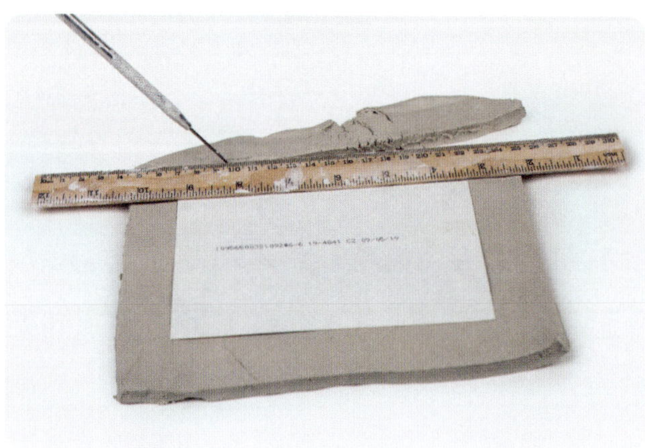

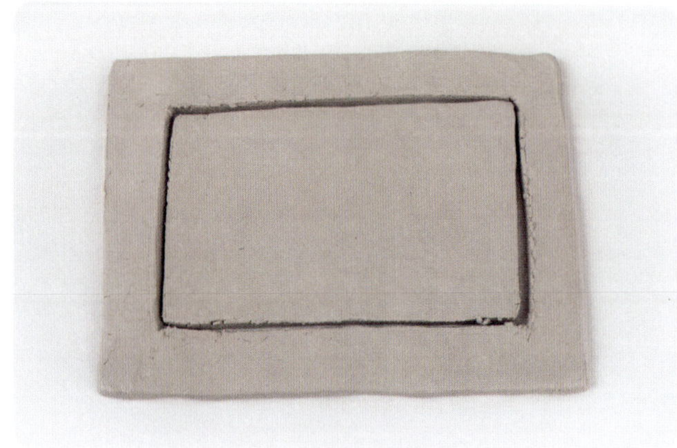

1. Roll out a slab. Place your photo on top of the slab. For each side of the photo, use a ruler to mark a point 1 inch (2½ cm) beyond the photo's edge. Use your needle tool to cut along that line.

2. Cut out the shape of your photo.

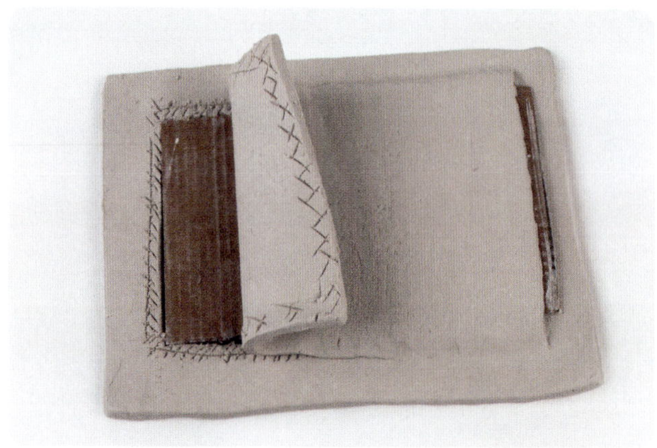

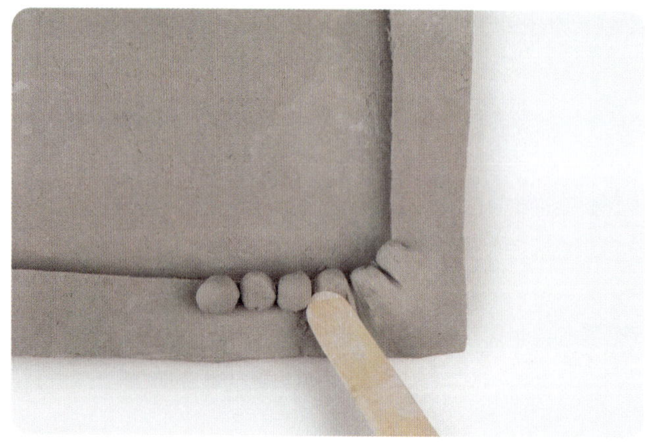

3. Roll out a thinner slab a bit larger than the shape of your photo. Cut out a piece of cardboard the size of your photo. Place the cardboard in the empty slot and put the thinner slab on top. Score and slip the thinner slab (see page 15) and the photo frame base, leaving one of the short sides open.

4. To create the frame's decorative border, score along the inside edge of your frame's front side. Roll out small balls and connect them to the frame so that they're positioned about half on and half over the inside edge. Blend into the frame. Remove the cardboard.

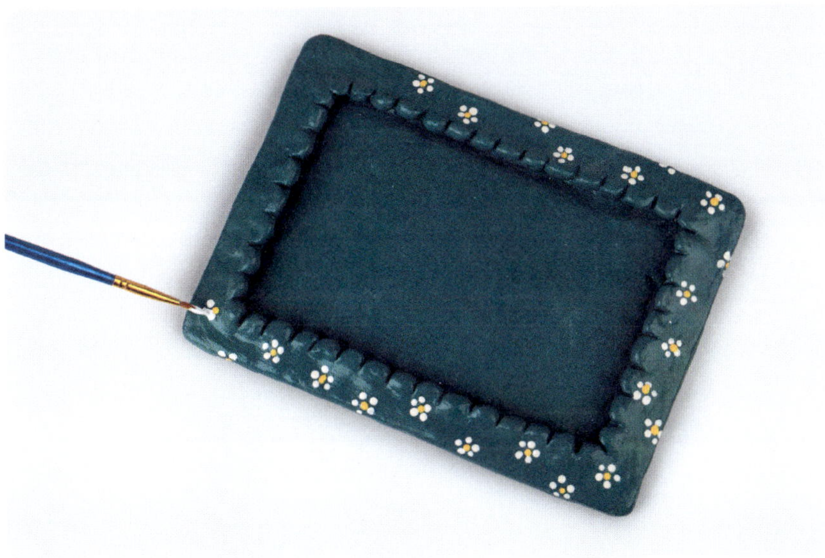

5. Once fully dry and cleaned up, paint the frame a base color and add a design of your choice, such as flowers. When the paint is dry, seal the piece with Mod Podge to finish.

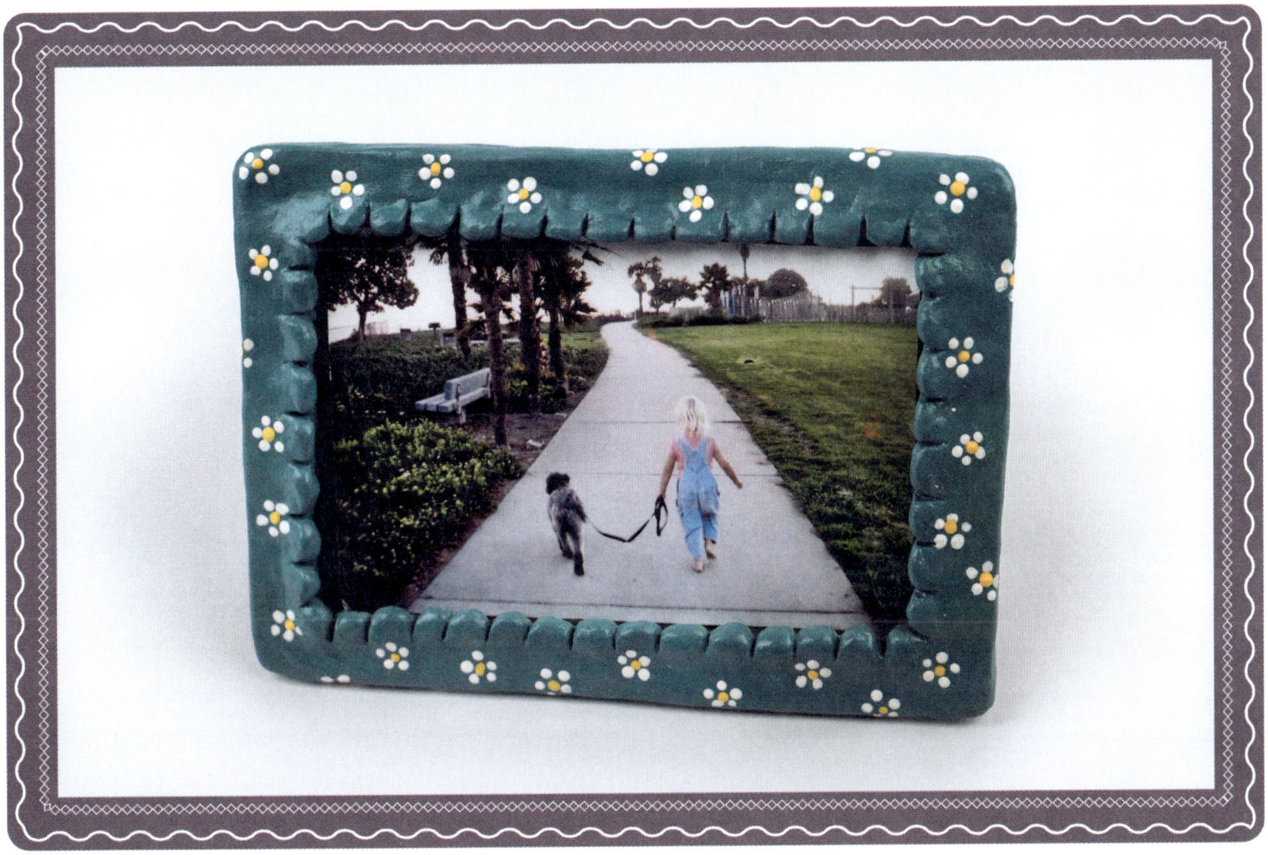

Small Vase

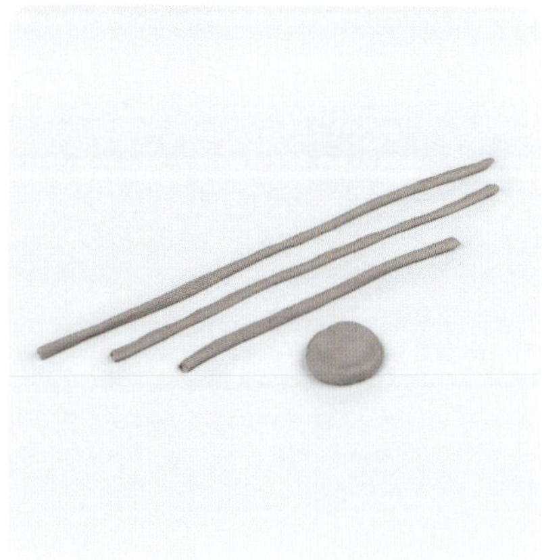

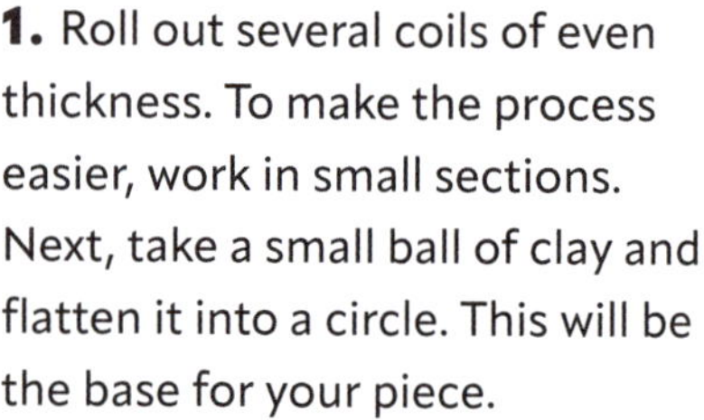

1. Roll out several coils of even thickness. To make the process easier, work in small sections. Next, take a small ball of clay and flatten it into a circle. This will be the base for your piece.

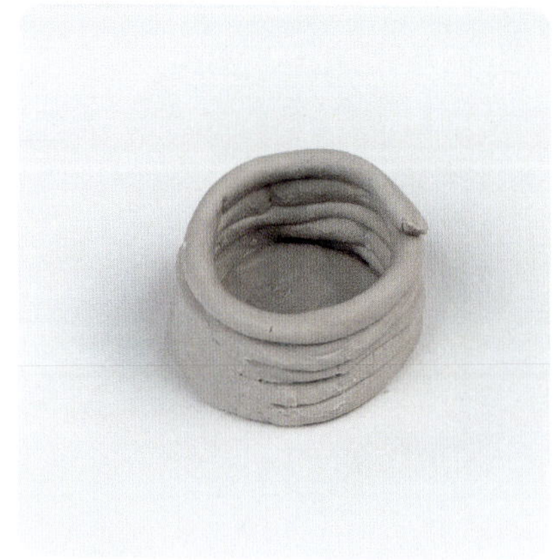

2. Begin to wrap your coils around the base, adding one coil at a time and continuing upward in a stack. Using a flat wooden tool or your dampened fingers, smooth the coils together.

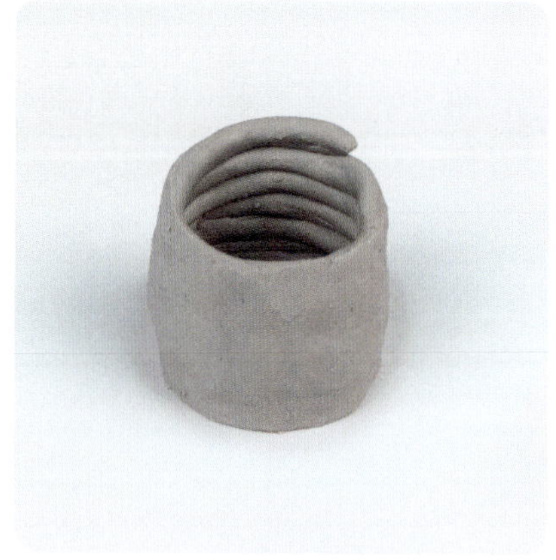

3. Once your vase's body is about 2 inches (5 cm) tall, create a bulbous shape by inserting your middle finger inside the vase and using your middle finger and thumb to gently press the sides of the vase outward.

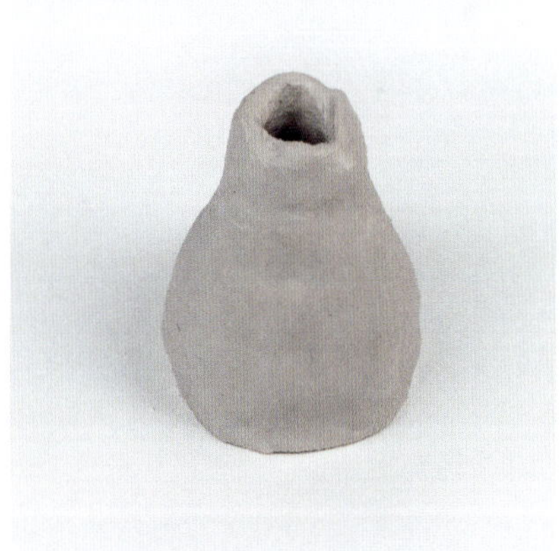

4. Continue making, placing, and smoothing coils, narrowing near the top to create the neck.

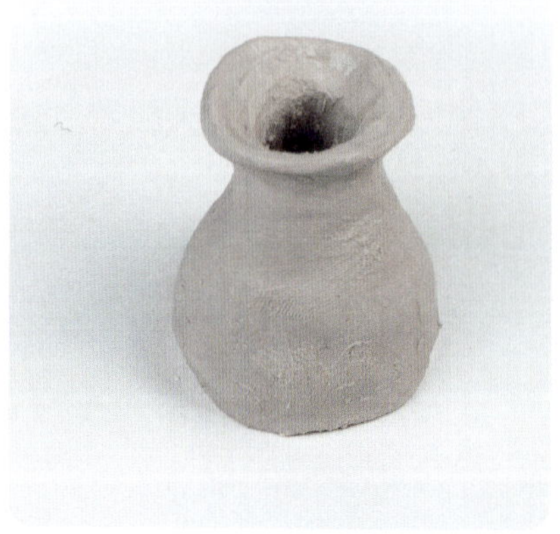

5. Add one or two final coils around the outer edge of the neck to form the lip of the vase.

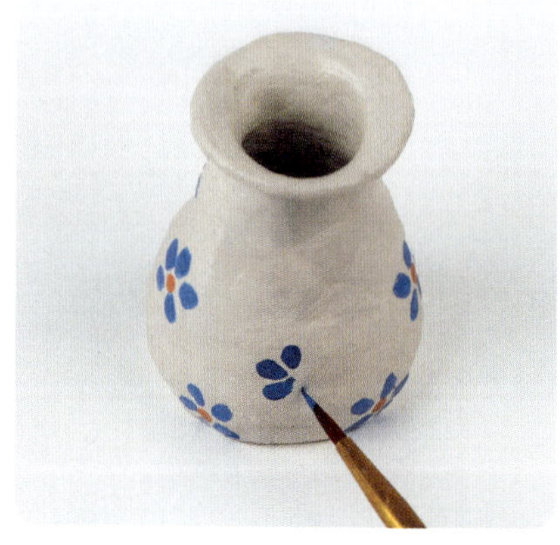

6. Once fully dry and smoothed, paint the vase a solid color, like off-white, and add a design of your choice, such as flowers. When the paint is dry, seal the piece with Mod Podge to finish.

TIP!

Don't smooth the inside of the vase, as it won't be seen and makes the structure harder to manipulate.

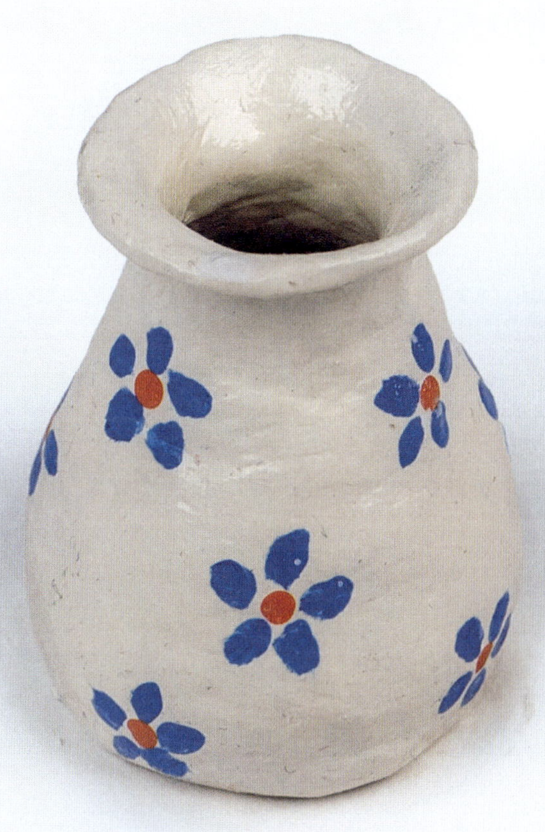

Hanging Planter

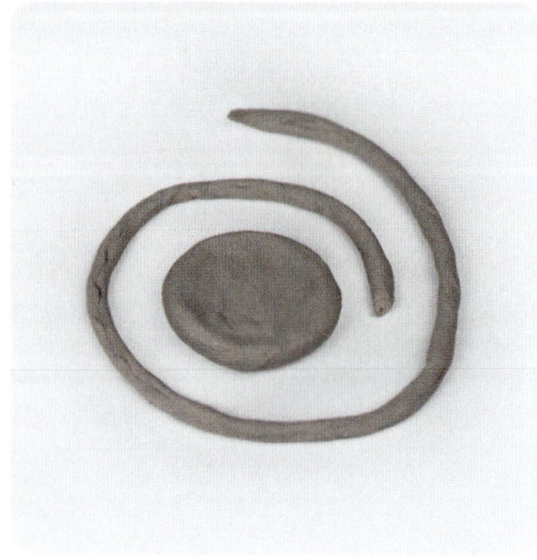

1. Roll out a small ball of clay and flatten it into a circle. Create a few coils about the thickness of your pinky finger.

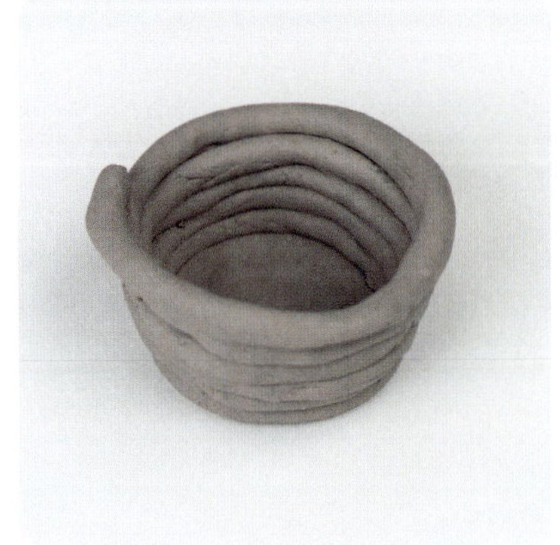

2. Start wrapping the coils around the circle, building upward and outward. Continue to roll out and wrap coils until you reach about 1½ inches (4 cm) tall. Smooth as you go.

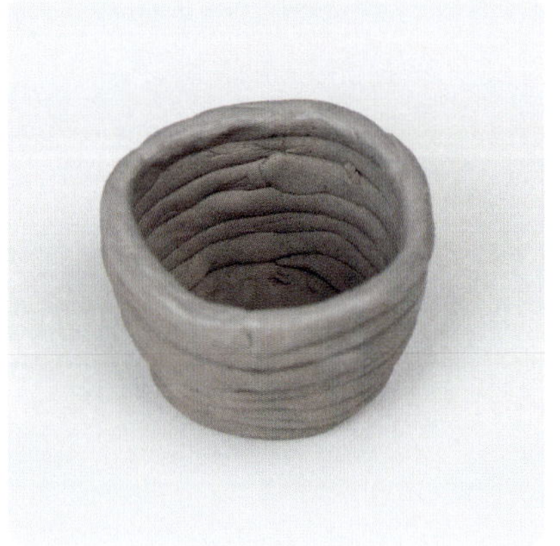

3. Continue creating and wrapping the coils, now stacking them directly on top of each other rather than angling them slightly outward as you did before.

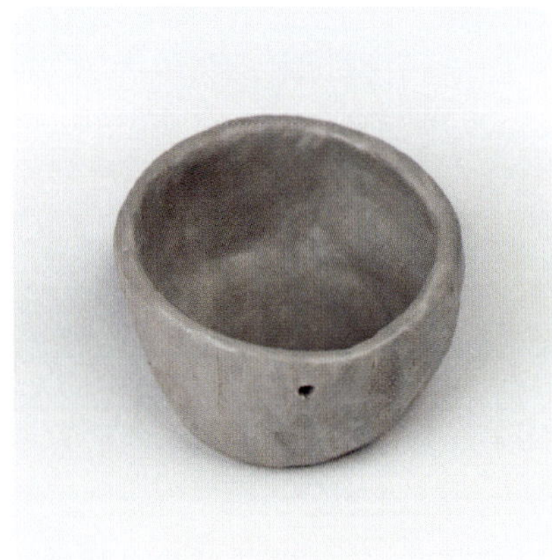

4. Smooth the interior and exterior while maintaining the structure. Use a needle tool to poke 2 holes on opposite sides of the upper half of the pot (make sure these are large enough for the string or ribbon to pass through).

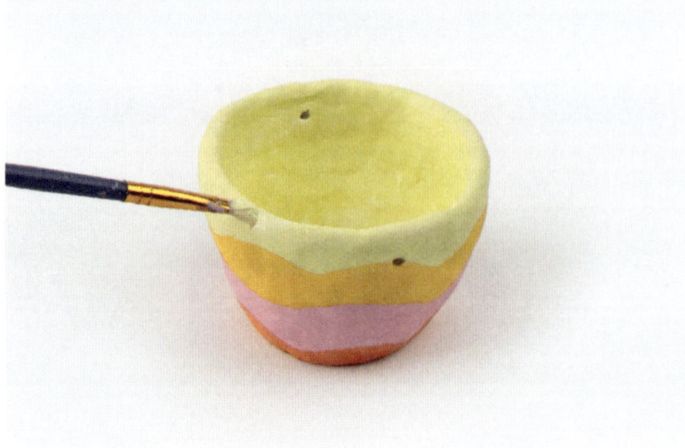

5. Once fully dry, paint your design. Seal the piece with Mod Podge. Loop 2 strings or ribbons through the holes and tie them on the inside of the planter to keep them in place. Tie the 2 together at the top to hang.

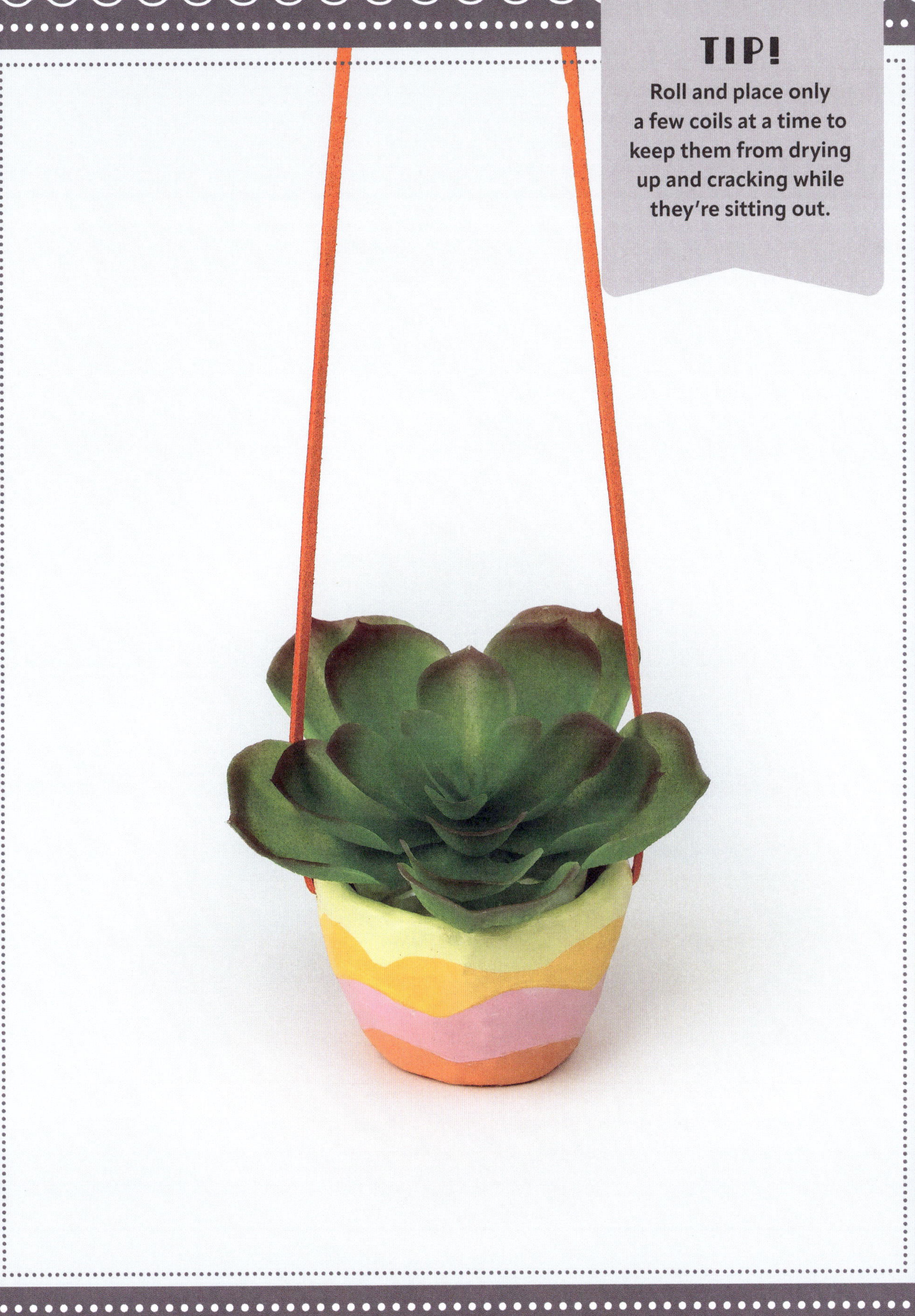

TIP!

Roll and place only a few coils at a time to keep them from drying up and cracking while they're sitting out.

Candlestick

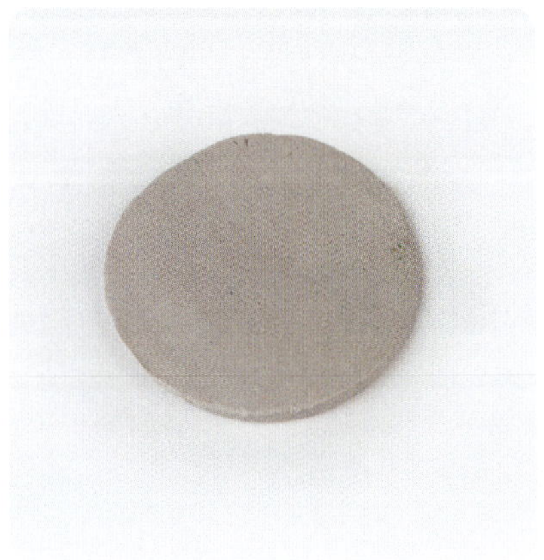

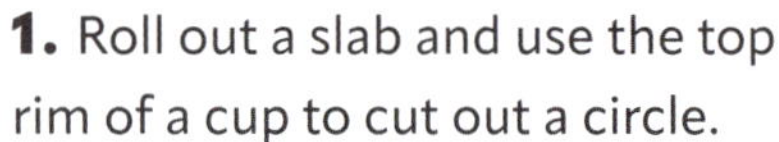

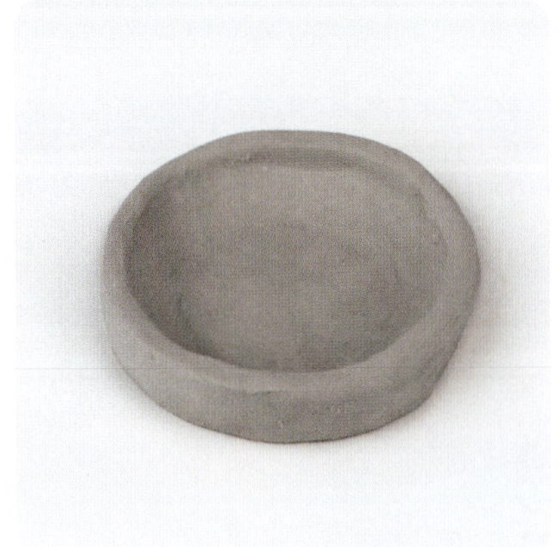

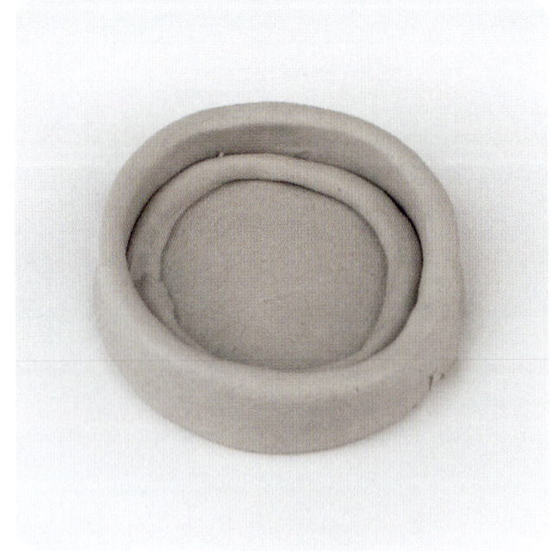

1. Roll out a slab and use the top rim of a cup to cut out a circle.

2. Roll out a long coil and flatten it, then wrap it around the perimeter of your circle. Create another coil about half the thickness of the first and wrap it around the inside of your first coil.

3. Blend and smooth the coils with your fingers or smoothing tool until you have a clean rim.

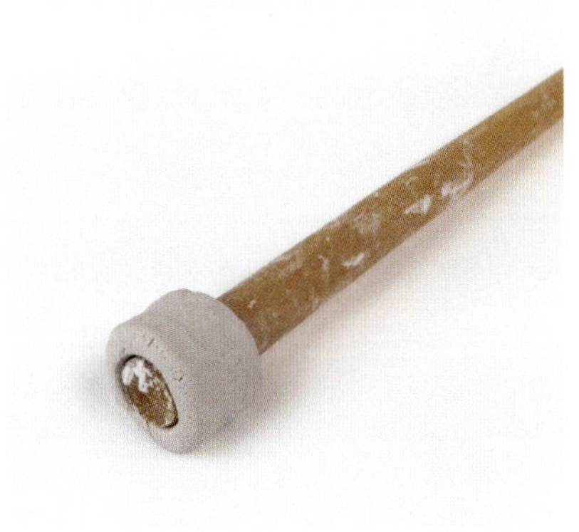

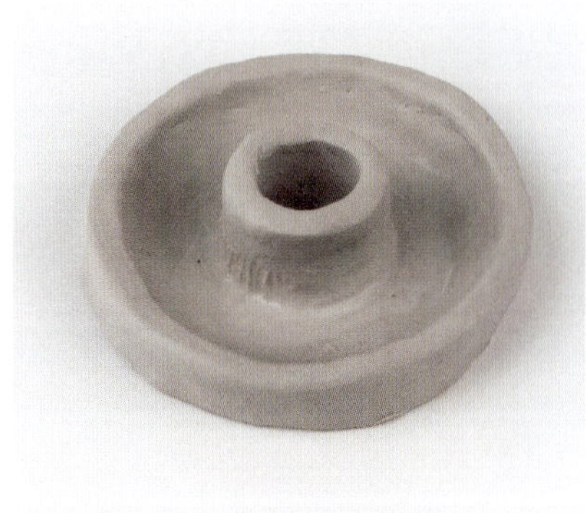

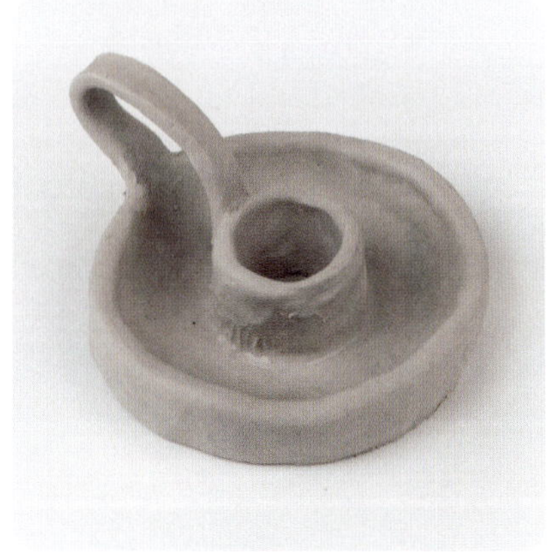

4. Roll out another coil similar in size to your first one, then flatten it. Wrap this flattened coil around the end of a candle to get the correct size and shape.

5. Remove the molded coil from the candle, score and slip (see page 15) the bottom of it, and attach it to the middle of the base.

6. Roll out another, thinner coil and shape it into a handle. Connect one end to the side of the outer rim and the other end to the inner candle holder.

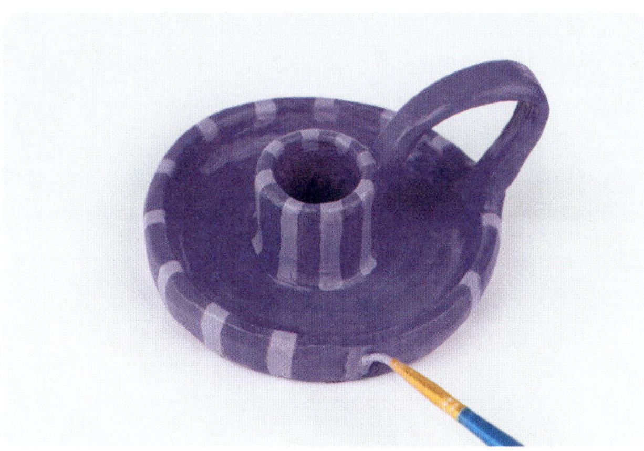

7. Once fully dry and smoothed, paint the piece a base color and add a design of your choice. When the paint is dry, seal the piece with Mod Podge to finish.

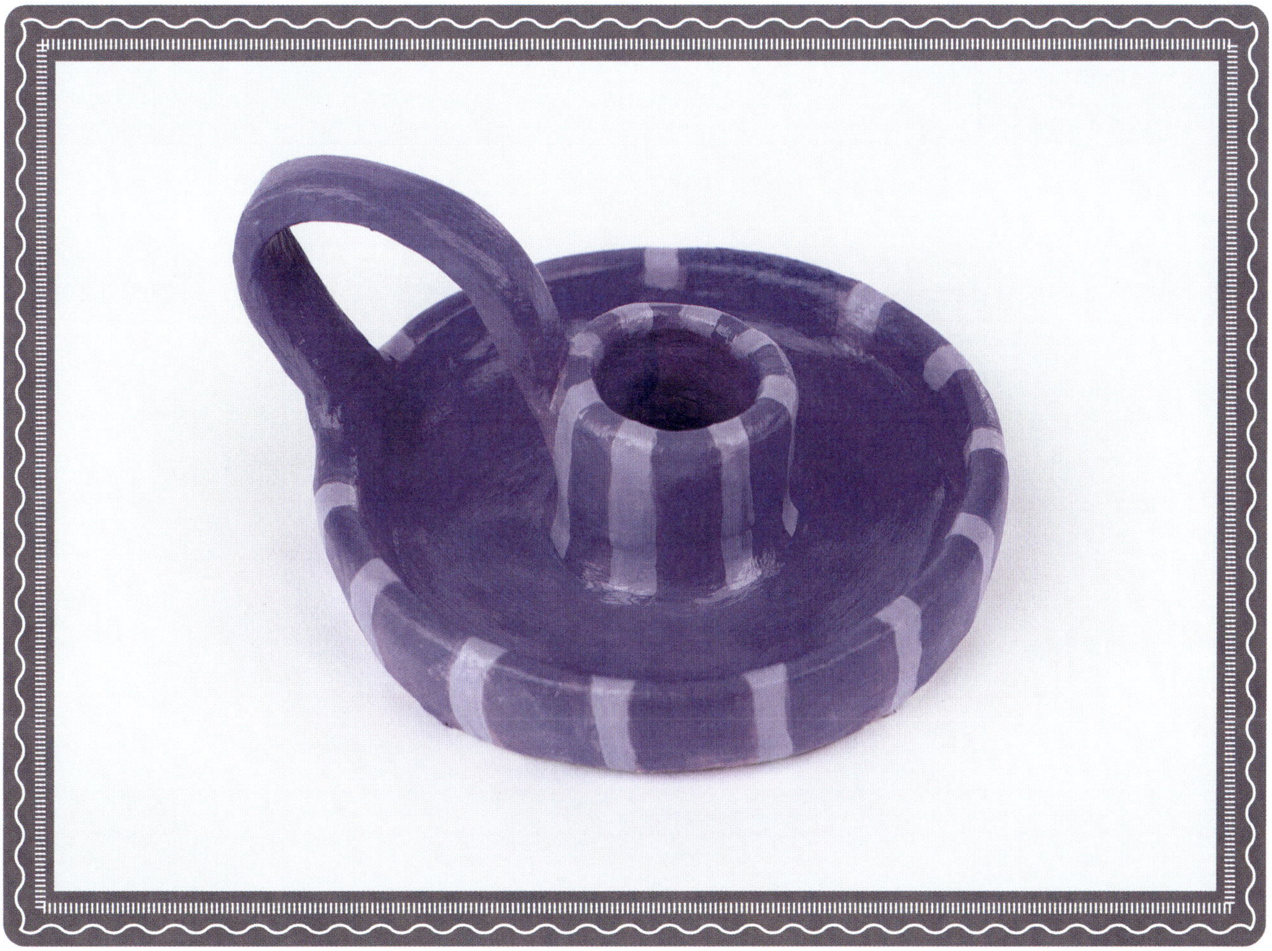

Incense Holder

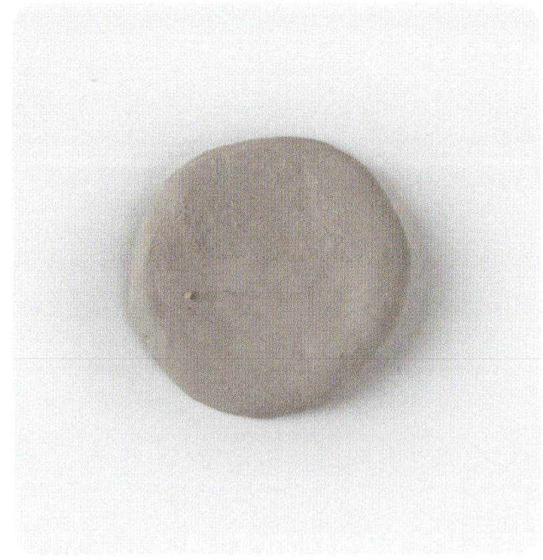

1. Roll out and flatten a ball to create your base.

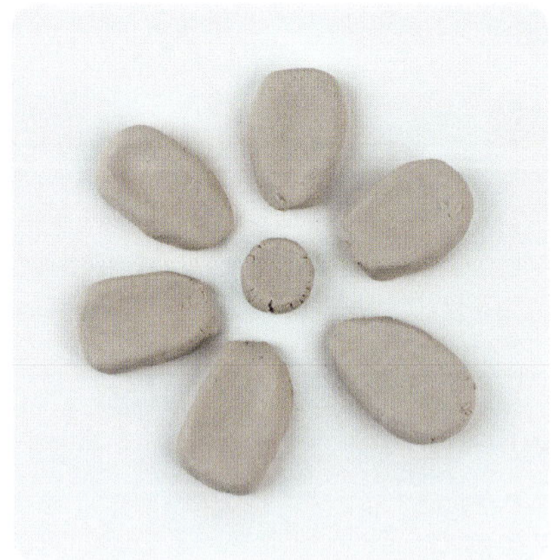

2. Sculpt 6 flat petal shapes and a smaller flattened ball.

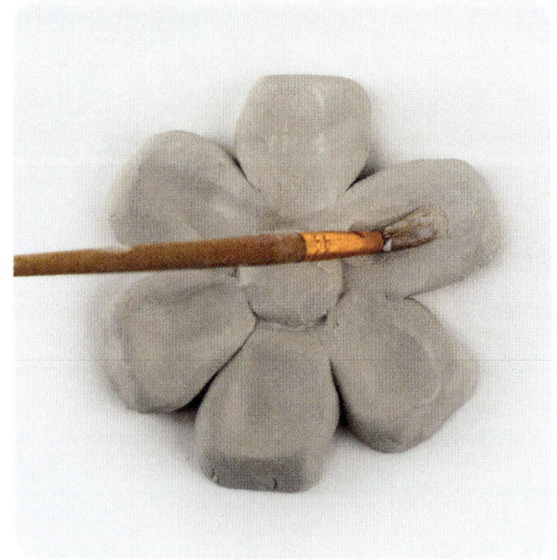

3. Connect the flattened ball to the center of your base and add the petals around the perimeter. Use a wet brush to create divots in each petal.

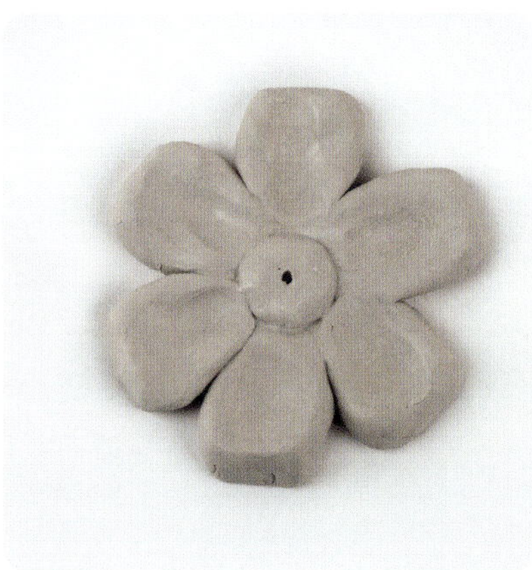

4. Use your needle tool to add a hole to the center of the flower.

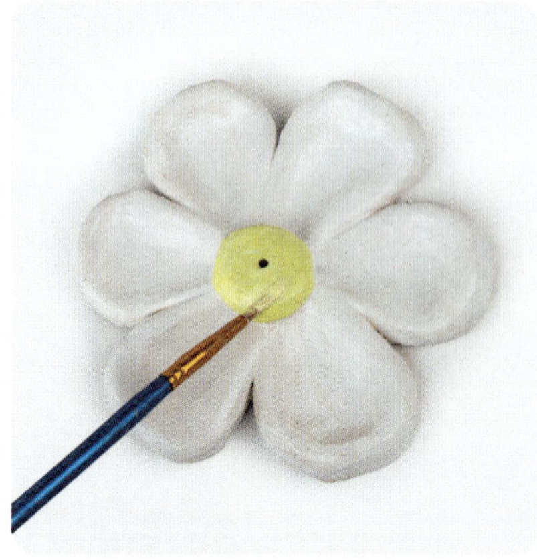

5. Once fully dry, paint the center yellow and the petals a different solid color. When the paint is dry, seal the piece with Mod Podge to finish.

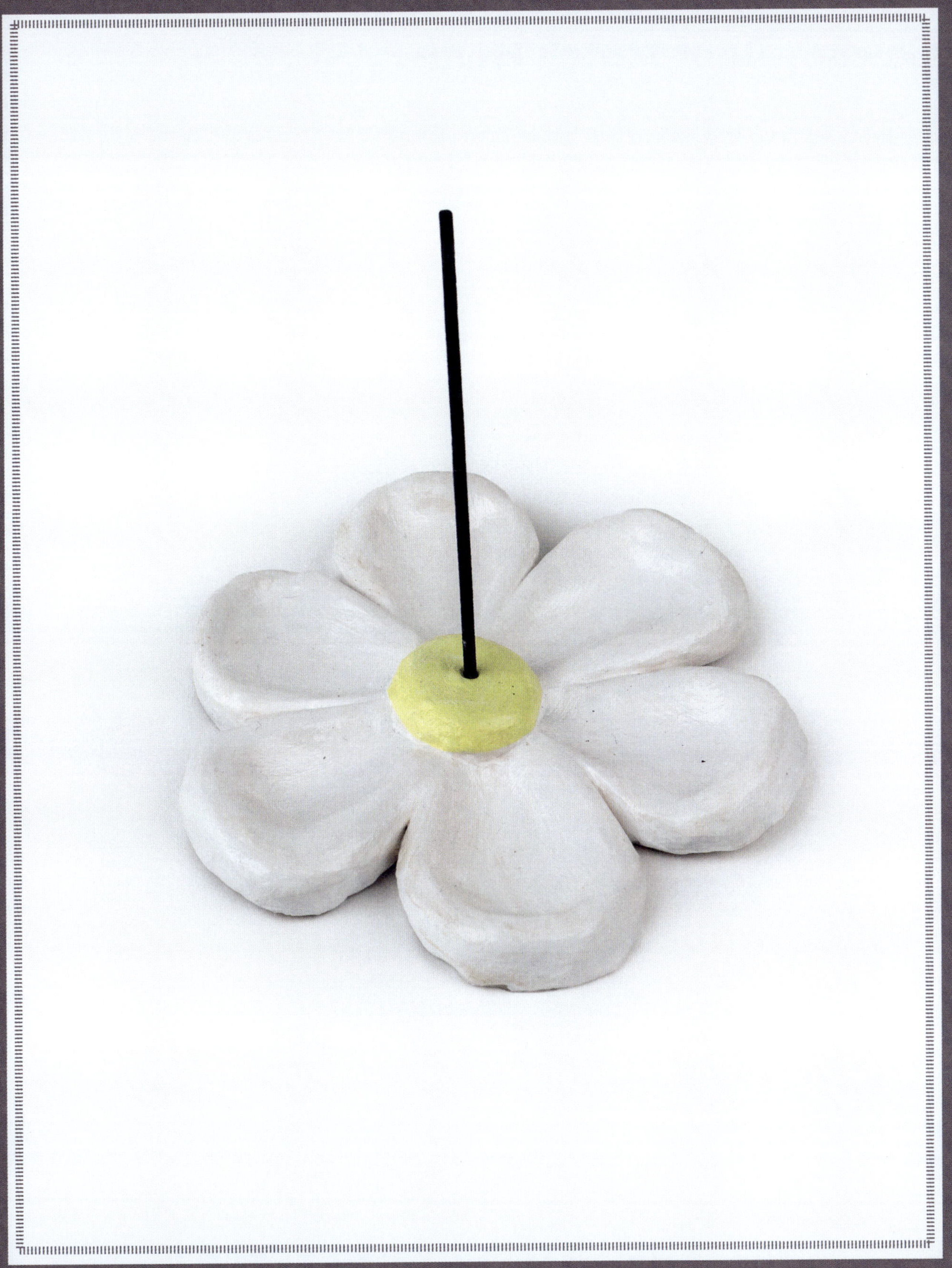

Cowboy Boot Match Holder

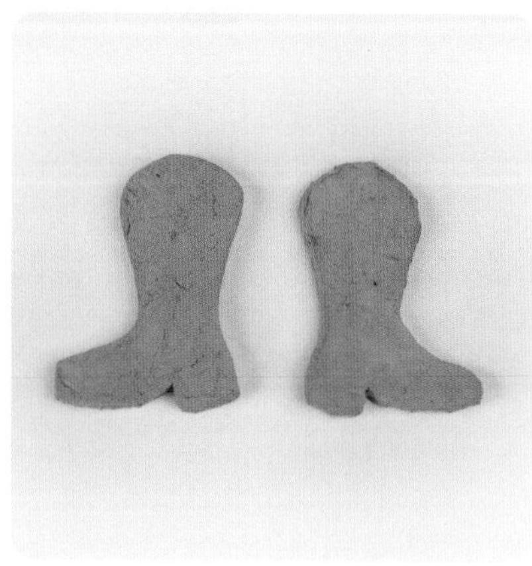

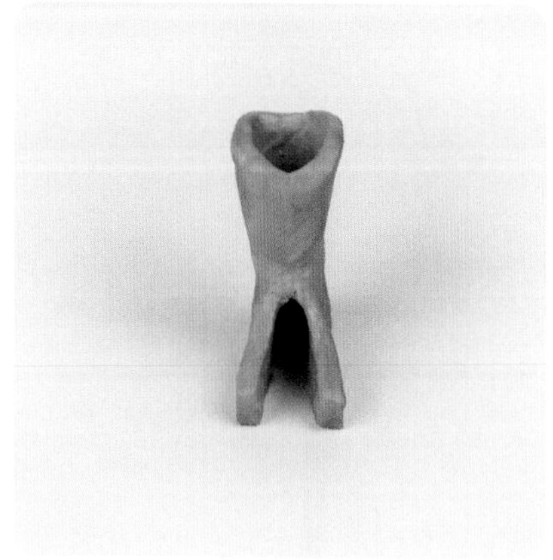

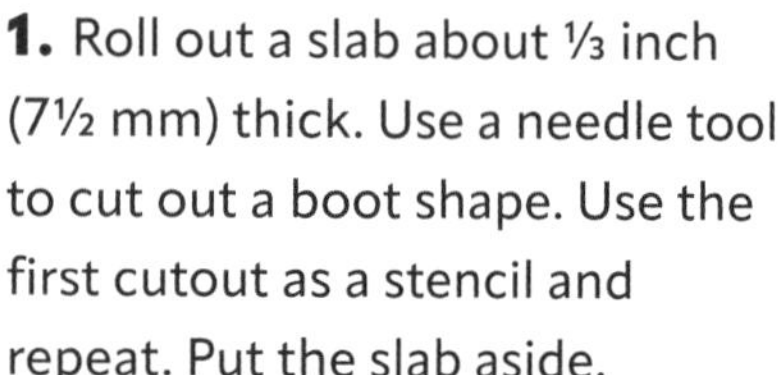

1. Roll out a slab about ⅓ inch (7½ mm) thick. Use a needle tool to cut out a boot shape. Use the first cutout as a stencil and repeat. Put the slab aside.

2. Attach the two pieces together all the way down the back of the boot. Then attach the two pieces at the front, stopping just before the foot of the boot curves forward. Insert your pointer finger into the top of the boot as you go to create a tube shape.

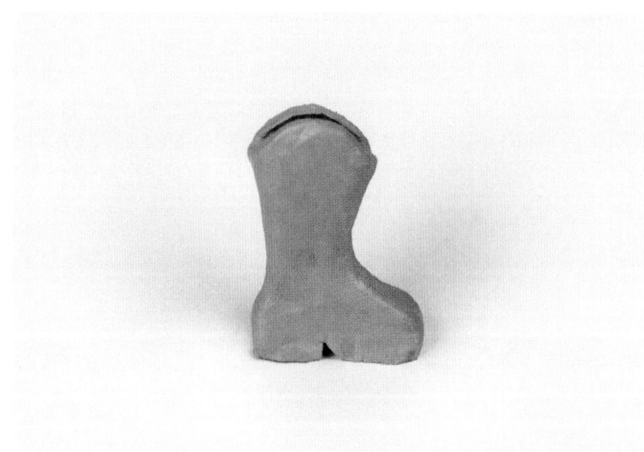

3. Cut out a strip from your slab the size of the gap at the top of the foot. Place the strip in the opening then connect and smooth it while maintaining the slope and squared tip of the boot. Cut out another piece from your slab the length of the bottom of the boot, using the sole of the boot as a stencil. Attach to the bottom and smooth together. Use your needle tool to cut a small triangle out of the bottom to separate the heel from the toe section.

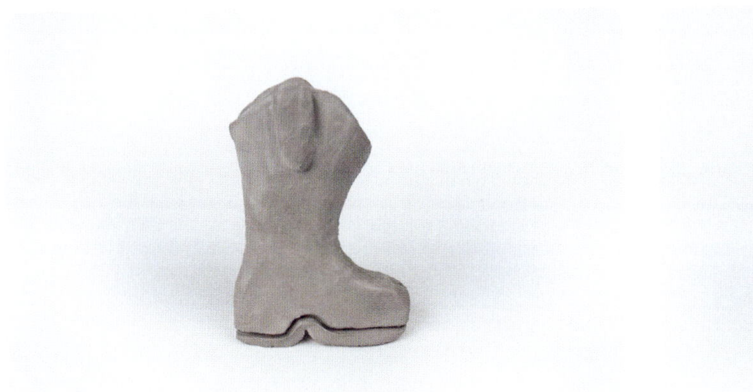

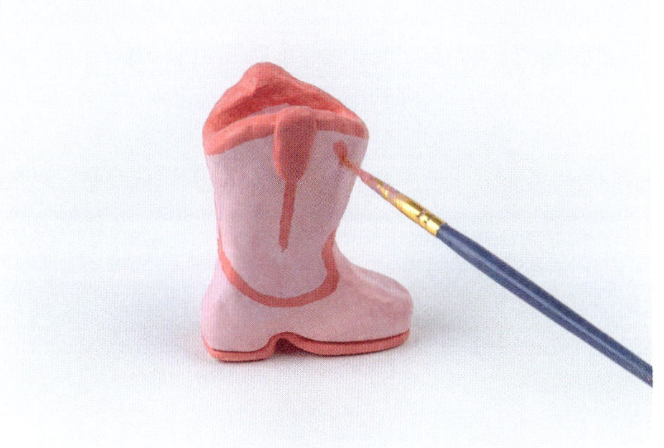

4. Add a small square to the bottom of the heel of the boot to slightly elevate it. Use a needle tool to define the bottom of the boot, following the shape of the heel and divot in the middle. Sculpt 2 small bits of clay into long ovals and attach them to either side for the boot pulls. Continue to pull and press the sides and bottom of the boot until you achieve your desired shape

5. Once fully dry, paint in whatever way you like. When the paint is dry, seal the piece with Mod Podge to finish.

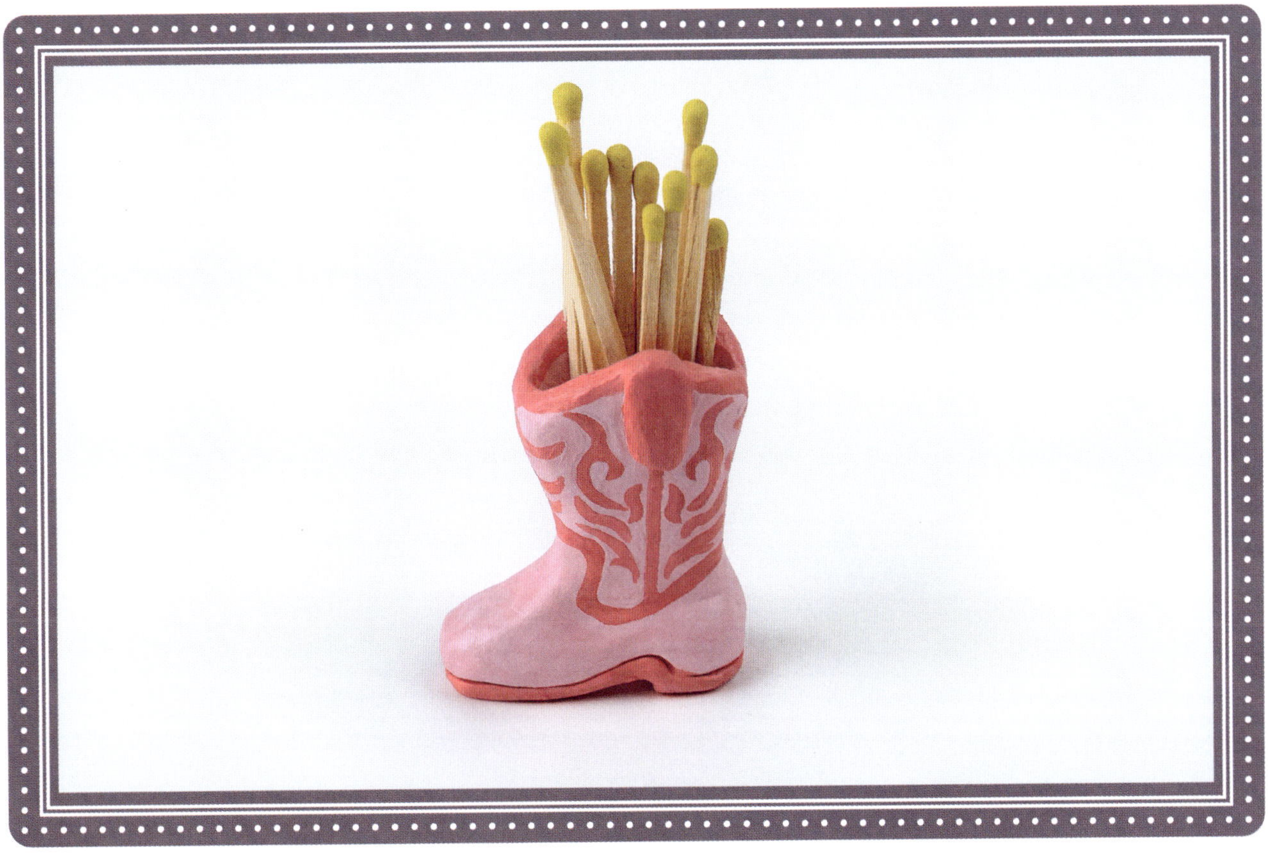

Earring Holder

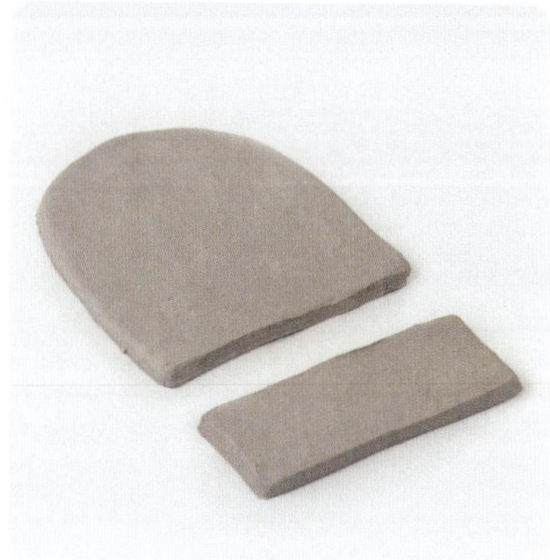

1. Roll out a slab. Cut out a rectangle with a rounded top. Cut out another shorter rectangle of the same width as the bottom of your first.

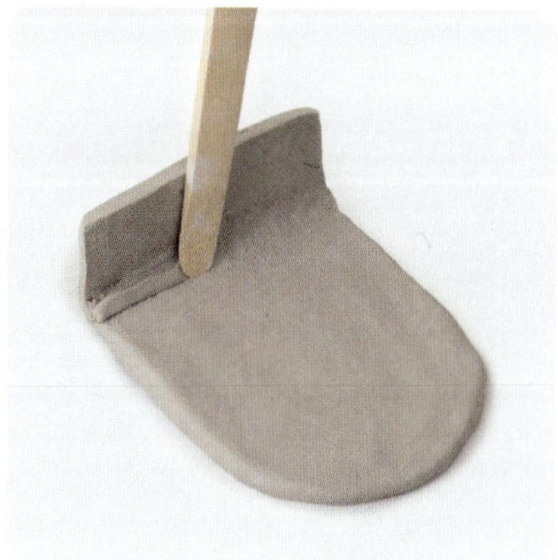

2. Score and slip the 2 pieces (see page 15) to create a 90-degree angle, pressing them together at the angle where they meet. Add a thin coil along the joint for strength. Smooth it out to blend the pieces. Round the corners of the smaller rectangle (now the base of the stand) to create a cohesive shape.

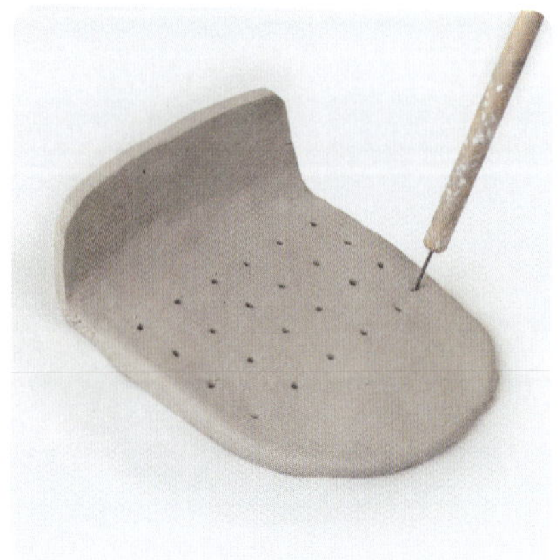

3. Lay your piece down on the longer, rounded side. Add your desired number of holes in a grid pattern using your needle tool. Rotate your needle tool once to widen each hole.

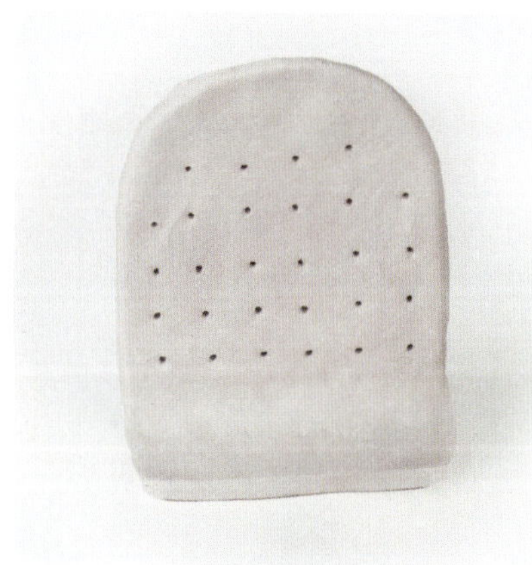

4. Allow the piece to fully dry face down. Rest the upright side (the base) against a solid object to keep it in place.

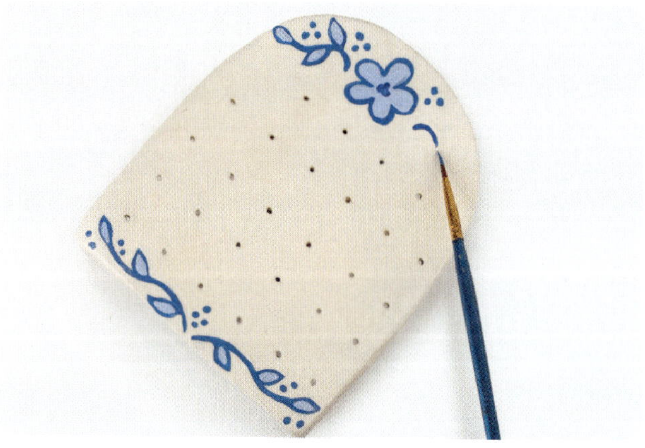

5. Once dry, smooth as needed, then paint the whole piece a background color and add a design of your choice to the front. When the paint is dry, seal the piece with Mod Podge to finish.

TIP!

If the paint blocks up the holes, use a needle tool to poke through the holes to clear them.

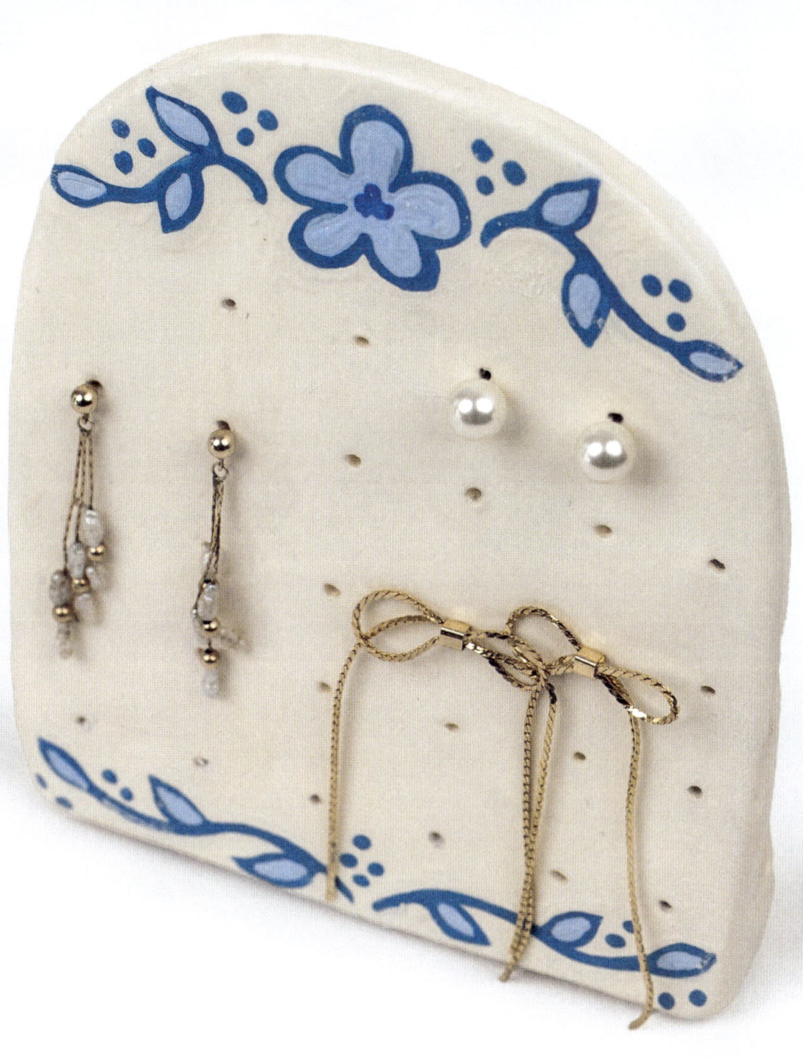

Pig Glasses Holder

1. Roll out a slab ½ inch (1 cm) thick. Use a needle tool to cut out a rounded rectangle large enough to hold a pair of glasses.

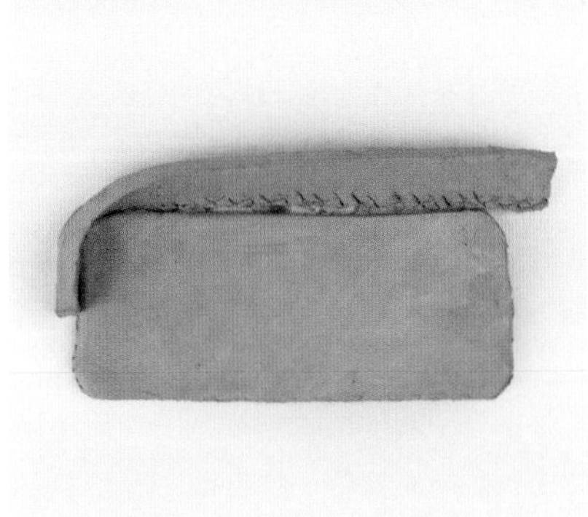

2. Cut multiple strips 1 inch (2½ cm) thick and long enough to wrap around the perimeter of the rectangle base. Connect them together along the base.

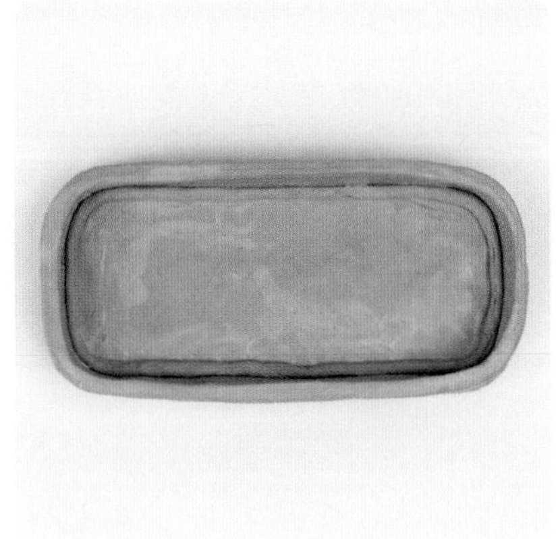

3. Roll out a thin coil and wrap it along the inside edge of the piece. Blend the coil into the sides and base of the piece.

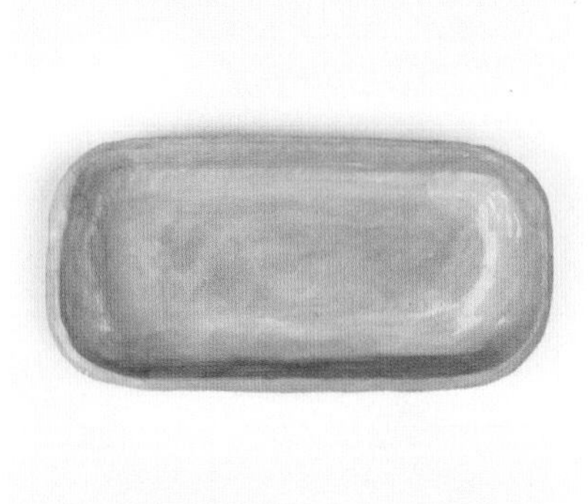

4. Use your thumb and pointer finger to gently curve the sides outward.

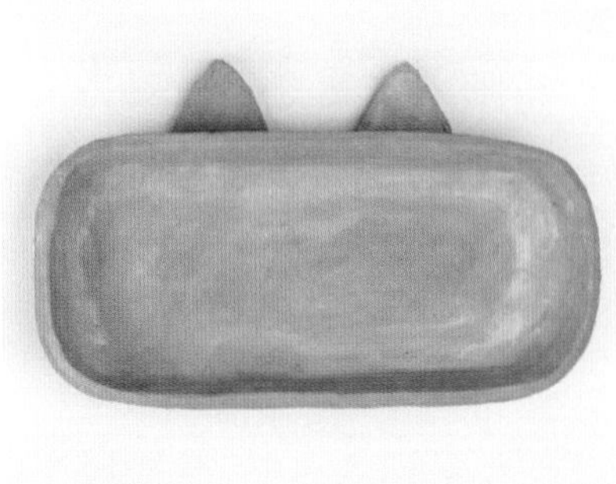

5. For ears, cut out two triangles from the slab and connect them to the top of the piece.

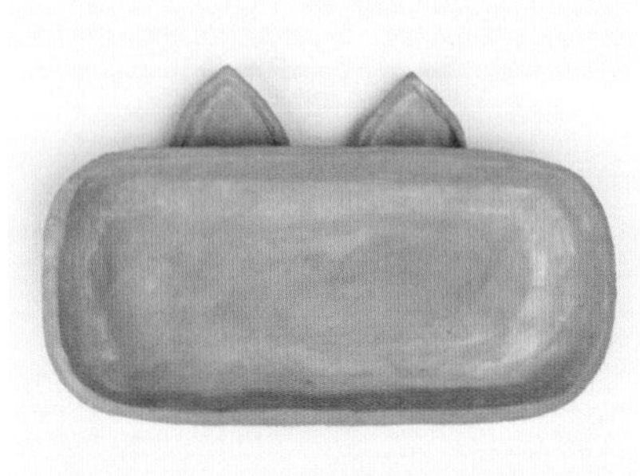

6. Roll out a slightly thinner coil and place it along the perimeter of the ears. Blend and smooth. Place your glasses in the tray to check the placement of the eyes and nose before you attach them.

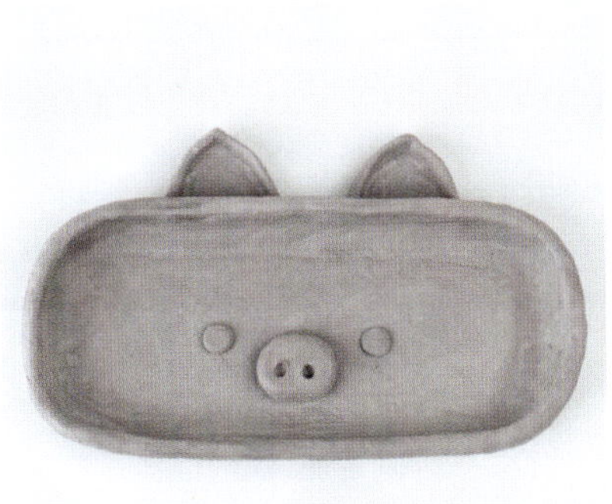

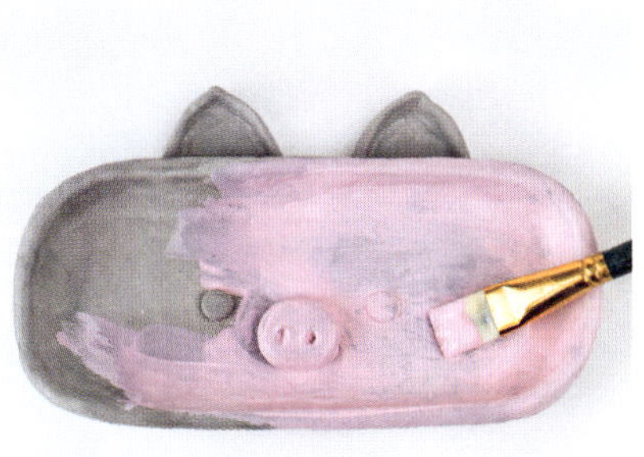

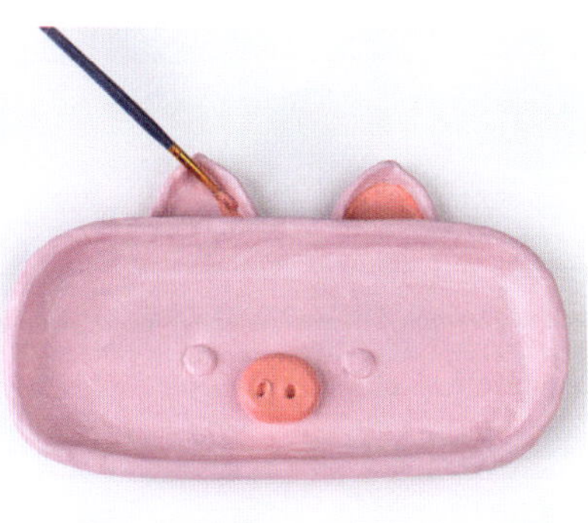

7. For the nose, flatten a small ball of clay and connect it to the lower center of the piece. Use a needle tool to make two nostrils. Flatten and attach two smaller balls of clay for eyes.

8. Once fully dry, paint the entire piece a base color like light pink.

9. Once dry, paint the nose and the insides of the ears dark pink, and add dark pink blush spots to the cheeks. Paint the eyes black. When the paint is dry, seal the piece with Mod Podge to finish.

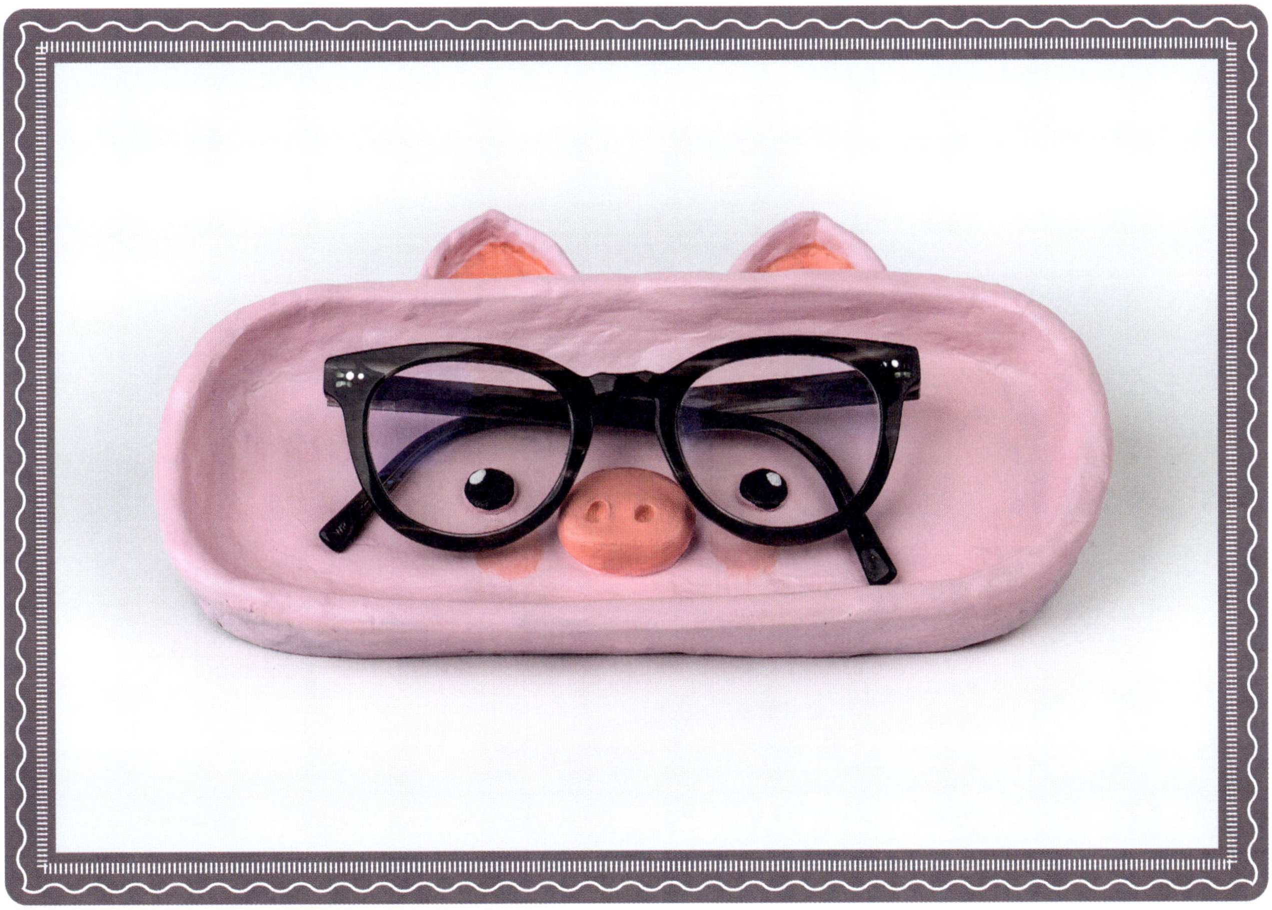

Paint Palette

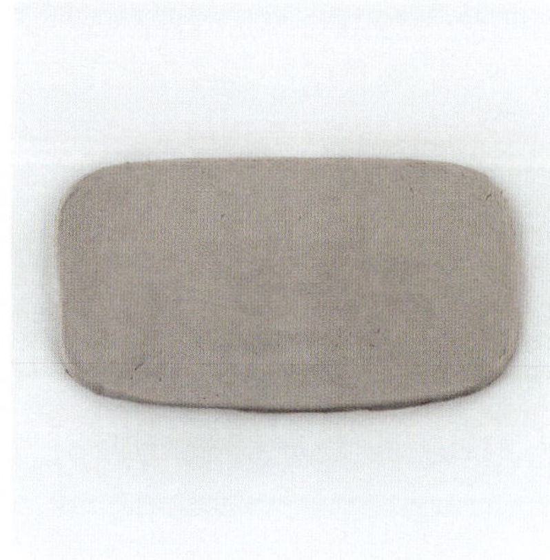

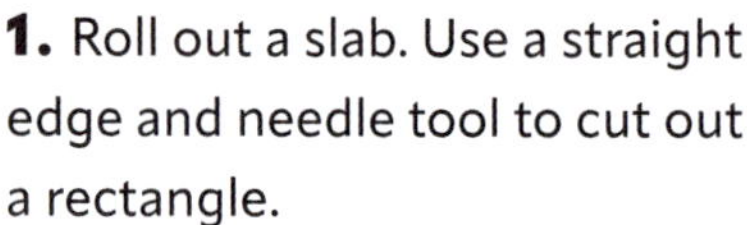

1. Roll out a slab. Use a straight edge and needle tool to cut out a rectangle.

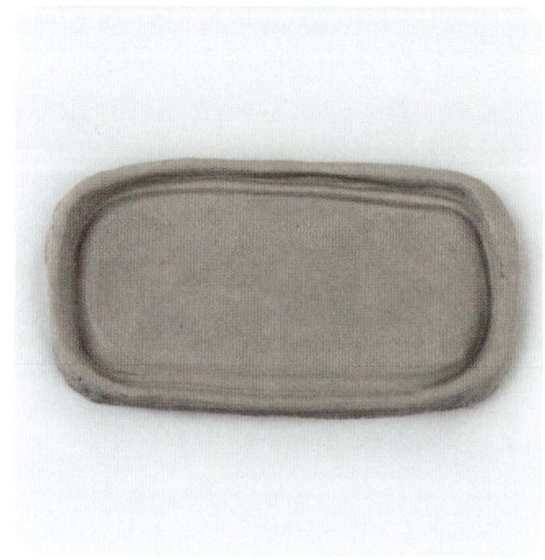

2. Roll out a coil and place it along the perimeter of the rectangle to create a rim. Smooth the coil into the base and use the back of a paintbrush to create a divot around the inside edge where the rim meets the base.

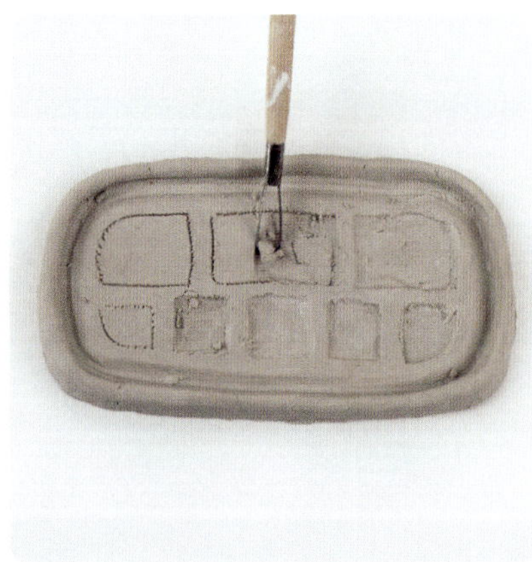

3. Allow the clay to partially harden and then mark and carve out the wells of the palette—be careful not to carve all the way through the base!

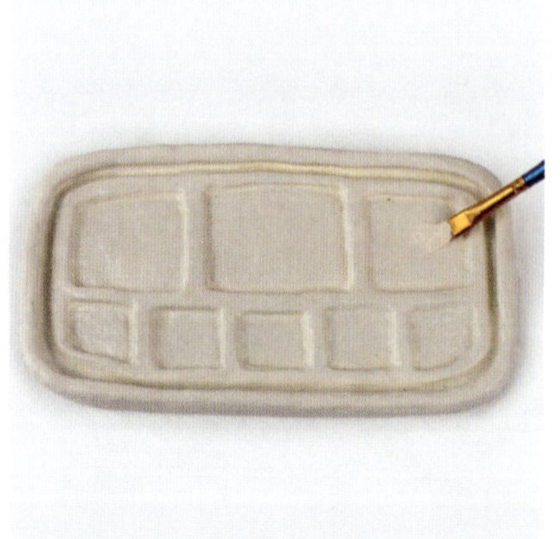

4. Once the piece is dry, clean up the edges of the wells and paint the whole thing a solid neutral color. When the paint is dry, seal the piece with Mod Podge—including the back side—to finish.

TIP!

You can use the palette with all paint types. Make sure to coat the full piece with Mod Podge to enable easy cleaning.

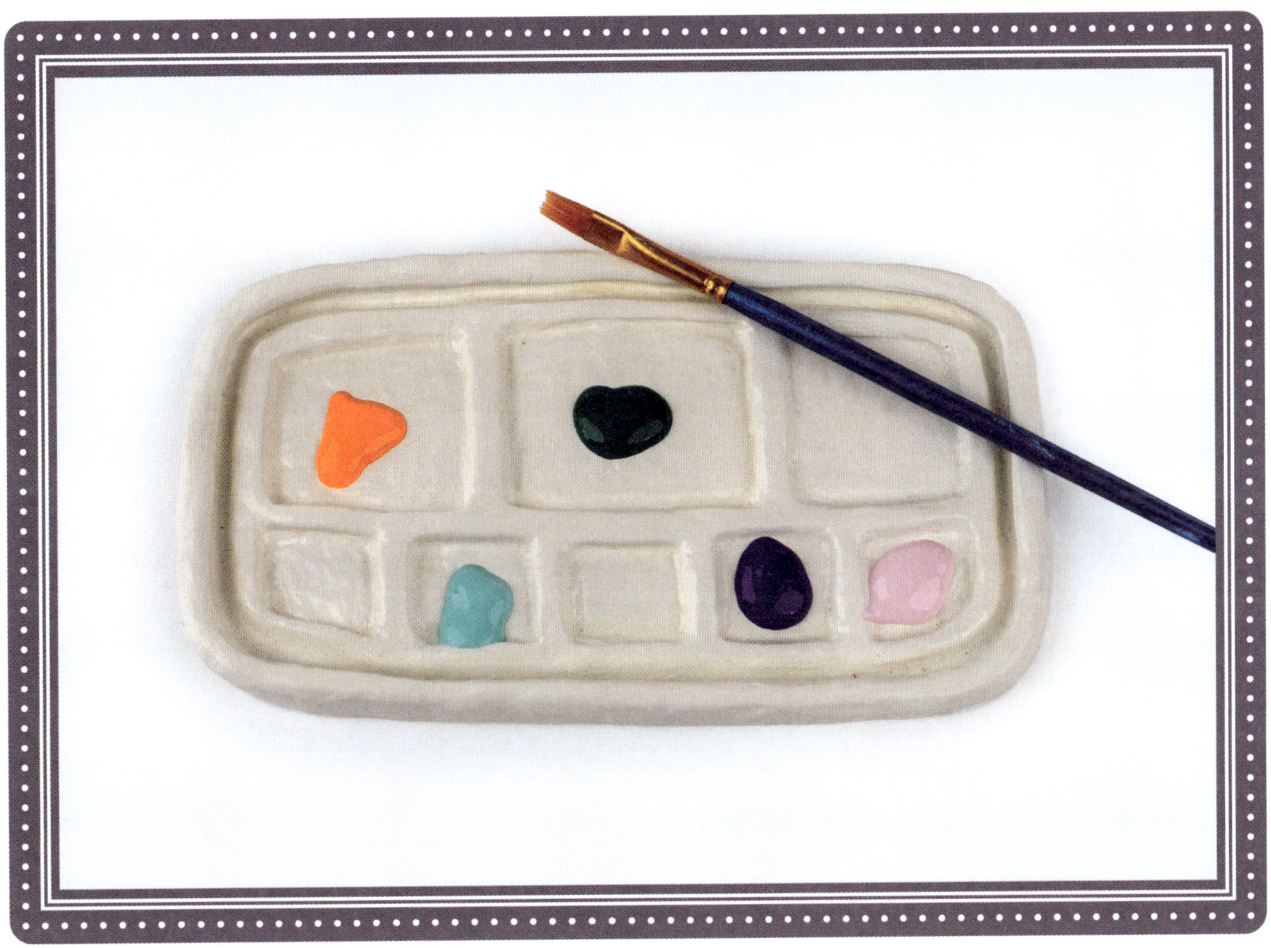

Paintbrush Holder

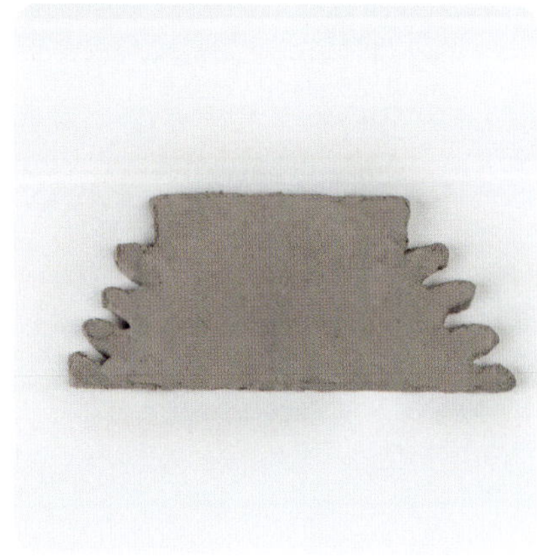

1. Roll out a slab ½ inch (1 cm) thick. Use your needle tool to cut out your base shape as pictured.

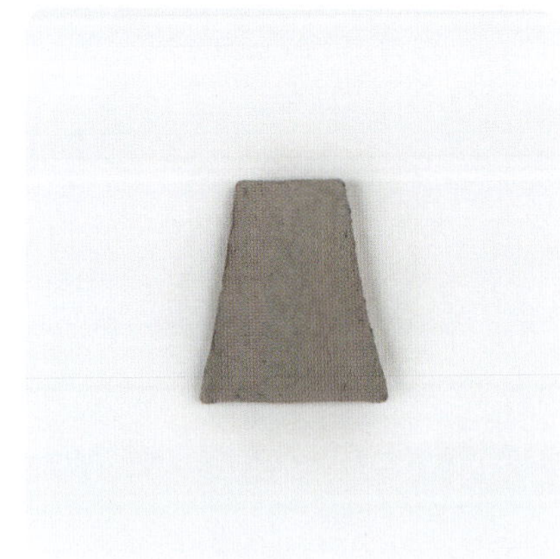

2. Cut out a piece of the slab in the shape of a trapezoid the same height as the first shape.

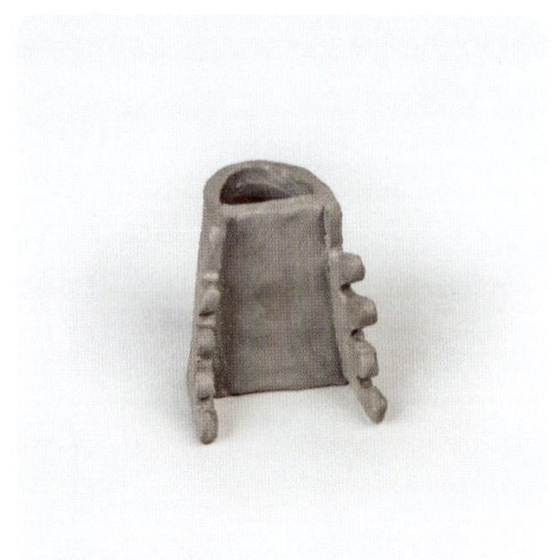

3. Gently curve the first piece toward yourself. Connect the second piece inside the first. Cut out a half circle the size of the bottom of the piece. Attach and smooth it to the base.

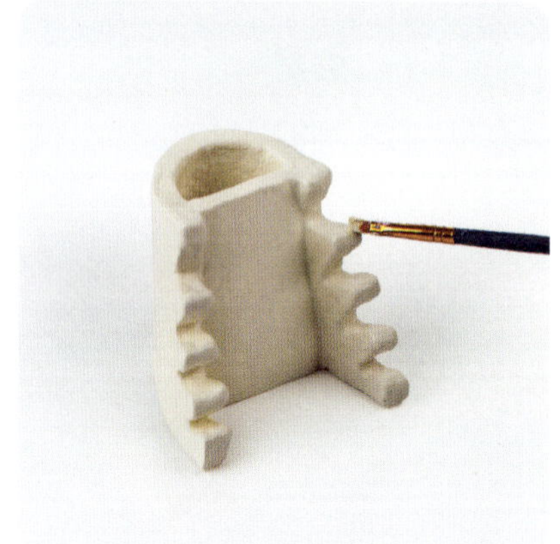

4. Once fully dry, paint the piece a base color and add whatever decoration you wish. When the paint is dry, seal the piece with Mod Podge to finish.

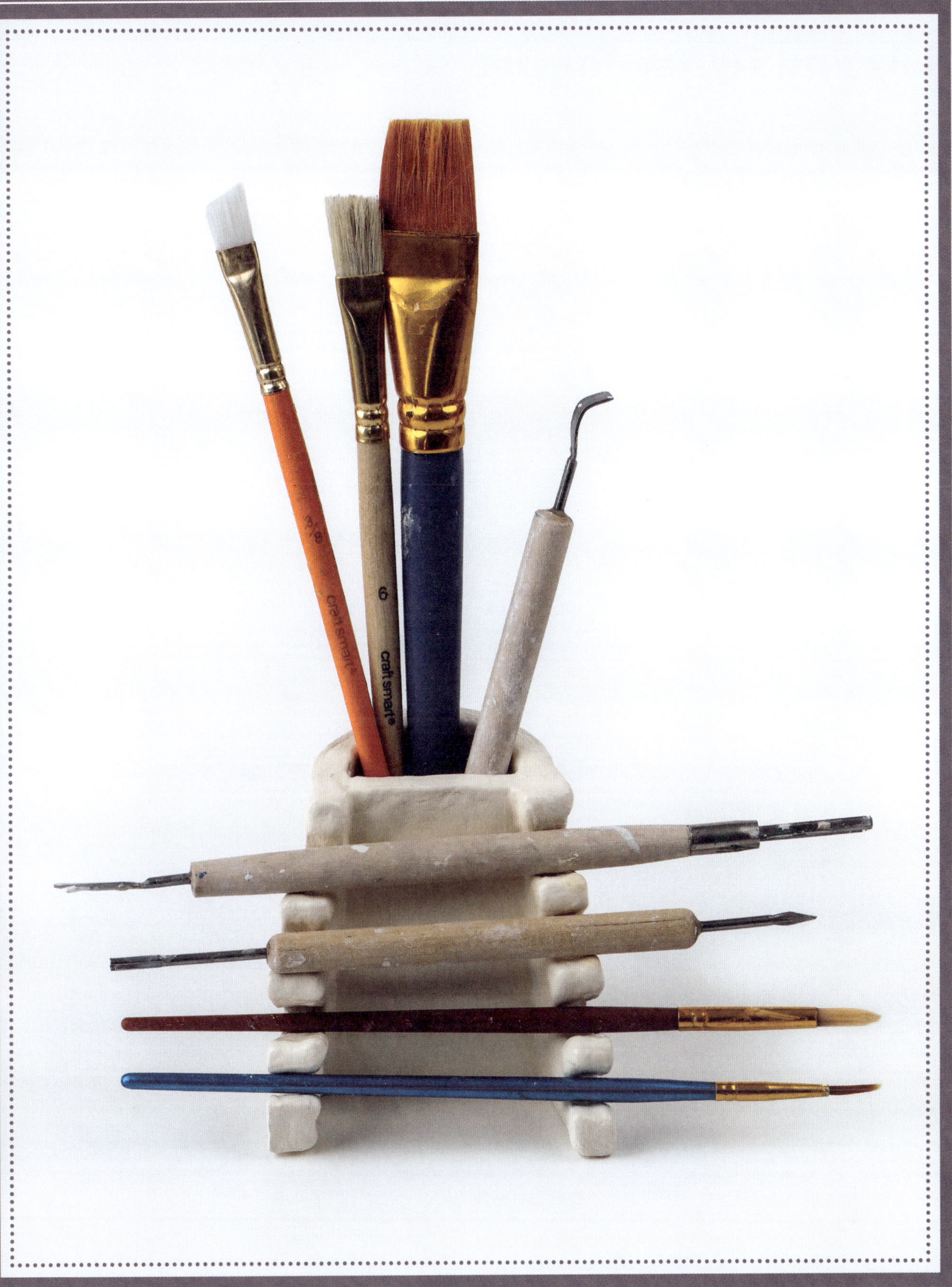
craft smart
6
craft smart®

Lily Pad Tic-Tac-Toe Set

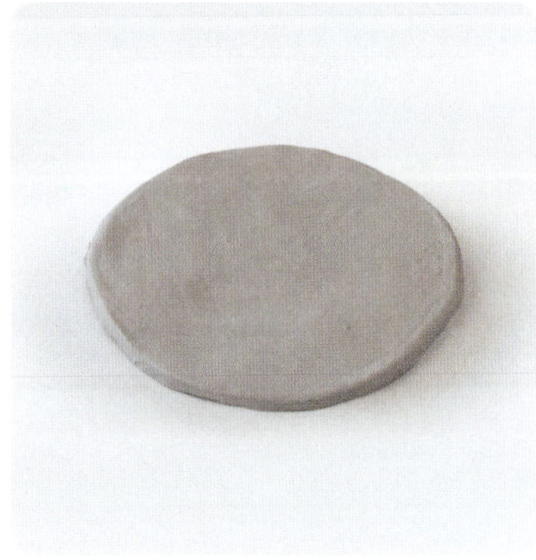

1. Roll out a slab about ¼ inch (6 mm) thick. Place a bowl upside down on the slab and use a needle tool to trace and cut out a circle.

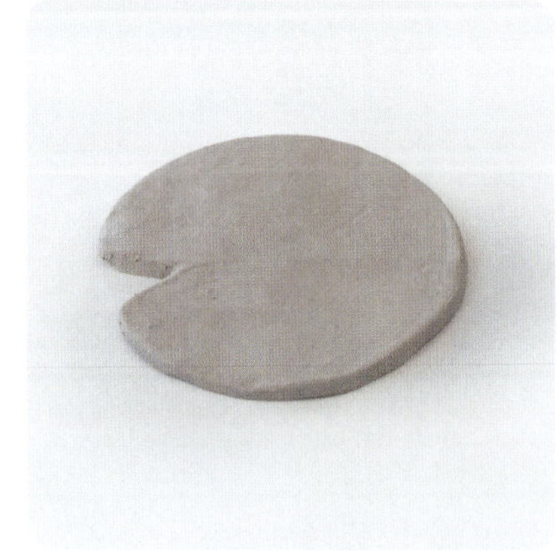

2. Cut a small triangle out of the side of the circle.

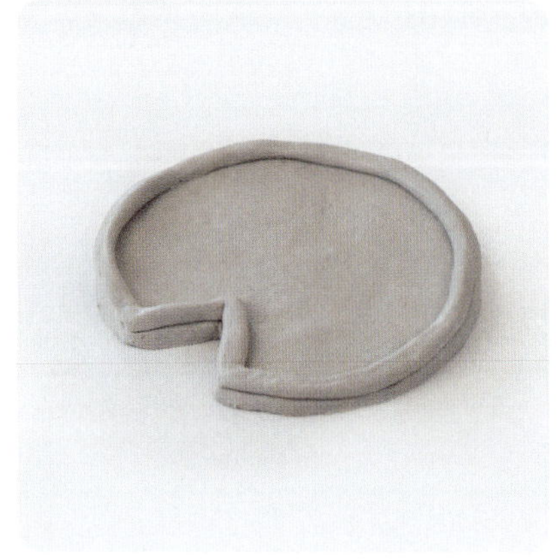

3. Roll out a thin coil and place it around the outer edge of your lily pad to form a rim.

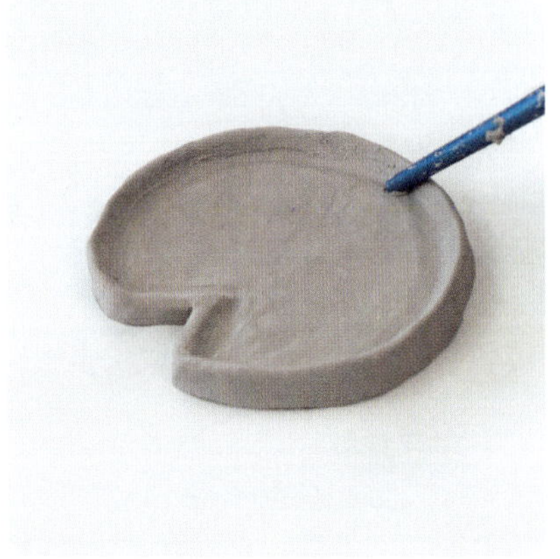

4. Add a bit of water and smooth the rim into the lily pad. Pinch the rim between your pointer finger and thumb to create a pointed edge. Run the back of a paintbrush around the inner perimeter to create a divot on the inside of the rim. Smooth the edges.

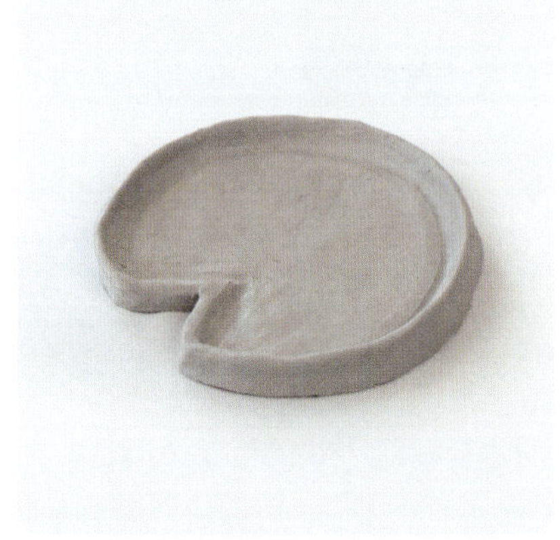

5. Use a curved carving tool to shape and round the outer edge of the lily pad by carving away clay from underneath the edge, working all the way around the pad. As you carve, smooth the area to create a rounded transition from the top to the base.

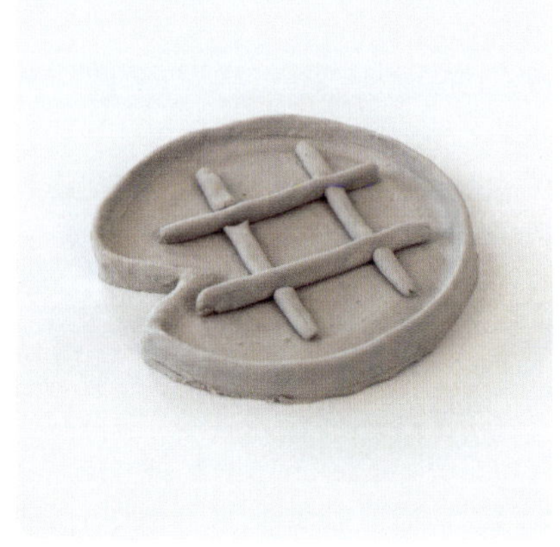

6. Roll out a coil the same thickness of the rim and then cut into 2 long and 6 short segments. Place pieces in a grid shape in the center of the lily pad.

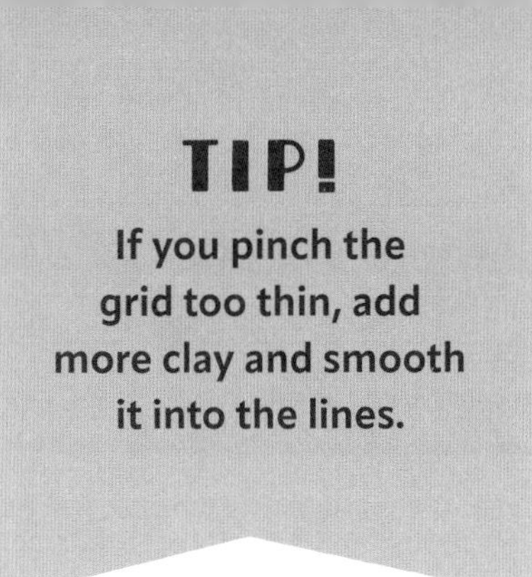

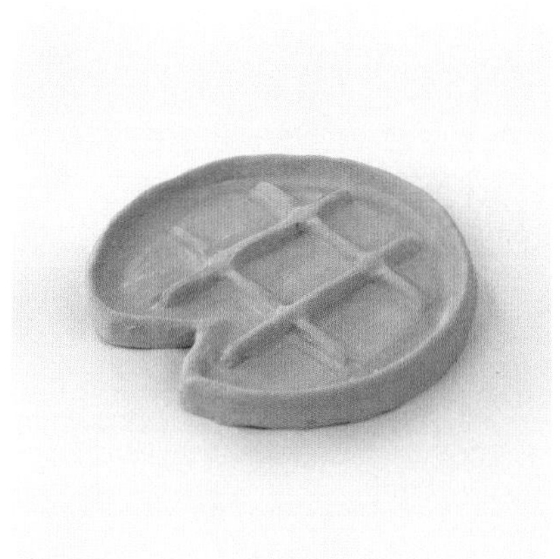

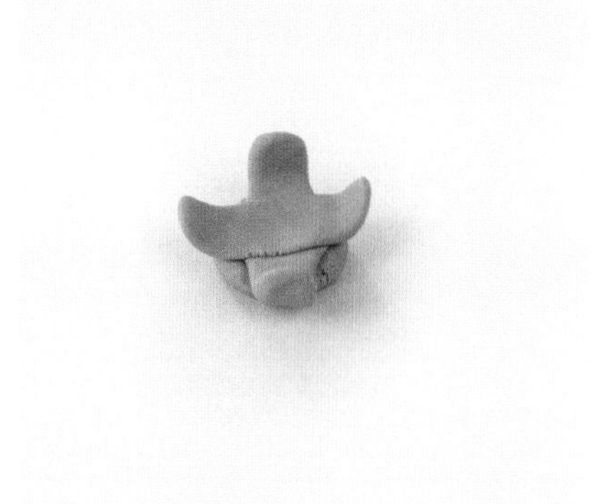

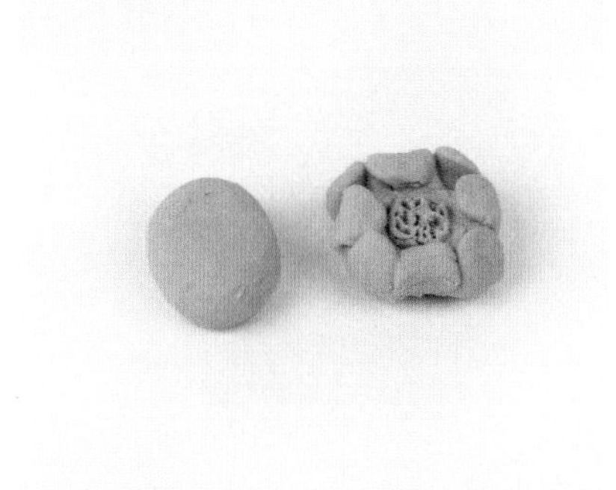

7. Smooth the coils into the base of the lily pad. Pinch the tips of the grid with your pointer finger and thumb to create a point that mimics the edge of the lily pad.

8. To sculpt the lotus flower–shaped playing pieces, flatten out a small ball for the base. Roll out and flatten 2 short coils, then place in an X shape on top of base. Repeat with 2 more coils layered over the first X to fill in the gaps and create 8 total petals.

9. Add a bit of clay to the center of the flowers and use your needle tool to add texture to it. Fold the petals inward. Repeat steps 8 to 9 for each flower playing piece. To create each ladybug playing piece, flatten a small oval.

Lily Pad Tic-Tac-Toe Set

Continued

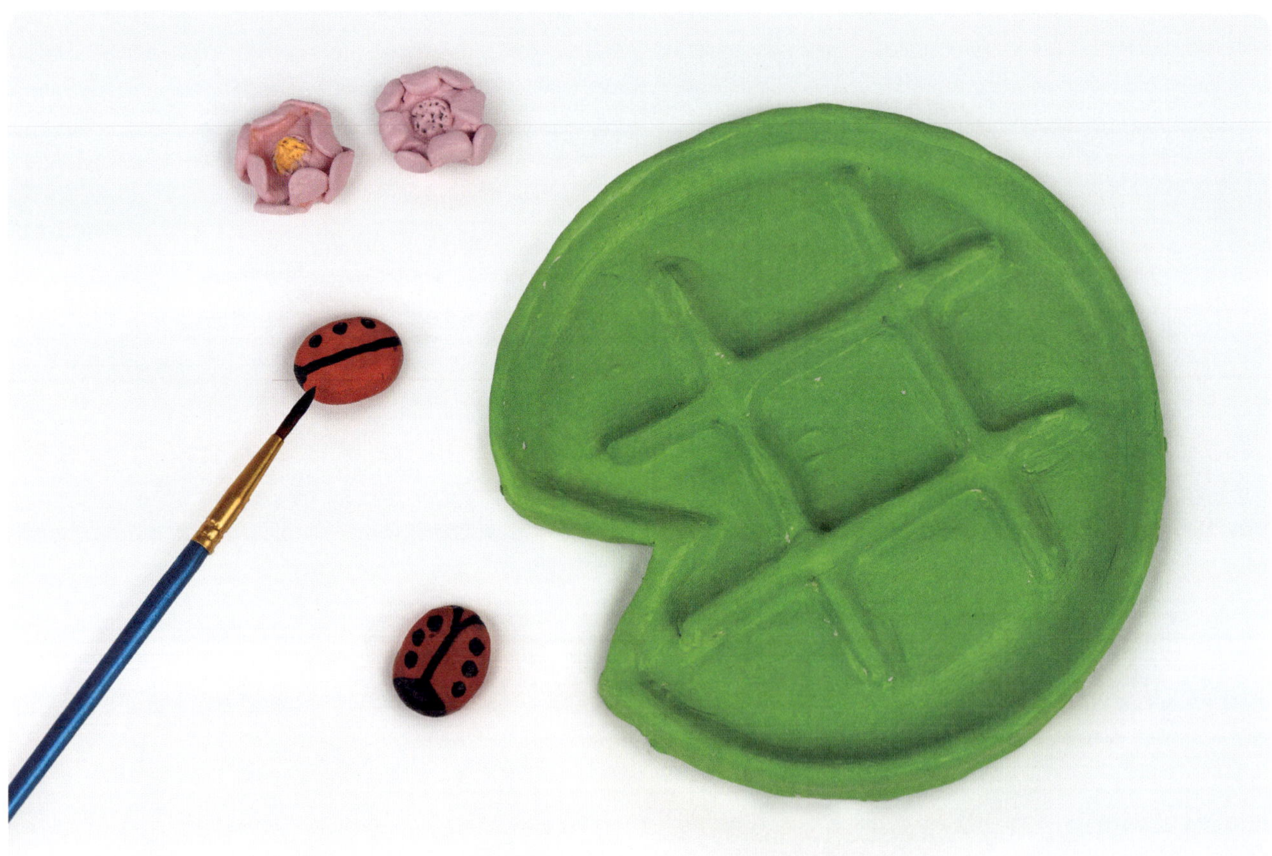

10. Once all pieces are dry, clean up the edges and the grid. Paint the lily pad green, the ladybugs red and black, and the flowers a different color, such as pink. When the paint is dry, seal with Mod Podge to finish.

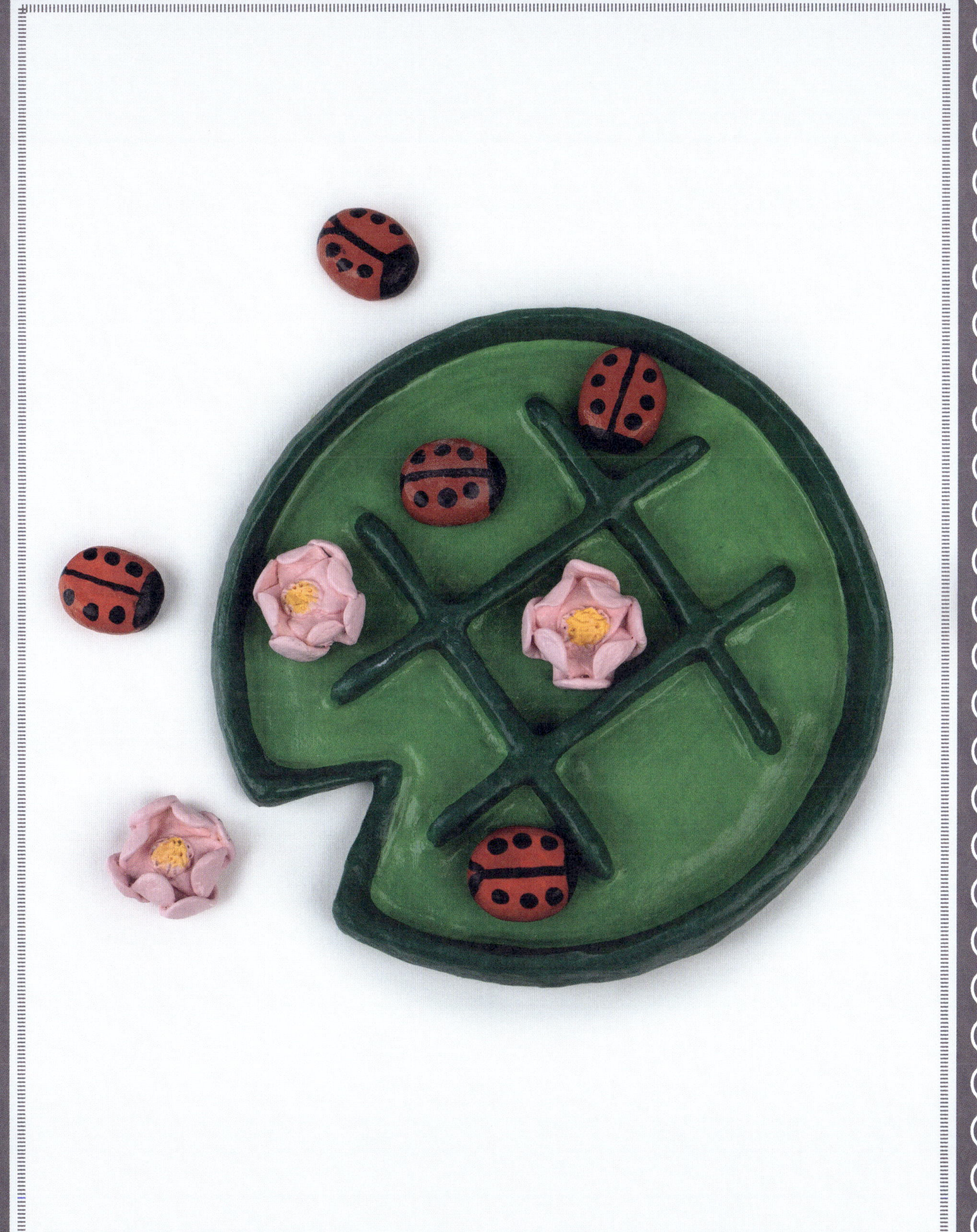

Holiday Ornaments

1. Roll out a slab. Cut out the shapes of your choice—cookie cutters are a great tool here!

2. After sculpting and cleaning up your design, use a needle tool to create a hole at the top of your ornament. Gently rotate the point to widen the hole.

3. Let the pieces dry, then paint. When the paint is dry, seal with Mod Podge. Thread a ribbon or string through the hole to finish.

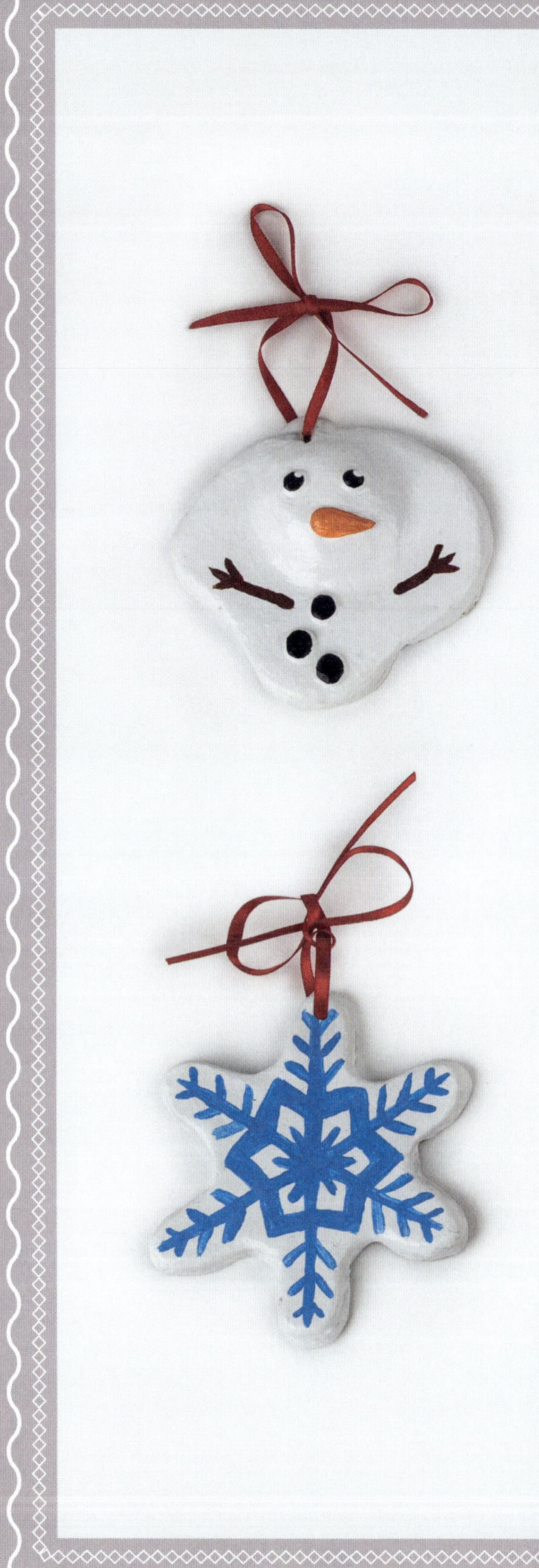

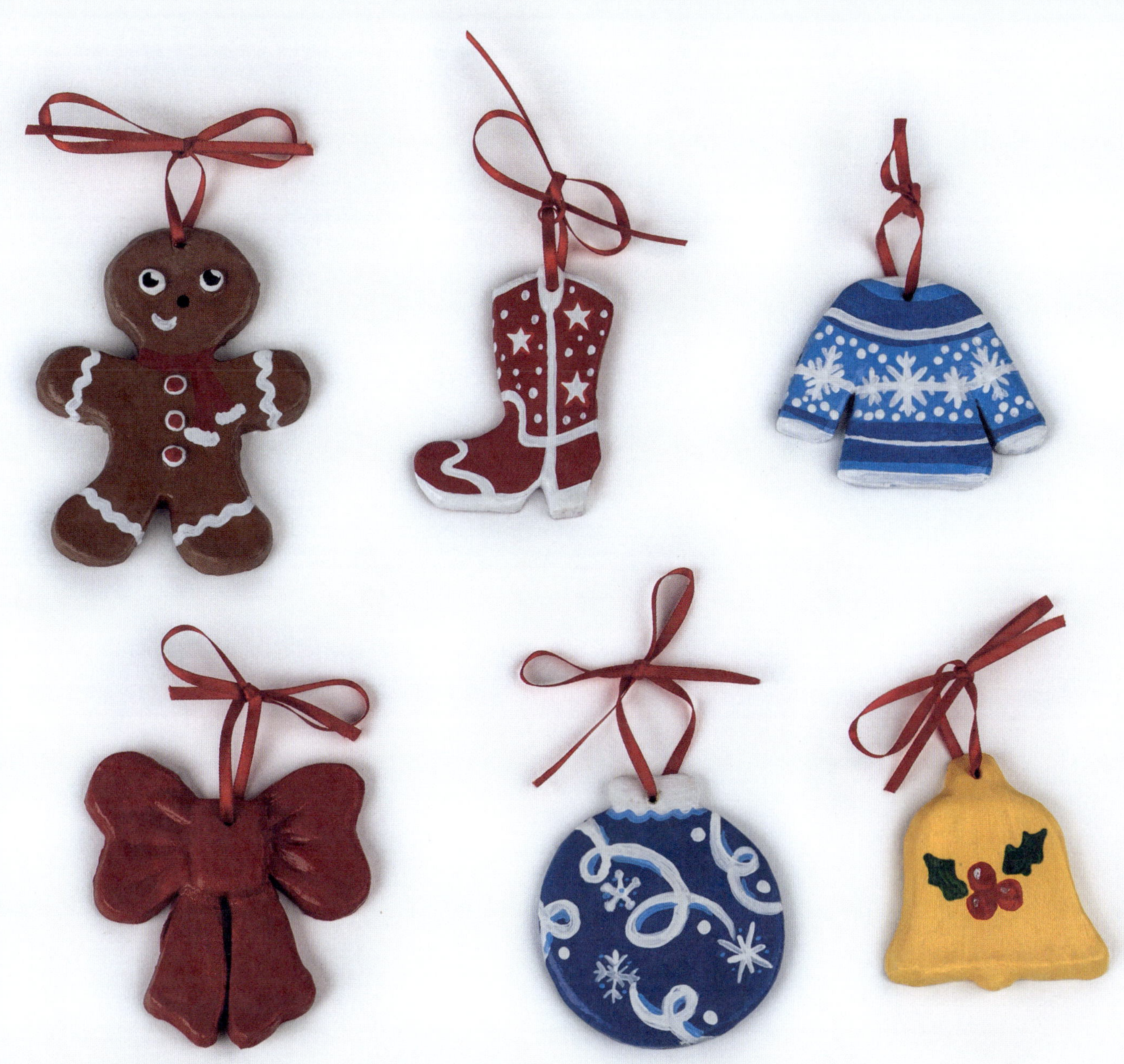

Charms

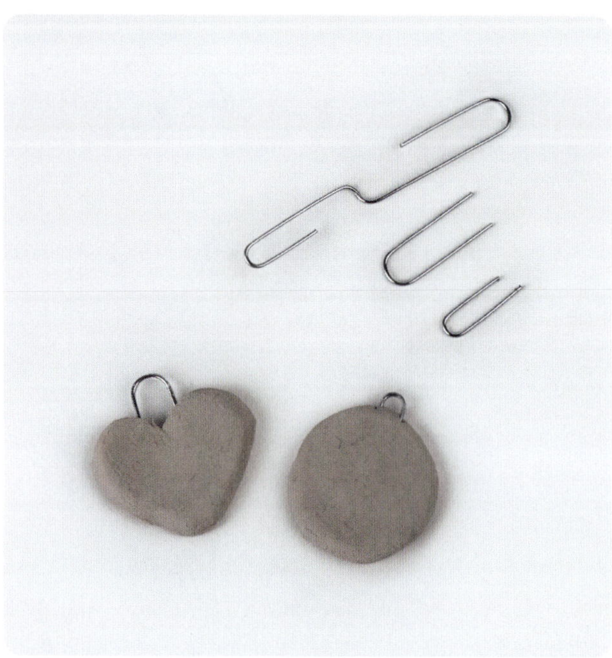

1. Cut small shapes out of a thin slab. Use a wet brush or sponge to smooth the edges.

2. Use wire cutters or strong scissors to cut off the rounded ends of paper clips. While the clay is still wet, insert the loop of wire into the clay at the top of the charm, making sure it isn't poking out the back. ←

3. Allow to dry fully, then paint to your liking. When the paint is dry, seal the pieces with Mod Podge to finish. ↓

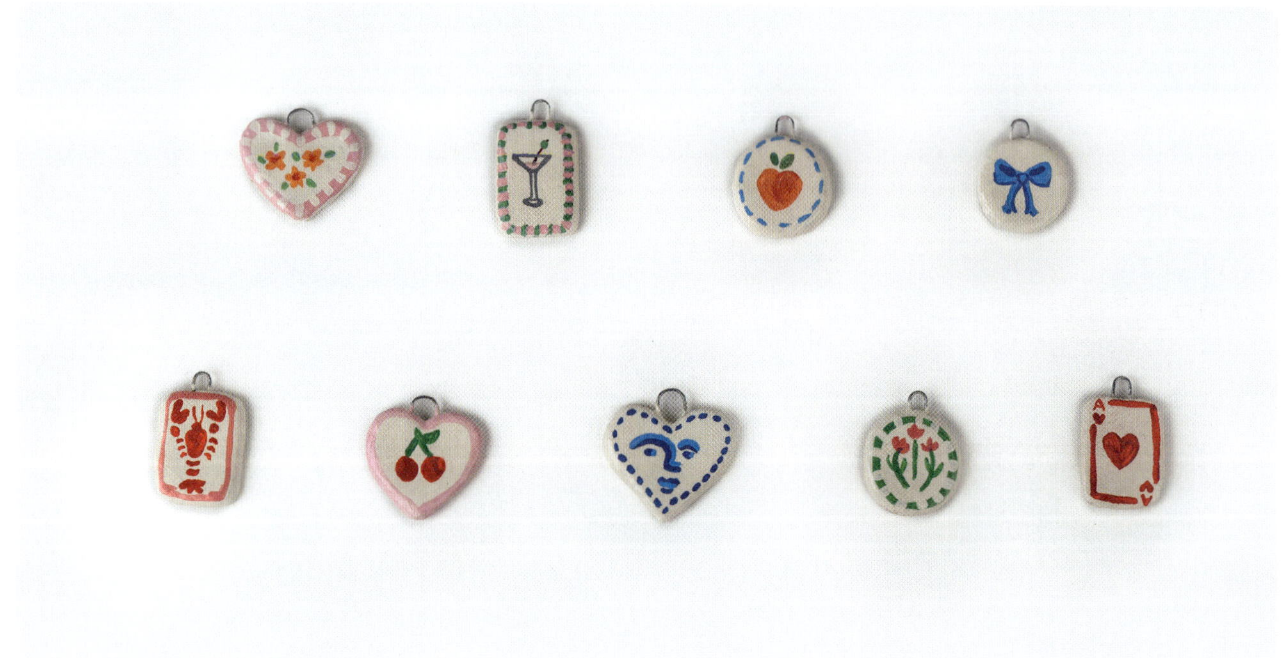

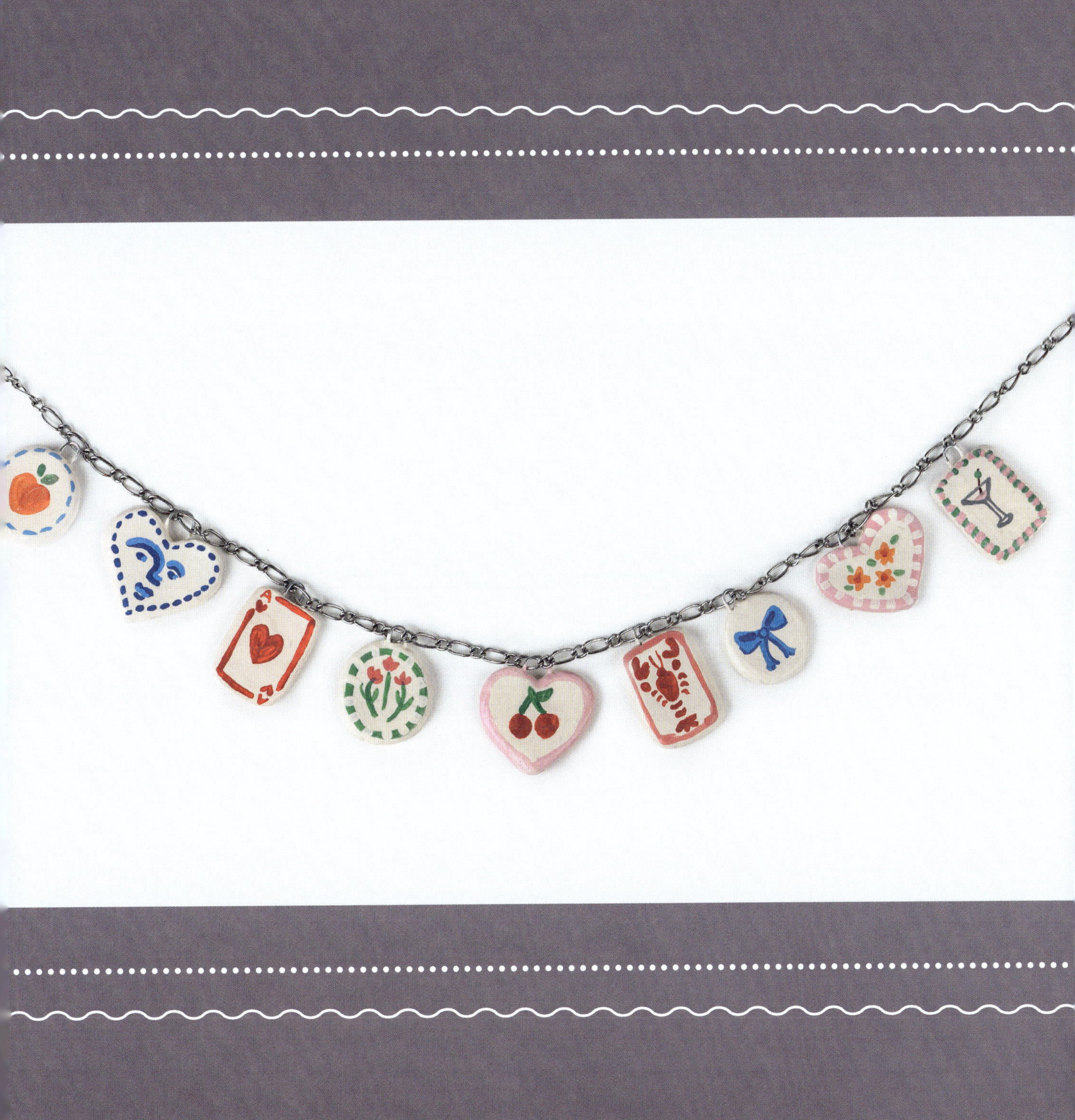

Buttons

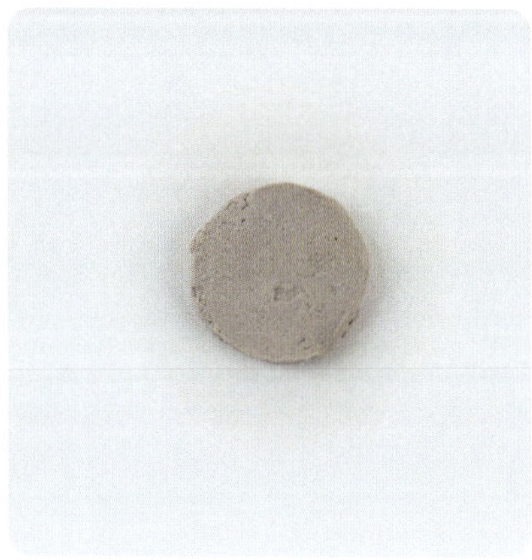

1. Roll out a slab and cut out a small circle.

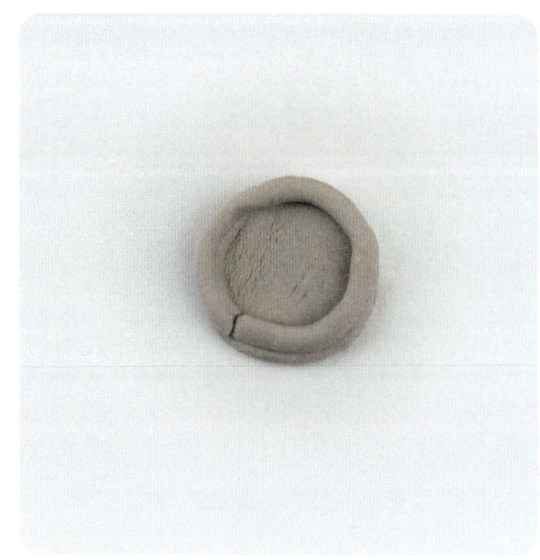

2. Roll out a thin coil and wrap it around the circle's perimeter.

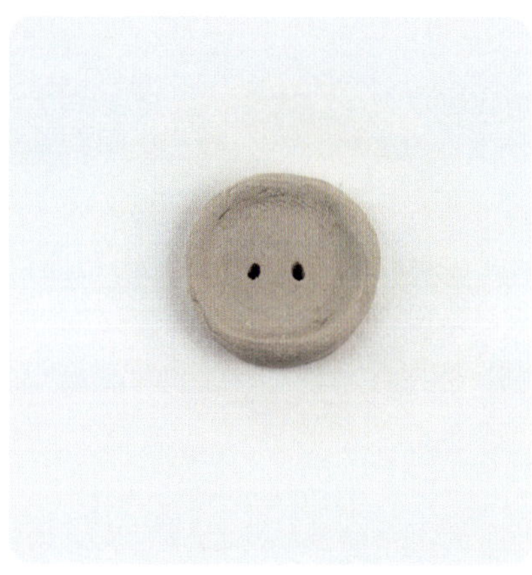

3. Smooth the coil into the base and use your needle tool to cut out holes in the center of the base.

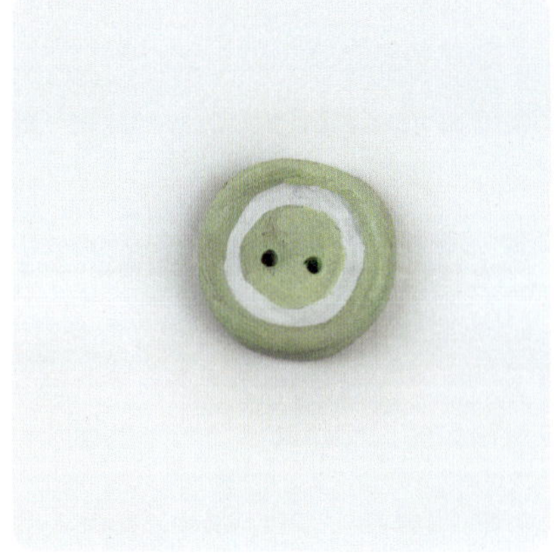

4. Allow to dry, then paint and decorate as desired. When the paint is dry, seal the piece with Mod Podge to finish.

TIP!

Instead of creating a circular base in step 1, cut out or craft other shapes, then follow steps 2 to 4 to make a variety of buttons. The possibilities are endless!

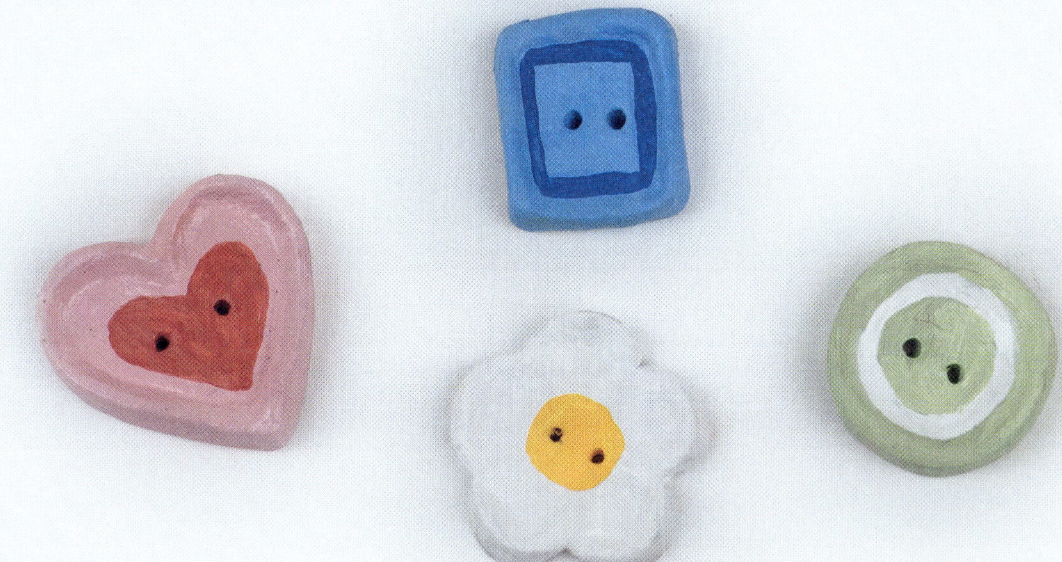

Wall Hanging Tutorial

1. Roll out a slab ½ inch (1 cm) thick. Using a small bowl and needle tool, draw a half circle onto the slab and carve it out. Cut the bottom into a rectangle shape.

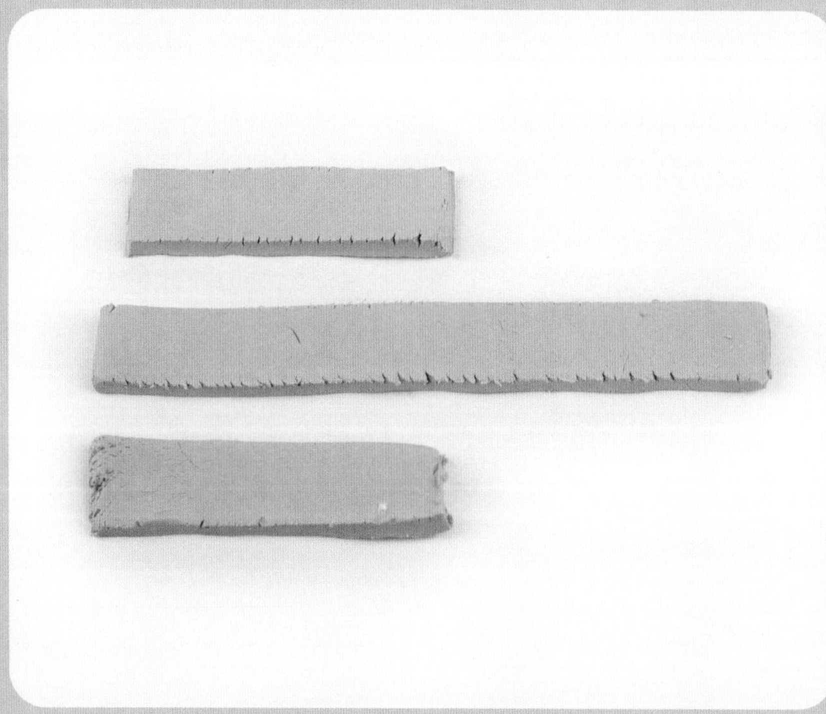

2. Cut strips from the slab long enough to wrap all the way around your shape. Attach the strips around the edge of the piece, leaving the straight bottom for last.

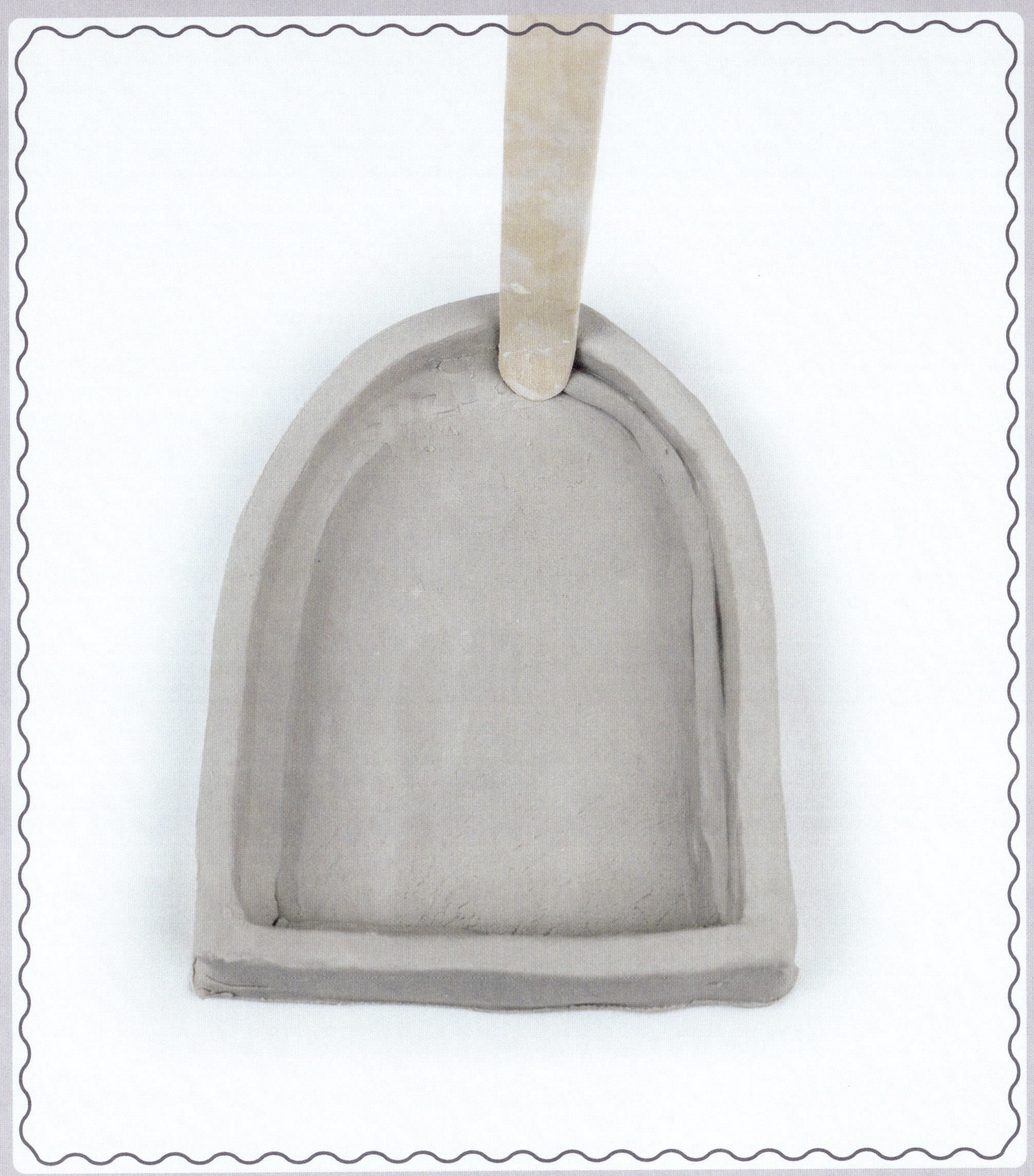

3. Roll out a thin coil long enough to stretch along the inner joint between the strips and the base. Smooth components together with a wet brush. Use your needle tool to create a hole in the top center of the piece.

Cozy Room Scene

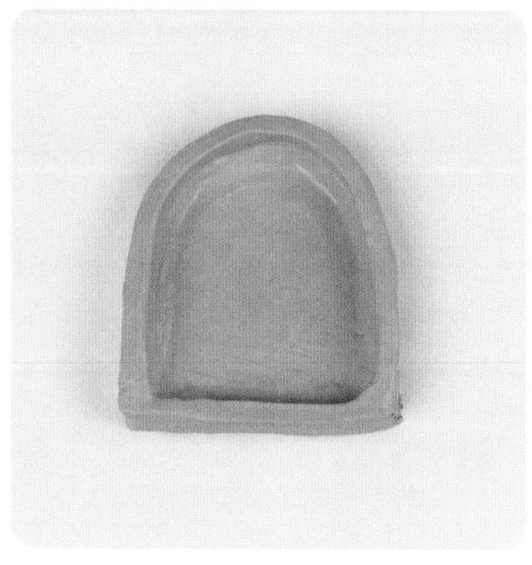

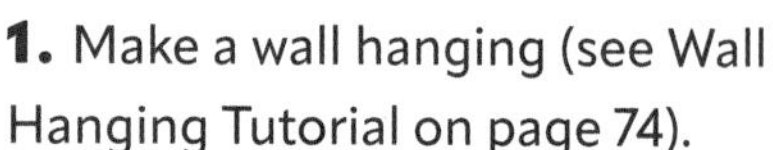

1. Make a wall hanging (see Wall Hanging Tutorial on page 74).

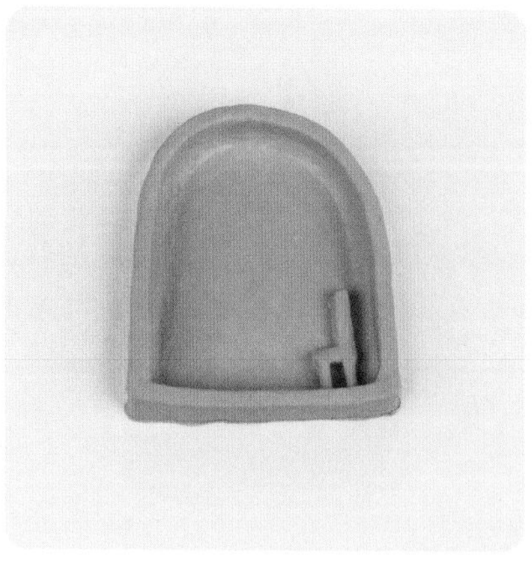

2. To form the chair in the scene, cut 2 small rectangles from a slab. Connect them to the base in an L shape in the right-hand corner. Roll out 2 thin coils long enough to stretch from the bottom of the chair to the "floor" at the bottom of the wall hanging. Attach there to complete the chair and create a 3D effect.

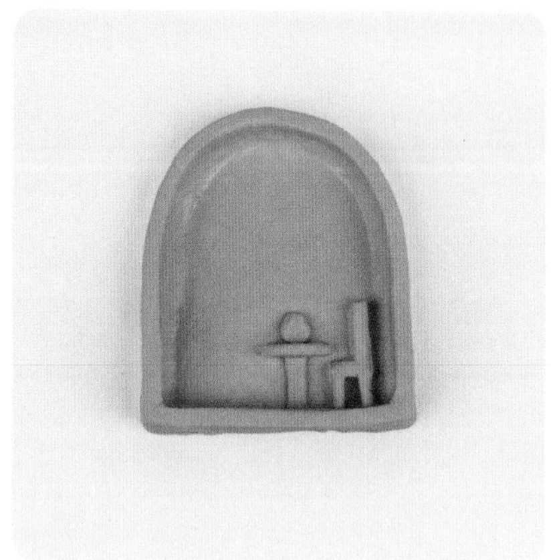

3. Cut a half circle out of the same slab and attach it to the middle of the wall hanging to create the tabletop. Add a thin flat coil from the "floor" to the bottom of the table. Sculpt a rounded vase shape from a small piece of clay and attach it to the top of your table.

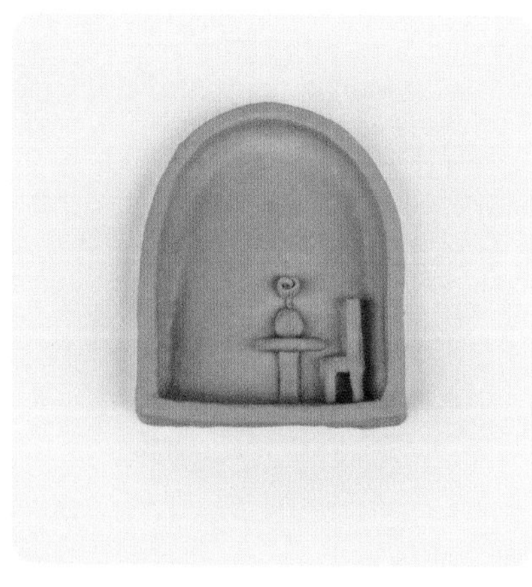

4. Roll out a very small coil and use a small section for the stem of a rose in the vase. Use the rest of the coil to make the rose by gently flattening it and rolling it up between your pointer finger and thumb. Attach it to the stem coming out of vase.

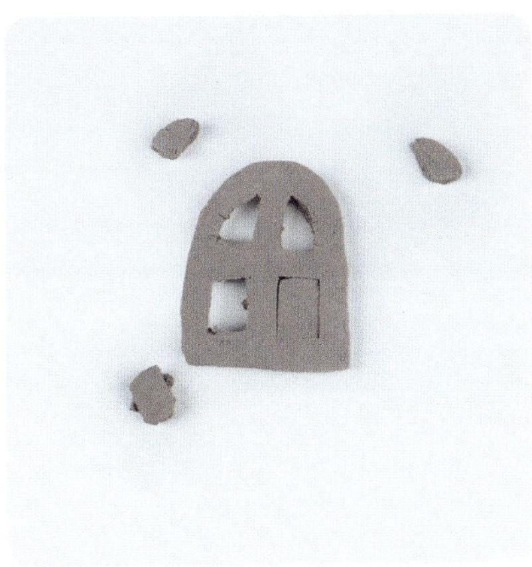

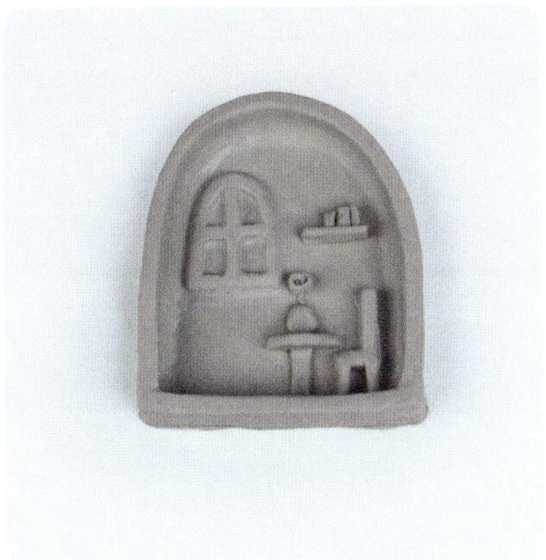

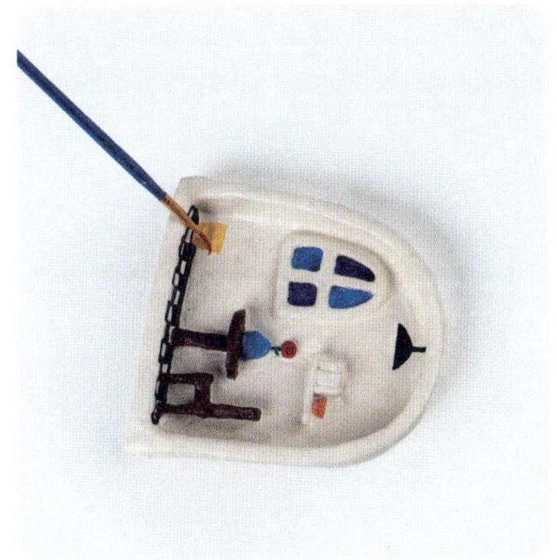

5. Roll out a thin slab. Use a needle tool to cut out a window shape with an arched top. Cut out 4 squares within the window for windowpanes. Attach it to the upper left side of the wall hanging.

6. Cut out a rectangle the thickness of your table and chair. Attach it above the table to create a shelf. Add books of varying thicknesses and heights using extra clay from your slabs.

7. Allow the piece to dry, then smooth and touch up details. Paint the wall hanging a solid base color and paint the other elements as desired. Add other painted details to the scene. When the paint is dry, seal the piece with Mod Podge to finish.

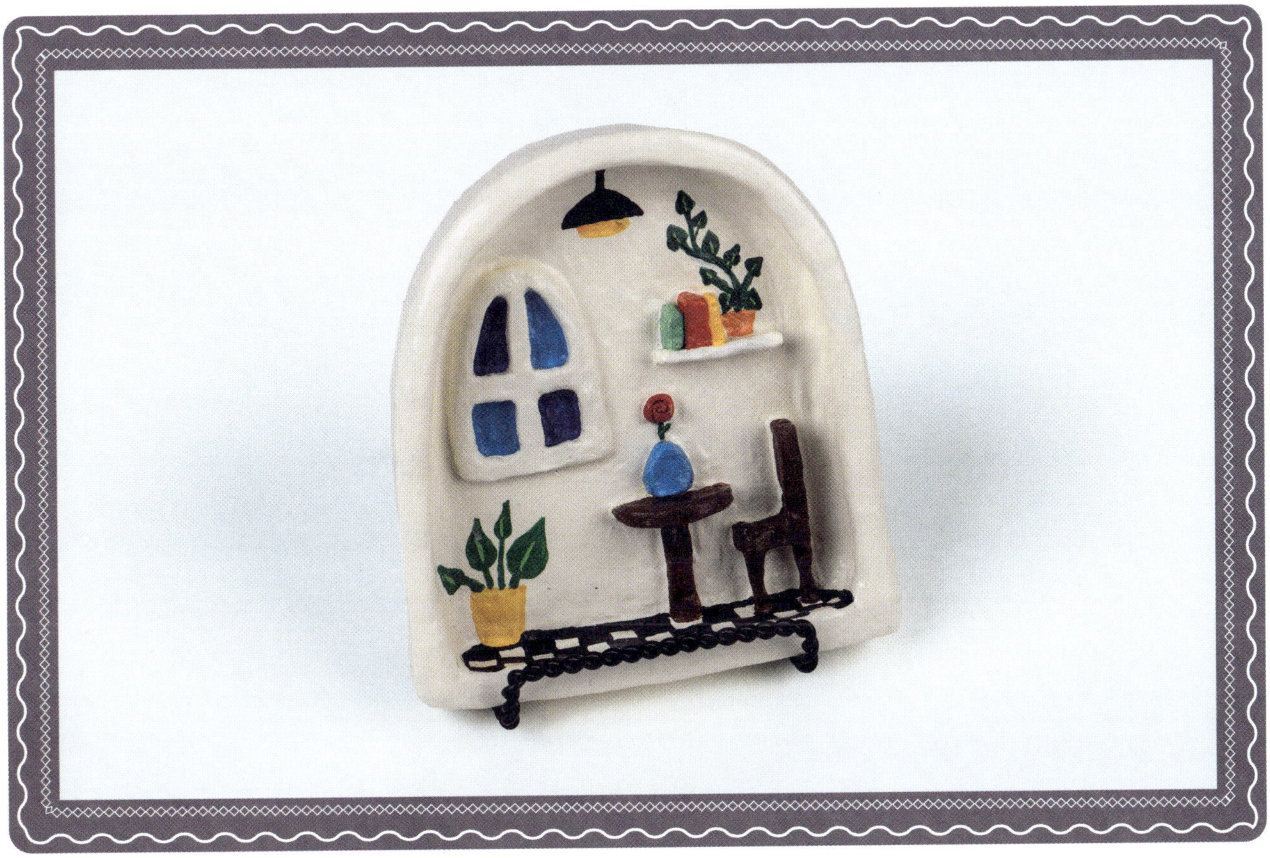

Vase in Front of Window Scene

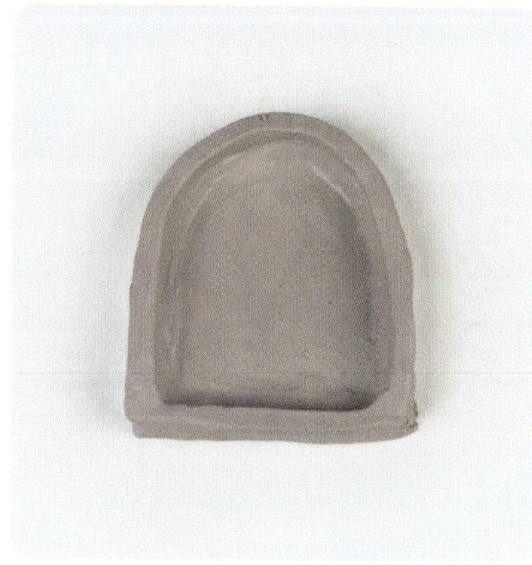

1. Make a small wall hanging (see Wall Hanging Tutorial on page 74 and size it down).

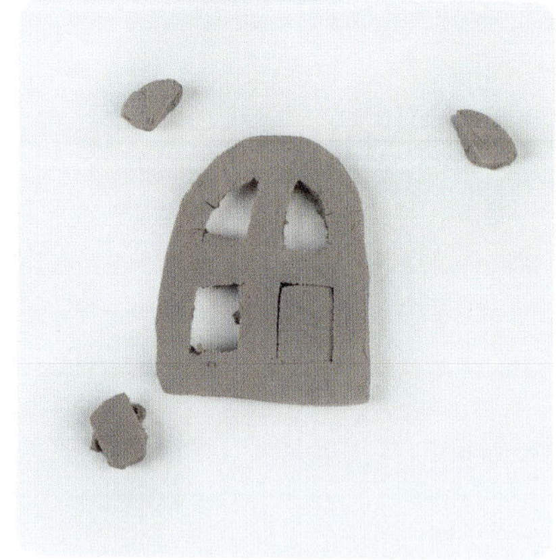

2. Roll out a thin slab. Cut out an arched shape to create a window. Cut 4 small squares out for the windowpanes.

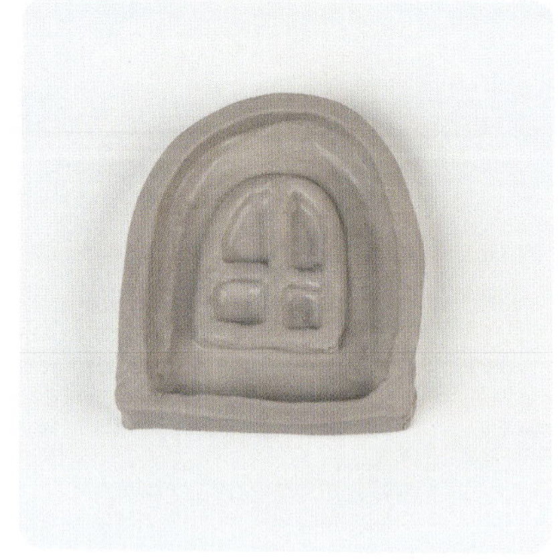

3. Score and slip (see page 15) one side of the window and connect it to the center of the wall hanging base.

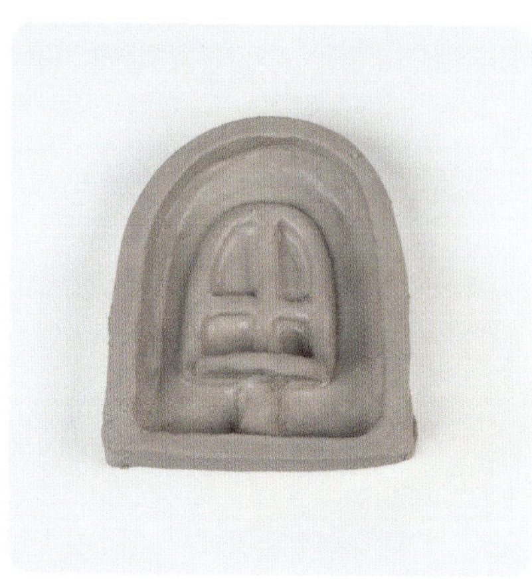

4. To make a table, cut out a half circle and connect it to the bottom of the window. Add a short coil from the table to the floor.

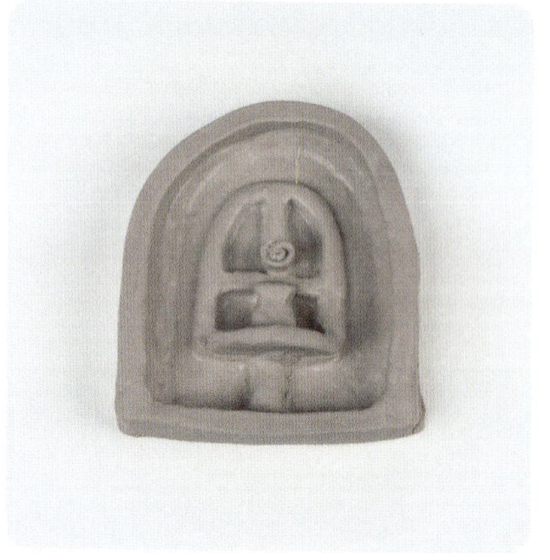

5. Sculpt a teardrop shape for the vase. Attach it to the middle of the window, with its base connected to the tabletop. Roll a coil into a rosebud and add it above the vase, leaving a small space between them to paint a stem.

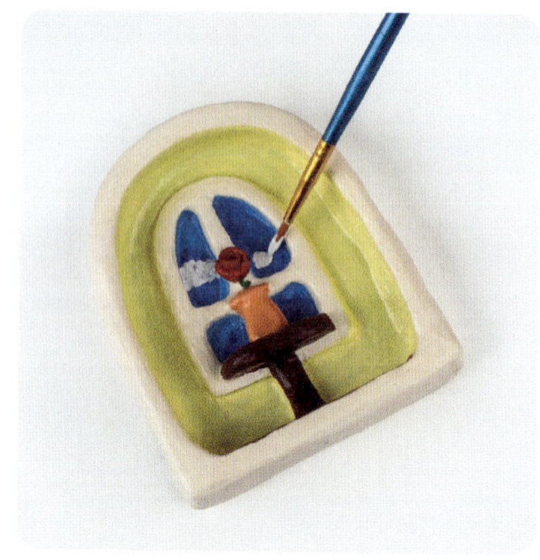

6. Once dry, smooth the piece, touch up details, and paint as desired. When the paint is dry, seal the piece with Mod Podge to finish.

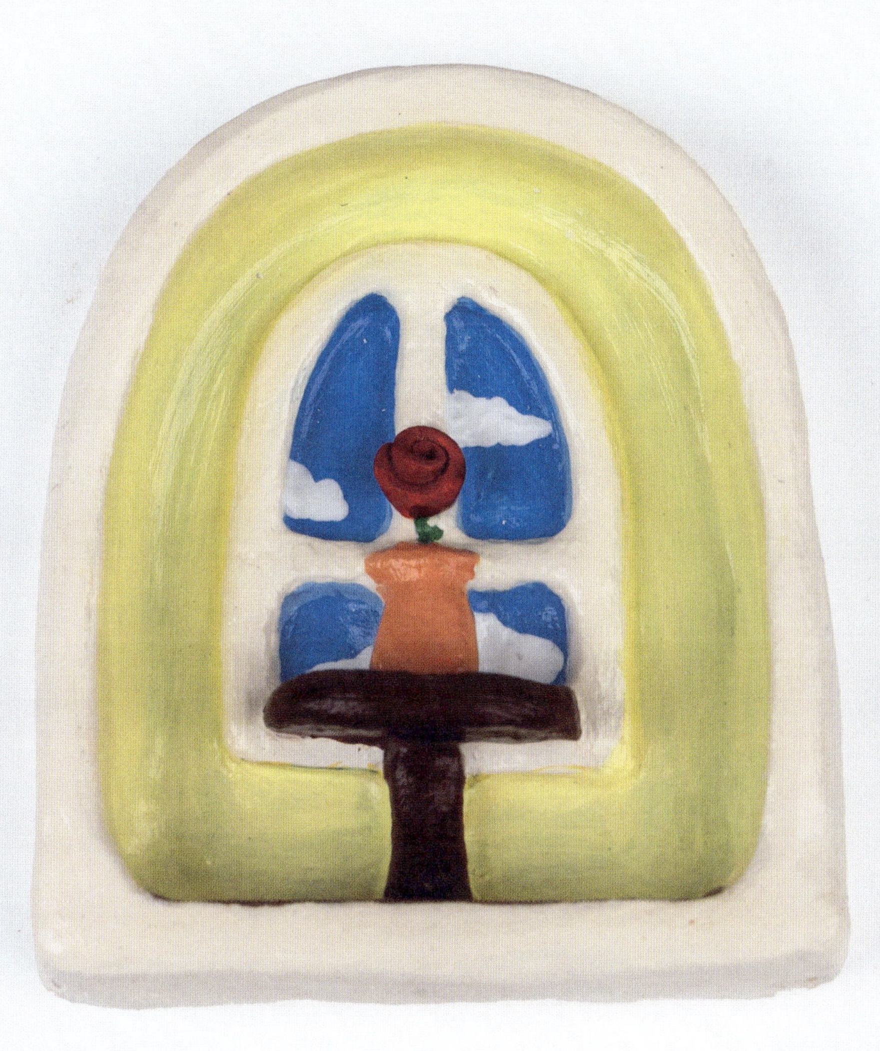

Wall Vase

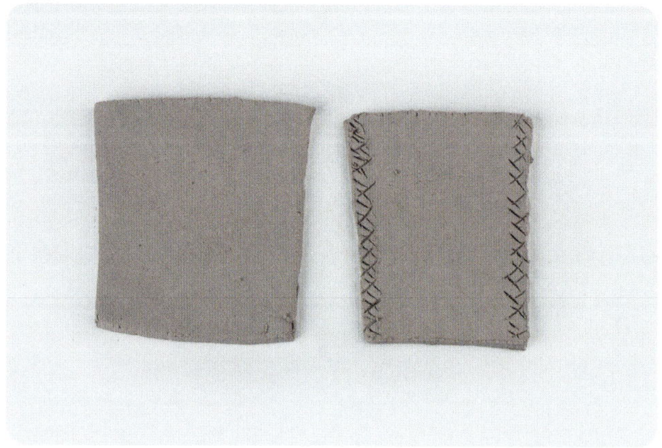

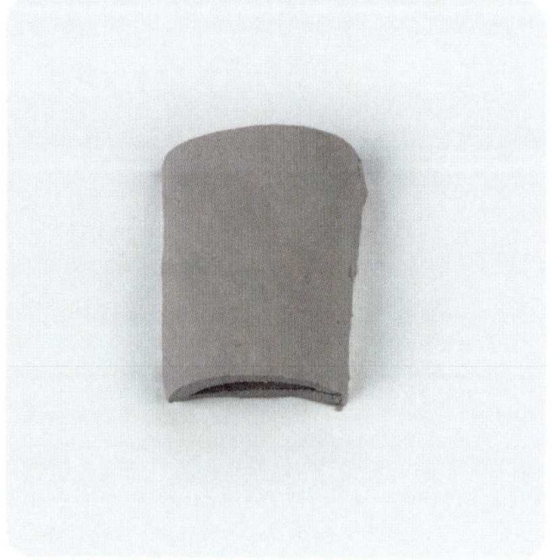

1. Roll out a slab. Use a straight edge to cut out a rectangle that widens on one end. Cut out another rectangle about 1 inch (2½ cm) wider on each side than the first. Score and slip the connection points (see page 15).

2. Place a scrunched-up piece of paper in the middle of the first rectangle. Gently place the second rectangle on top and connect the sides together.

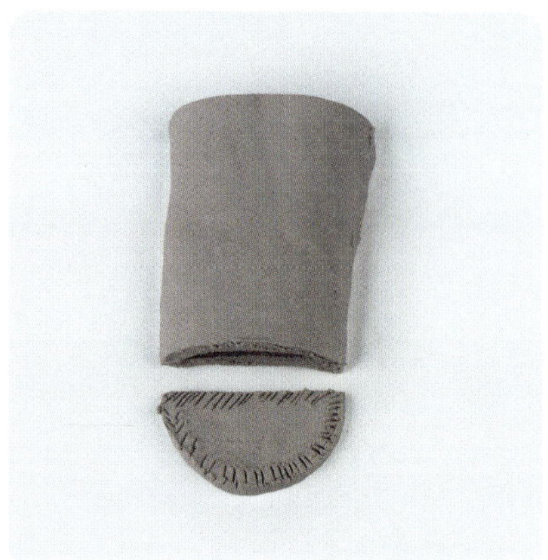

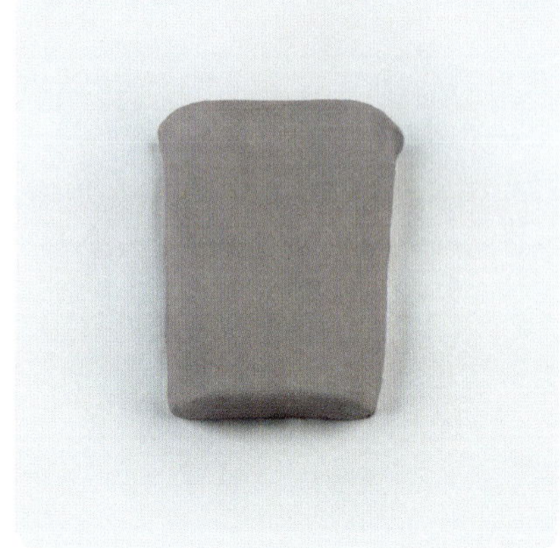

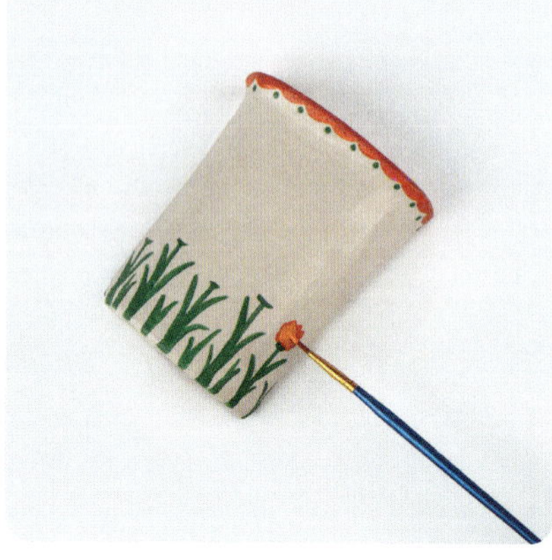

3. Cut out a half circle the size of the hole at the bottom of the vase (the narrow end) from the slab and attach it there.

4. Use a wet sponge to smooth and shape the vase. Curl the lip out by pinching it between your pointer finger and thumb while pulling slightly outward. Once the piece feels like it won't collapse in on itself, carefully remove the paper through the top. Use a needle tool to create a hole on the back of the vase.

5. Once dry, paint the vase a base color like off-white and add a design of your choice. When the paint is dry, seal the piece with Mod Podge to finish.

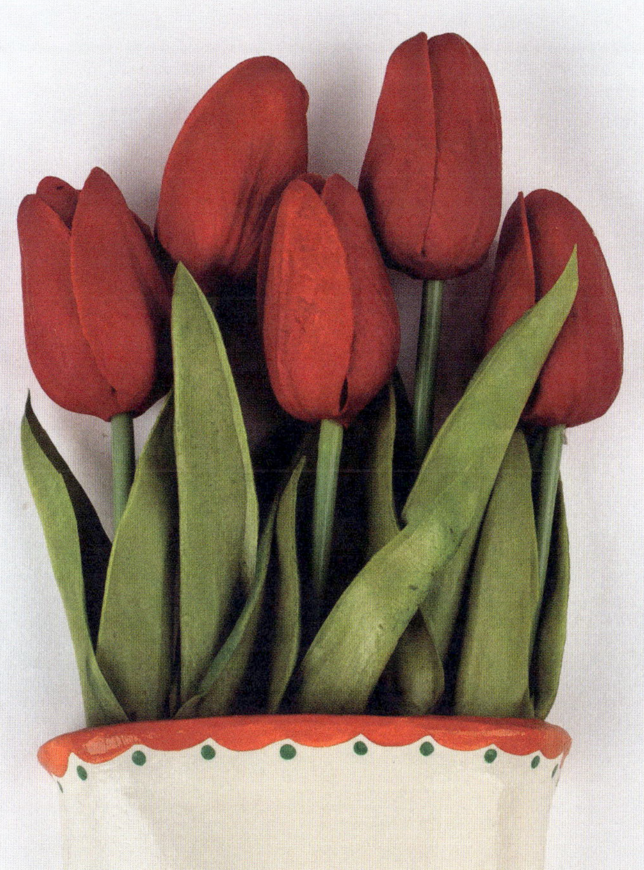
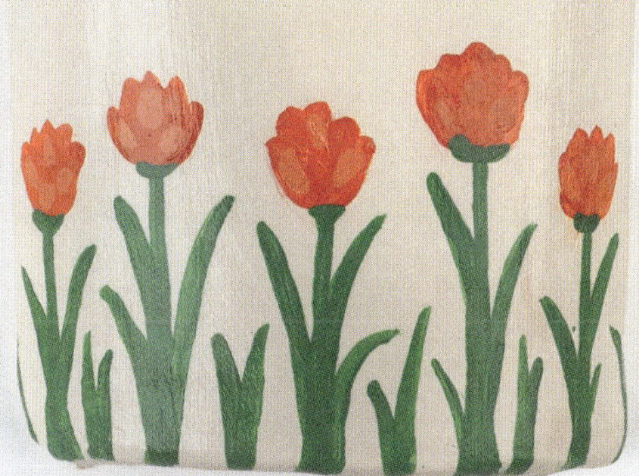

Trinket Shelf

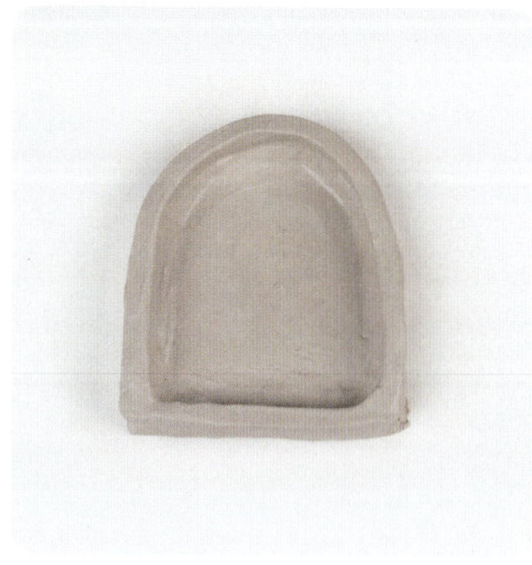

1. Create a wall hanging (see Wall Hanging Tutorial on page 74).

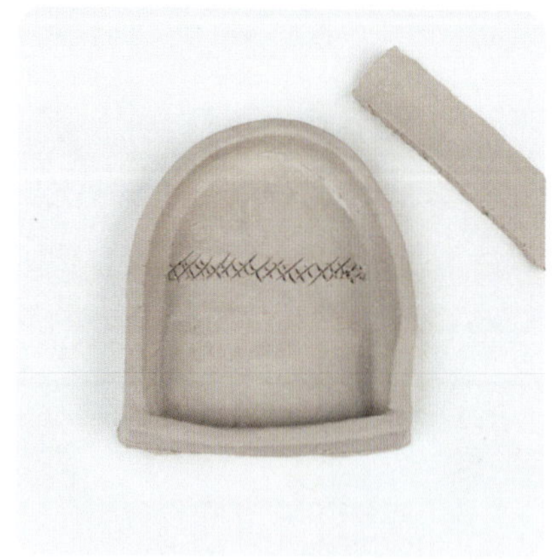

2. Roll out a slab and cut out a rectangle the width and depth of the middle of your wall hanging. Score and slip (see page 15) the connection points.

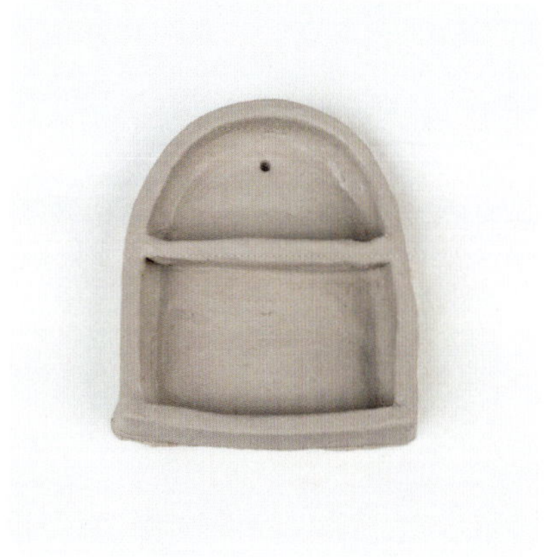

3. Attach the rectangle to the center of the wall hanging to create a shelf. Make a coil and place underneath the shelf, then connect and smooth to reinforce.

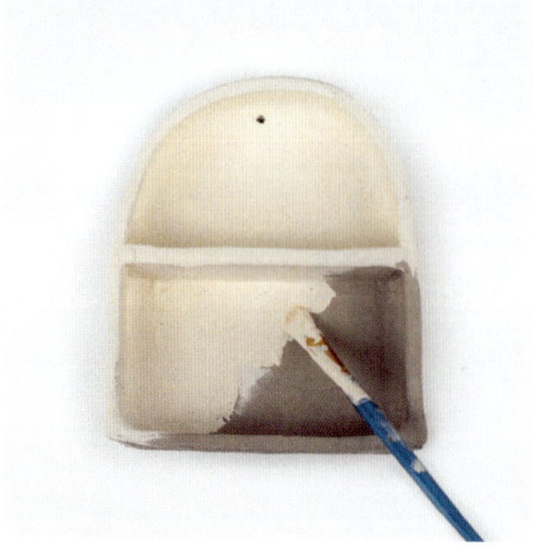

4. Once fully dry and smoothed, paint a solid color like off-white. When the paint is dry, seal the piece with Mod Podge to finish.

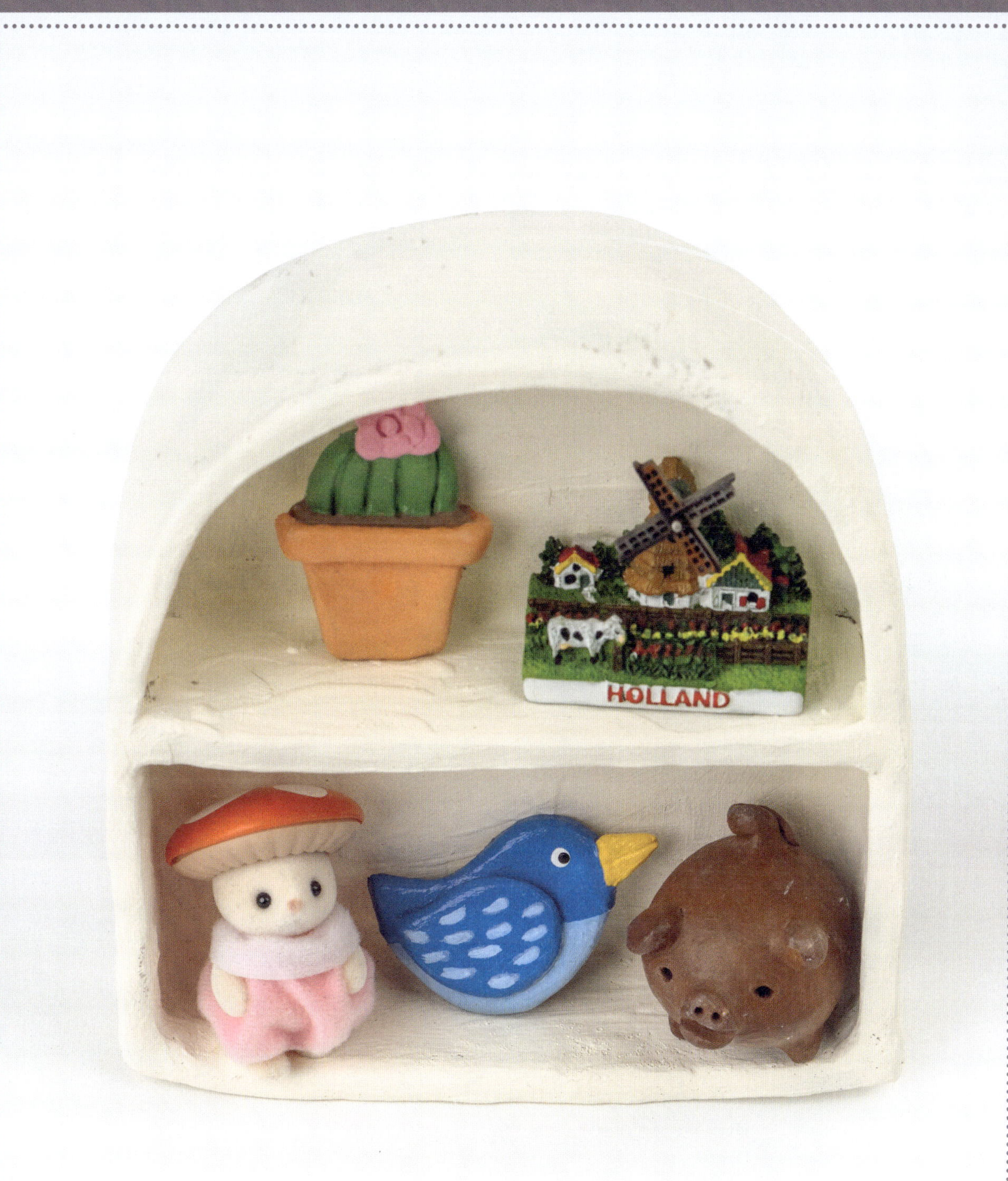
HOLLAND

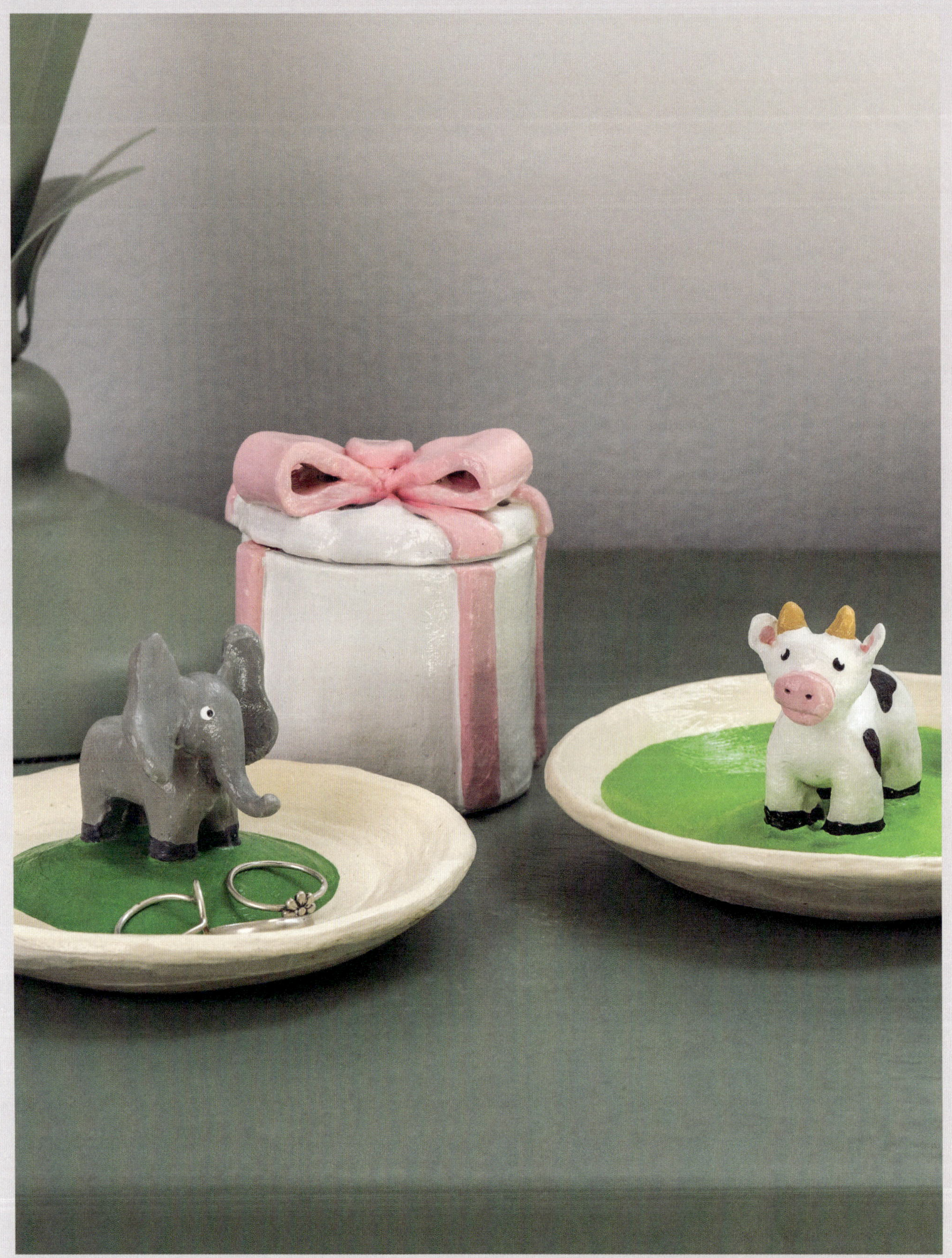

FOR YOUR TRINKETS

Small Dish Tutorial

1. Roll out a slab ½ inch (1 cm) thick. Obtain a bowl to use as a mold, with a bottom rim the size of the dish you'd like to make. Cut out a circle the size of that bottom rim.

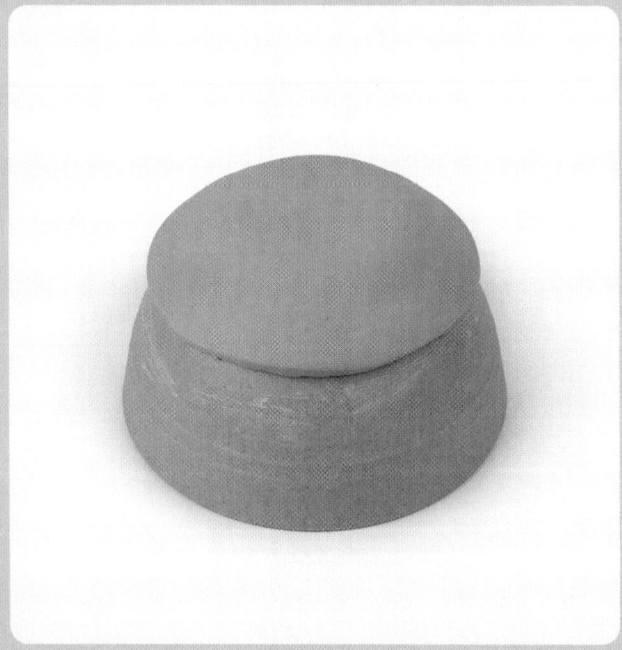

2. Use a wet sponge to smooth the edges of the circle and then mold it to the bottom of the bowl.

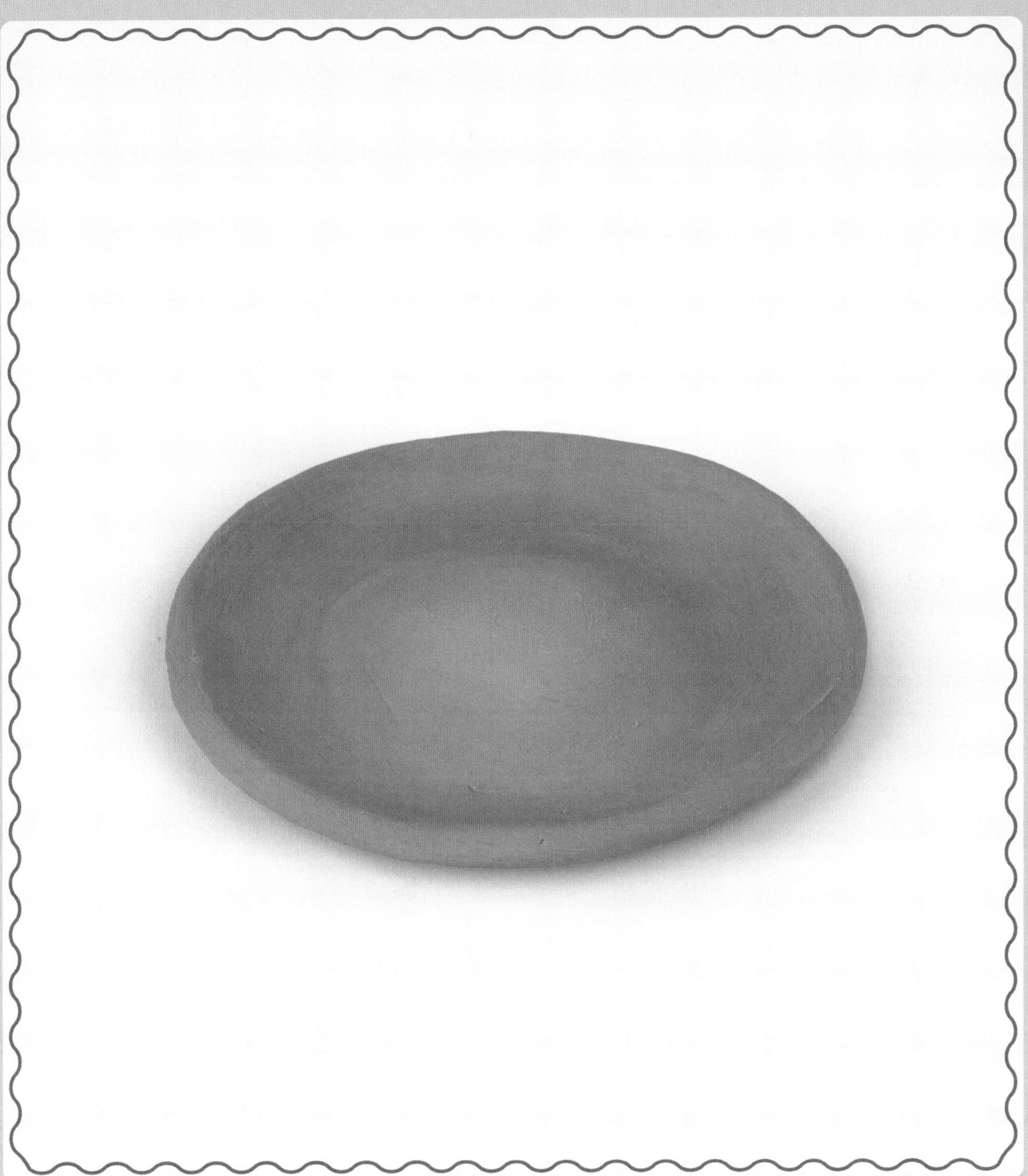

3. Allow to dry until leather hard (see Glossary on page 22). Gently remove from the bowl and place upright. Clean up edges and smooth the middle.

Cat Dish

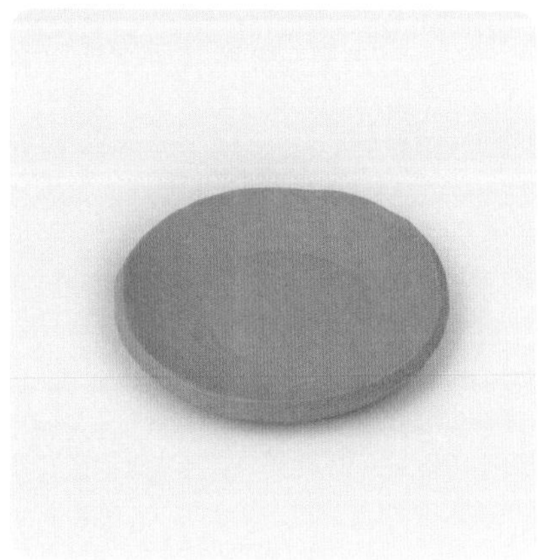

1. Create a dish (see Small Dish Tutorial on page 86).

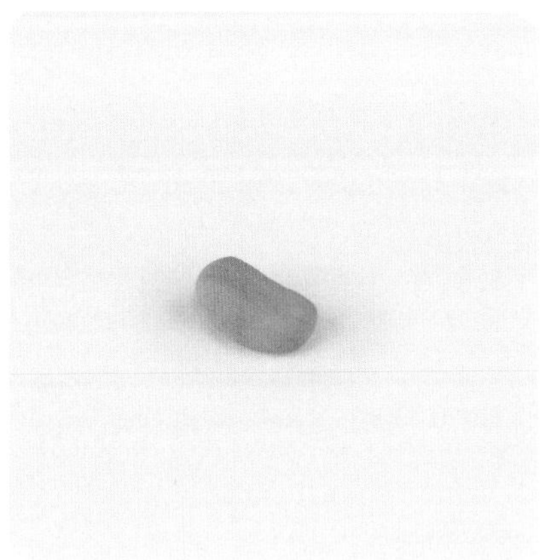

2. To form the cat, sculpt a bean shape from a small ball of clay. Gently pull up one end about ½ inch (1 cm) to suggest a raised posture.

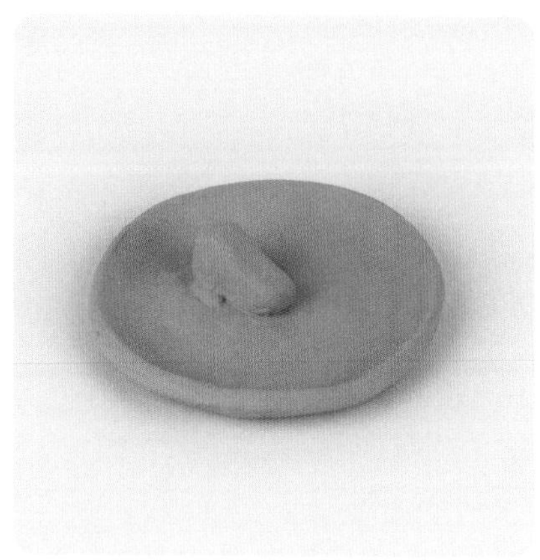

3. Shape 2 small clay balls and stack them beneath the lifted end as hind legs. Attach the cat's body to the center back of the dish. Smooth the components together to make the legs seem to peek out from beneath the cat's body.

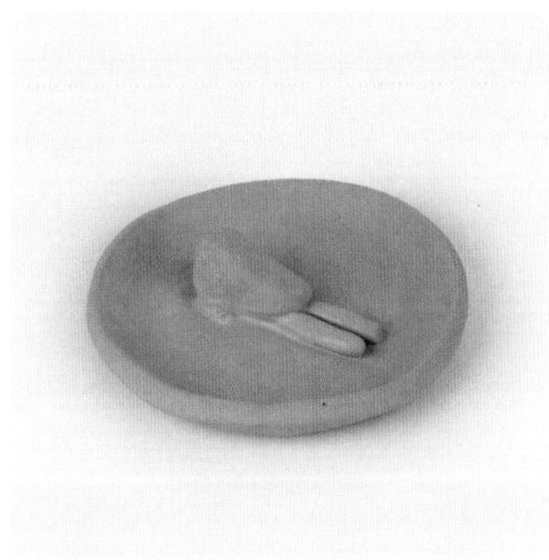

4. Roll out a thin coil and cut it into 2 outstretched legs, rounding them at one end. Connect them to the front end of the body.

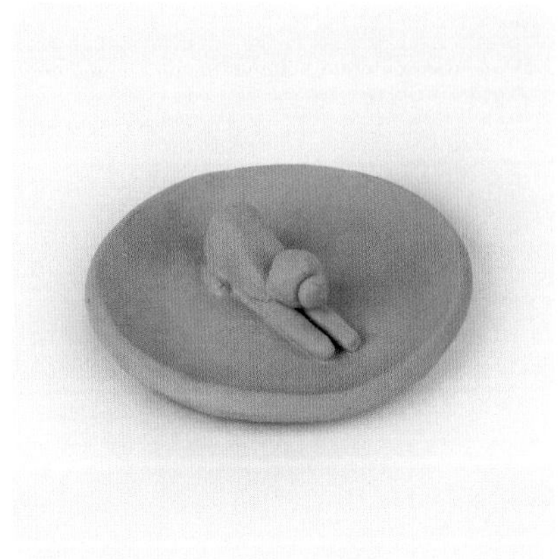

5. Roll out 2 balls, one smaller than the other, to form the head and the snout. Attach the larger ball to the front of the body and the smaller to the front of the first.

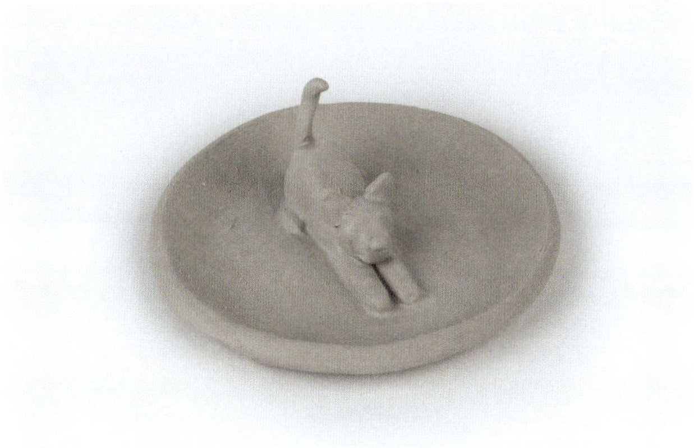

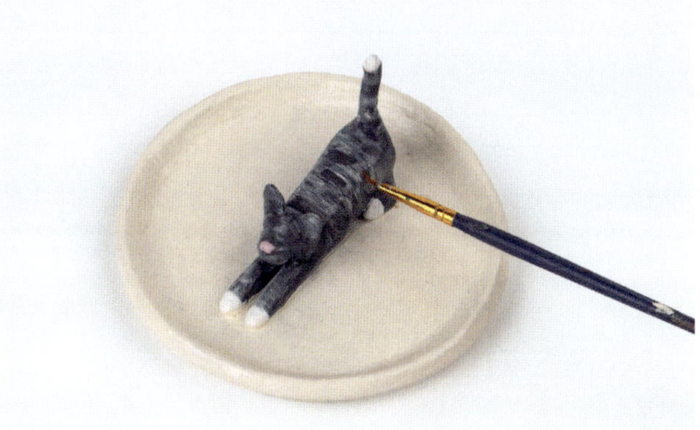

6. Roll out a coil and cut one end at an angle. Attach this tail by the angled end to the back of the body. Add a bit of clay at the connection point to secure and cover the seam. Bend the tip of the tail and add flattened bits of clay to the head for the ears and nose.

7. Allow the piece to dry, then touch up and smooth it. Paint the dish a solid base color and paint details, such as eyes, onto the cat, then paint the rest as desired. When the paint is dry, seal the piece with Mod Podge to finish.

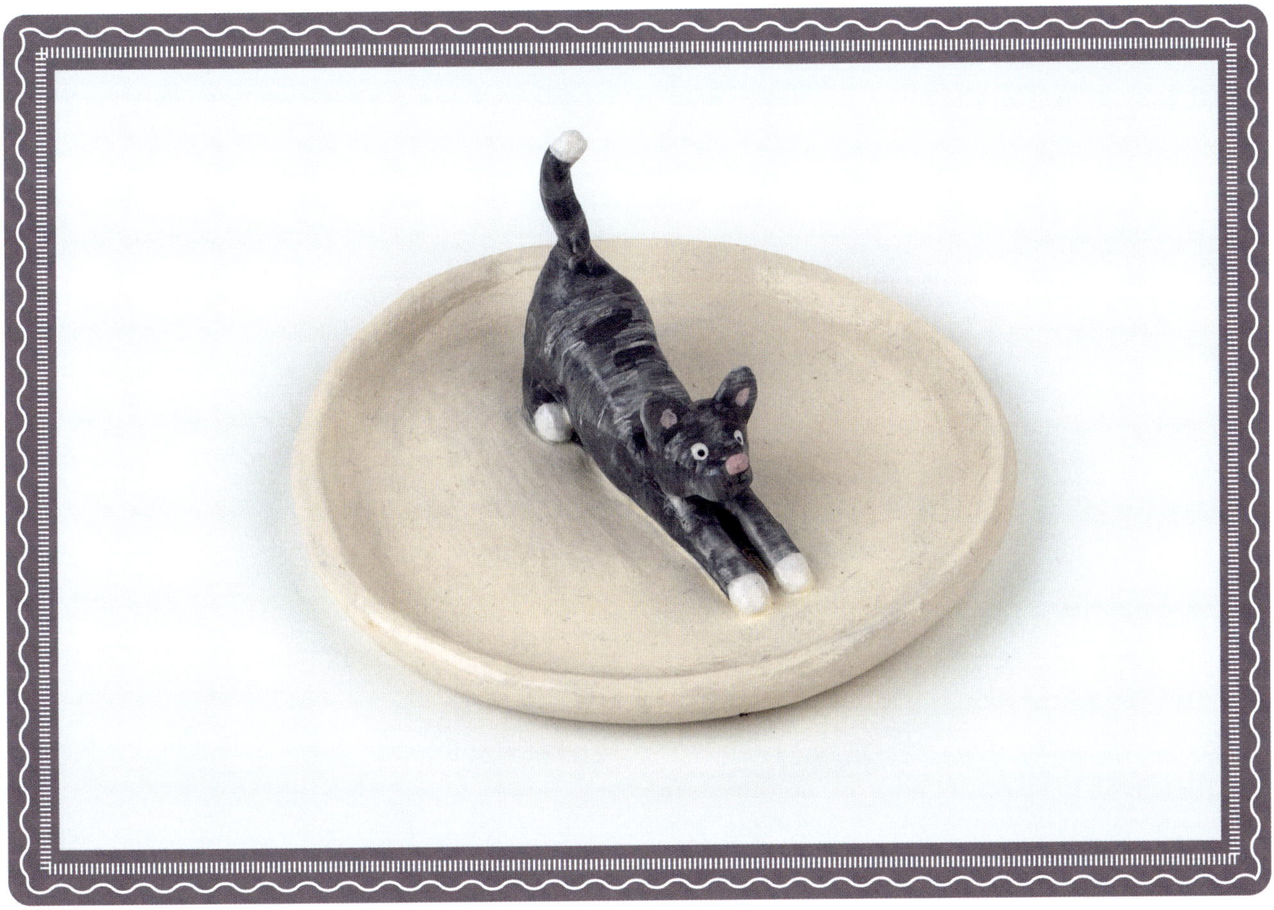

Dog Dish

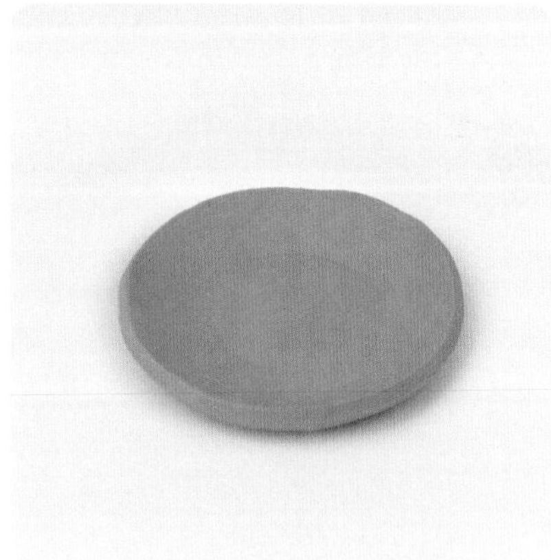

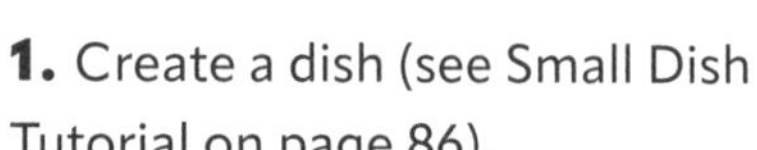

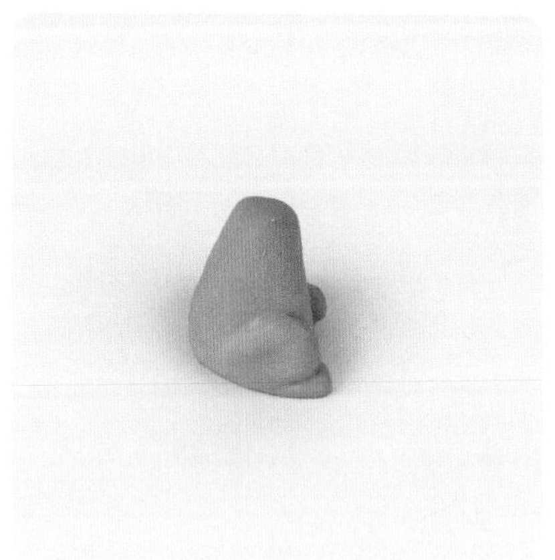

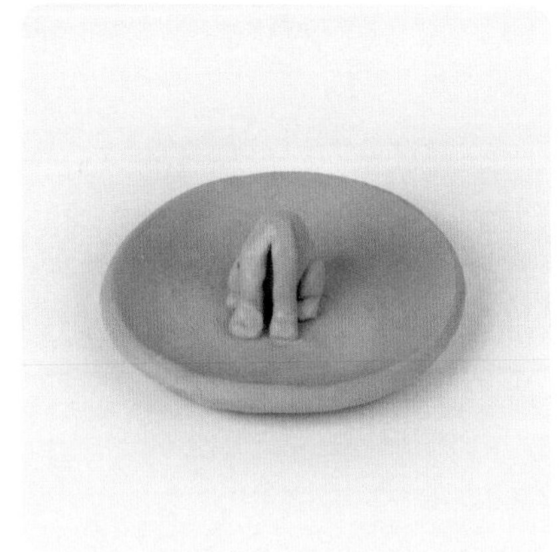

1. Create a dish (see Small Dish Tutorial on page 86).

2. To form the dog, sculpt an upright bean shape from a small ball of clay. Attach a flattened ball to each side of the bean's base as haunches, then add smaller rounded pieces of clay under the flattened balls to create feet.

3. Roll out 2 more coils for the front legs. Cut them slightly longer than the distance from the chest of the dog to the dish. Place them on the dish in front of your dog, leaving a bit folded out to create feet, and connect the other ends to the chest. Round out the feet.

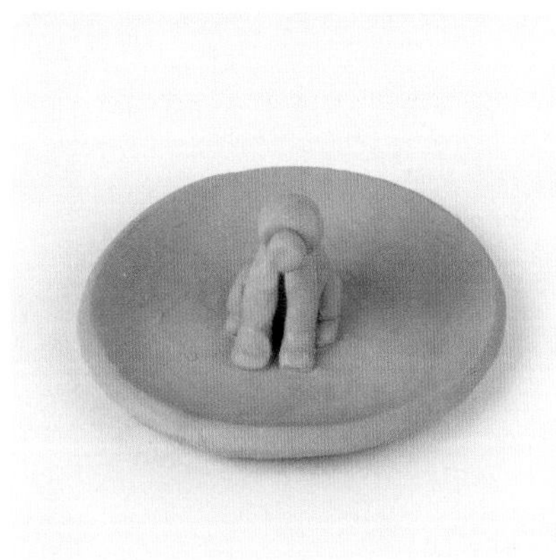

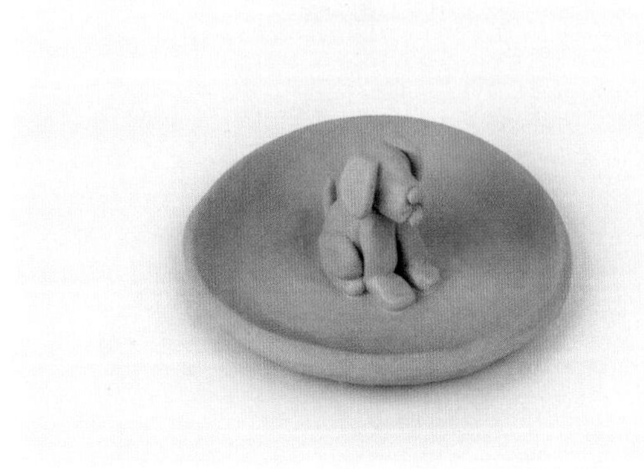

4. To make the head, roll out a small ball and connect it to the top of the body. Roll another ball and connect it to the front of the first to make a snout.

5. Smooth the balls together. Use the edge of your needle tool to cut out a mouth. Add flat round pieces to either side of the snout. Roll out and flatten multiple, different-sized balls to add a tongue inside the mouth, a nose, and a tail. Smooth out as needed.

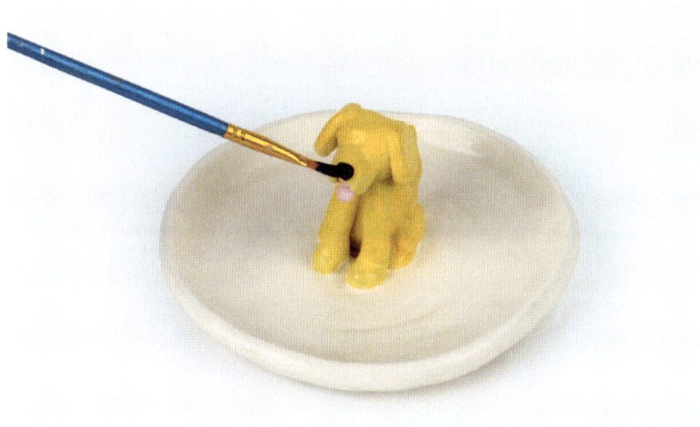

6. Once dry, paint the dish a base color and paint details like eyes onto the dog, then paint the rest as you like. When the paint is dry, seal the piece with Mod Podge to finish.

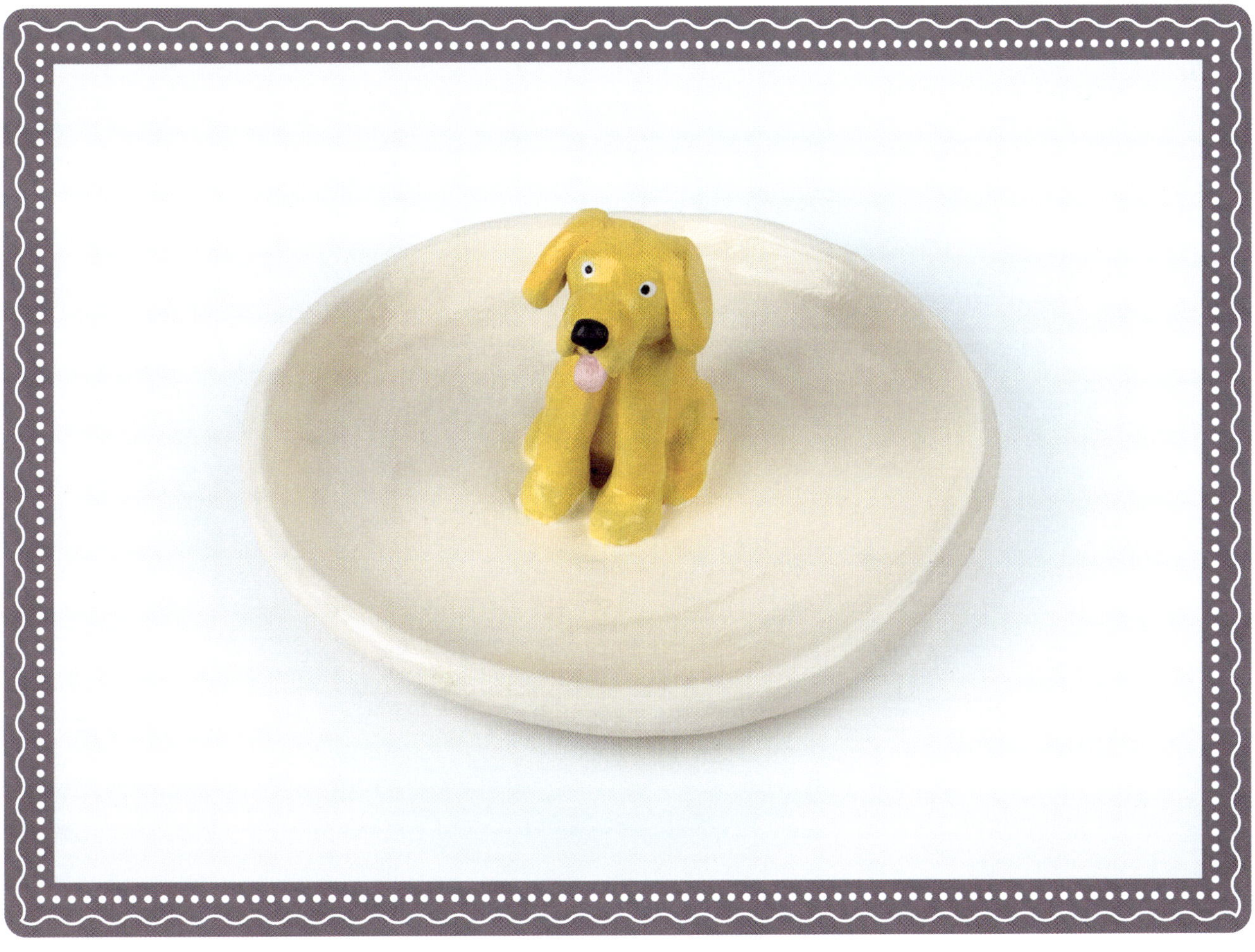

Cow Dish

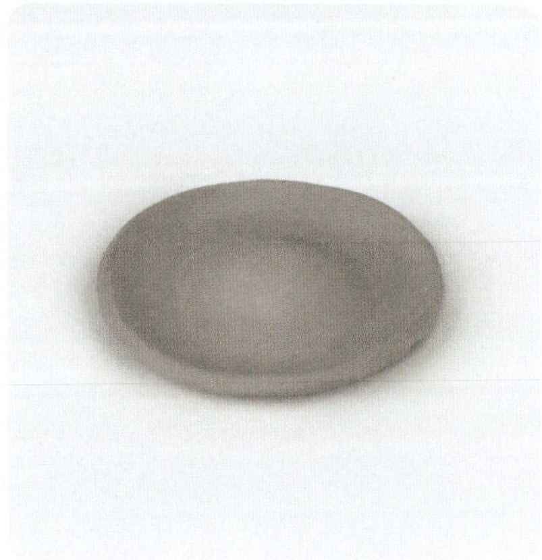

1. Make a dish (see Small Dish Tutorial on page 86) and add a ball of clay to the middle. Smooth its edges to create a lump in the center of your dish.

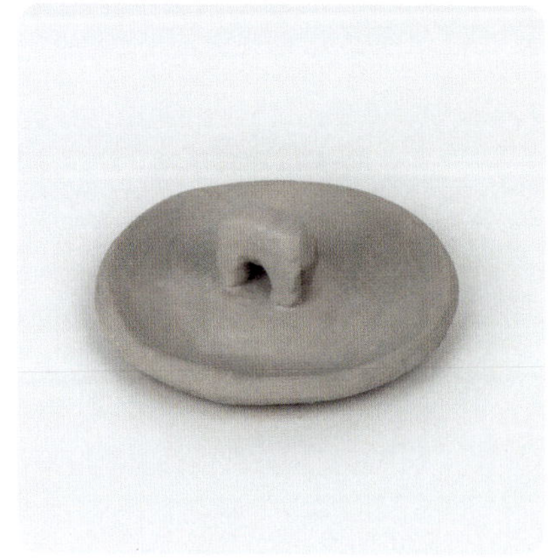

2. Create a log shape from a small ball of clay for the cow's body and then roll out a coil. Cut the coil into 4 stubs for legs. Connect the stubs to the body and attach the legs to the center of the mound in the dish.

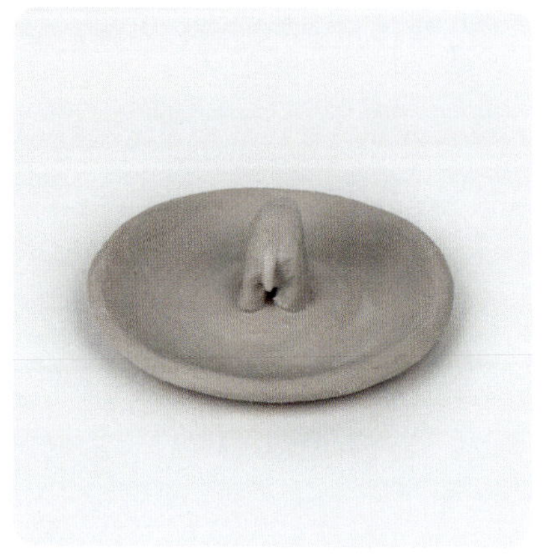

3. Roll out a small thin piece of clay and connect it to the back of the body for a tail.

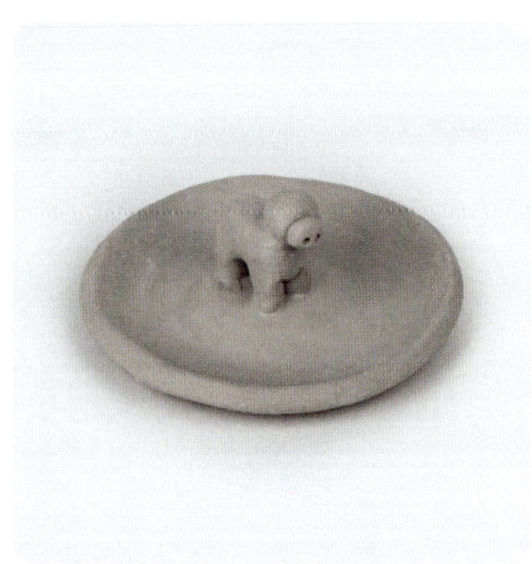

4. Add a ball to the front of the body for the head. Connect a smaller ball to the front of the first ball and use your needle tool to poke 2 holes in it for the nostrils.

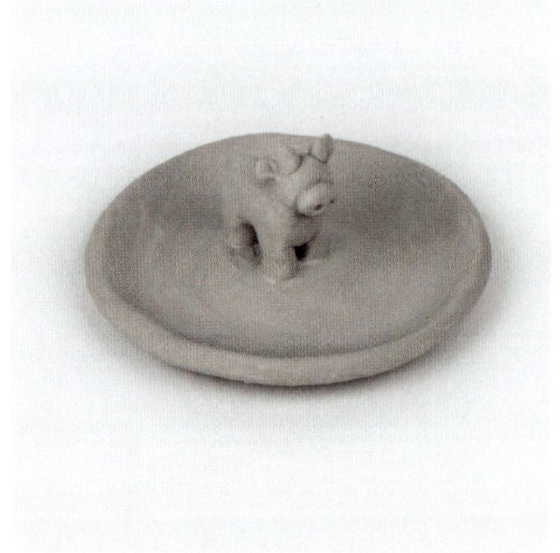

5. Roll out 2 small balls and flatten and pinch them into ear shapes. Connect these to the head. Create 2 pointed stubs and connect them to the head in between the ears.

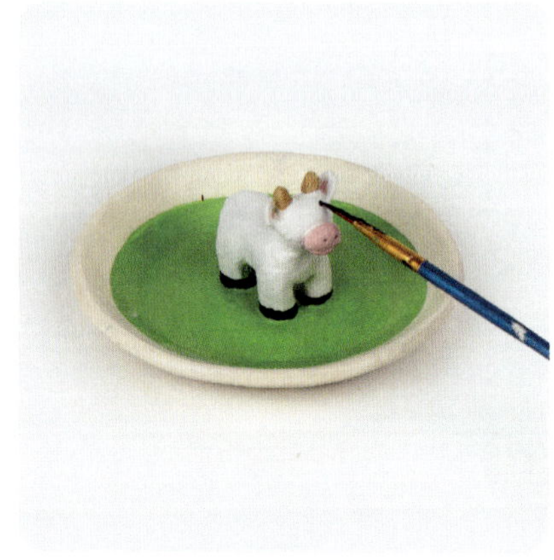

6. Once dry, clean up details and smooth the dish. Paint the center of the dish green with an off-white rim. Paint details like eyes onto the cow and paint the rest as desired. When the paint is dry, seal the piece with Mod Podge to finish.

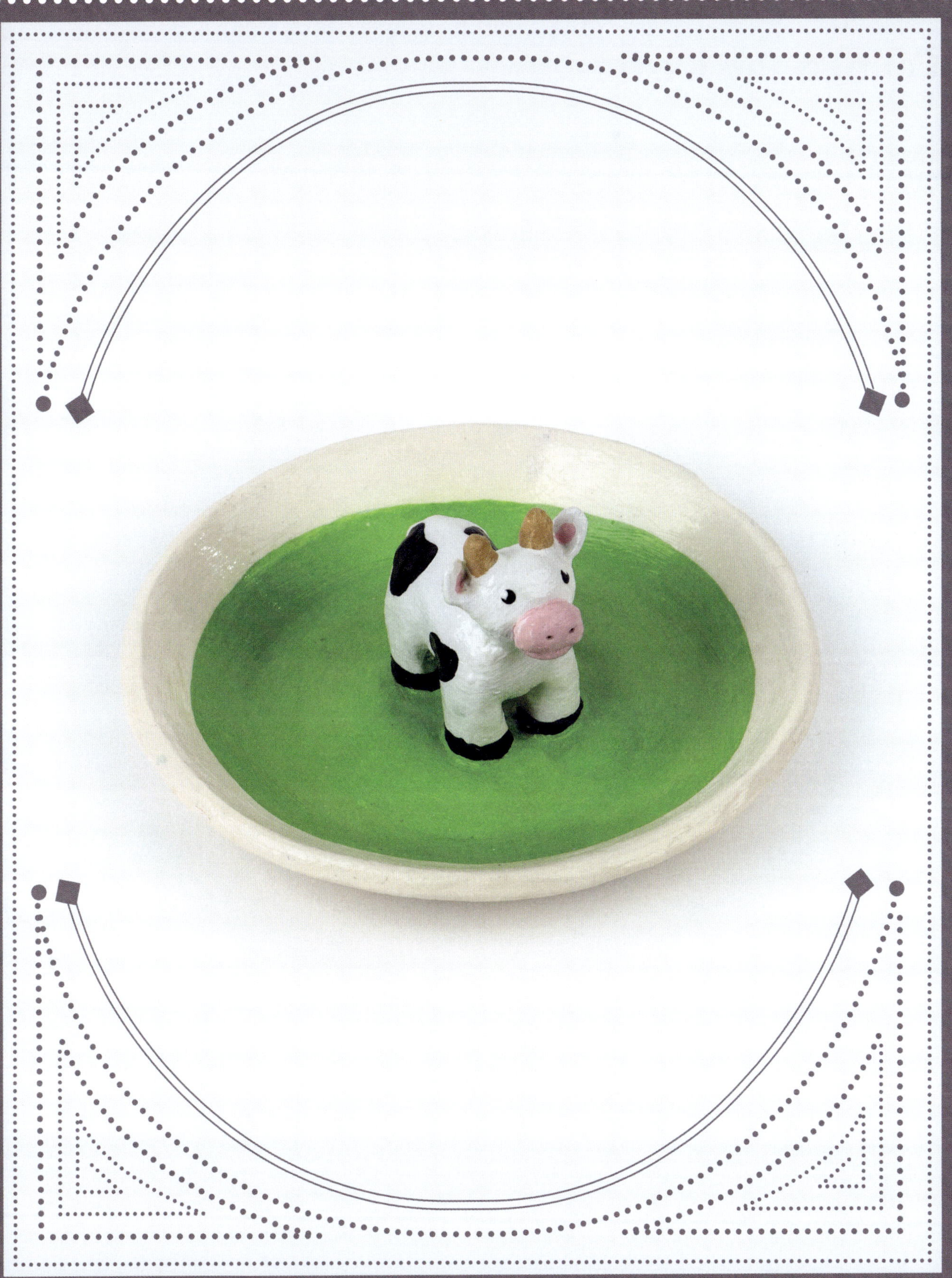

Guinea Pig Dish

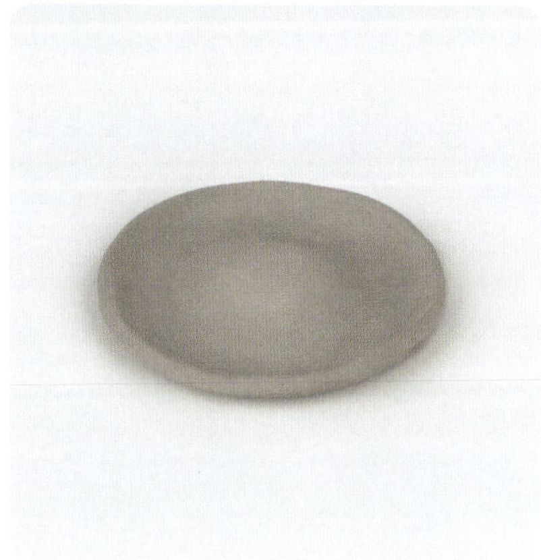

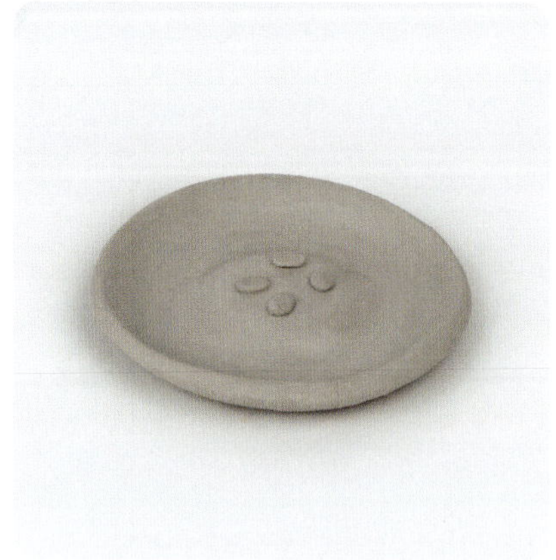

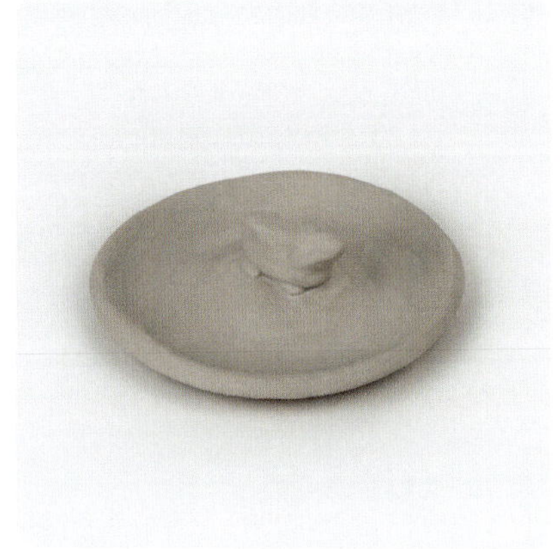

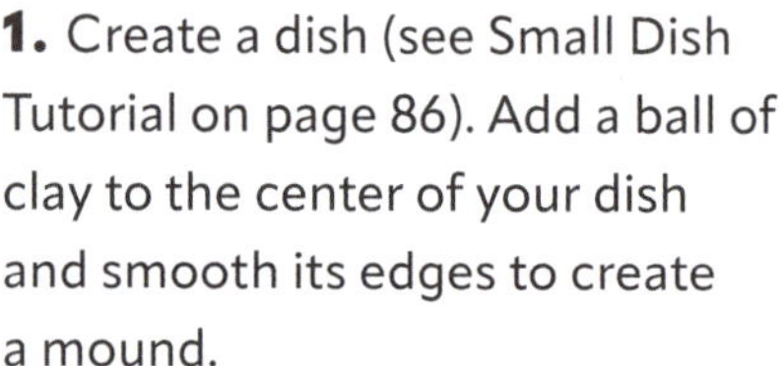

1. Create a dish (see Small Dish Tutorial on page 86). Add a ball of clay to the center of your dish and smooth its edges to create a mound.

2. Roll out 4 small balls for feet, flatten them, and position them in a square shape in the middle of the mound before attaching them there.

3. To form the guinea pig's body, sculpt a bean shape from a small ball of clay. Pull one end up and pinch it into a point (this will be the face). Connect the body to the top of the feet.

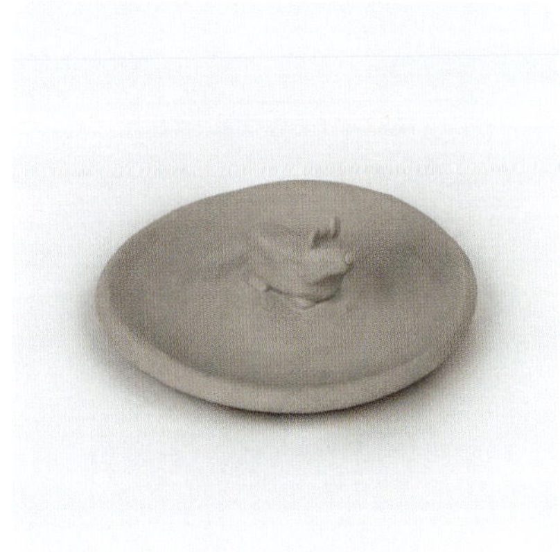

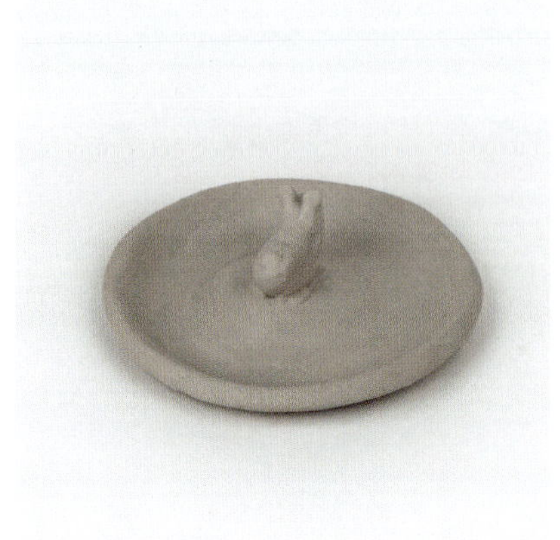

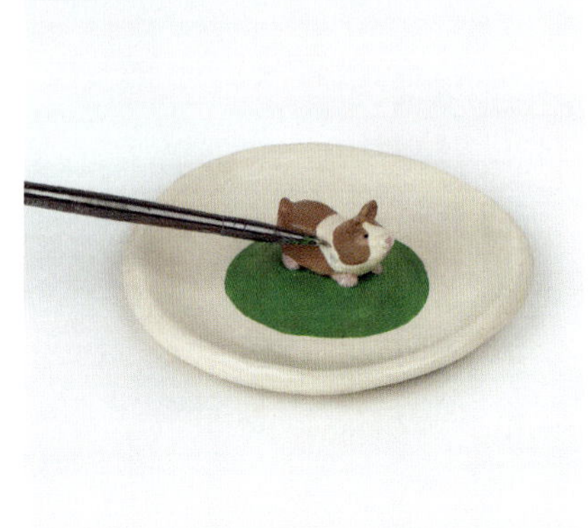

4. Roll out 2 small balls and flatten them. Pinch one end of each and connect them to the back of the head to create ears. Add a small ball of clay at the tip of the face for a nose.

5. Add a nub of clay to the back of the body for the tail and use a wet brush to smooth the body.

6. Once dry, smooth and touch up the piece. Paint the mound in the center of the dish green and the rest of the dish off-white. Add details like eyes to the guinea pig and paint the rest of it as you like. When the paint is dry, seal the piece with Mod Podge to finish.

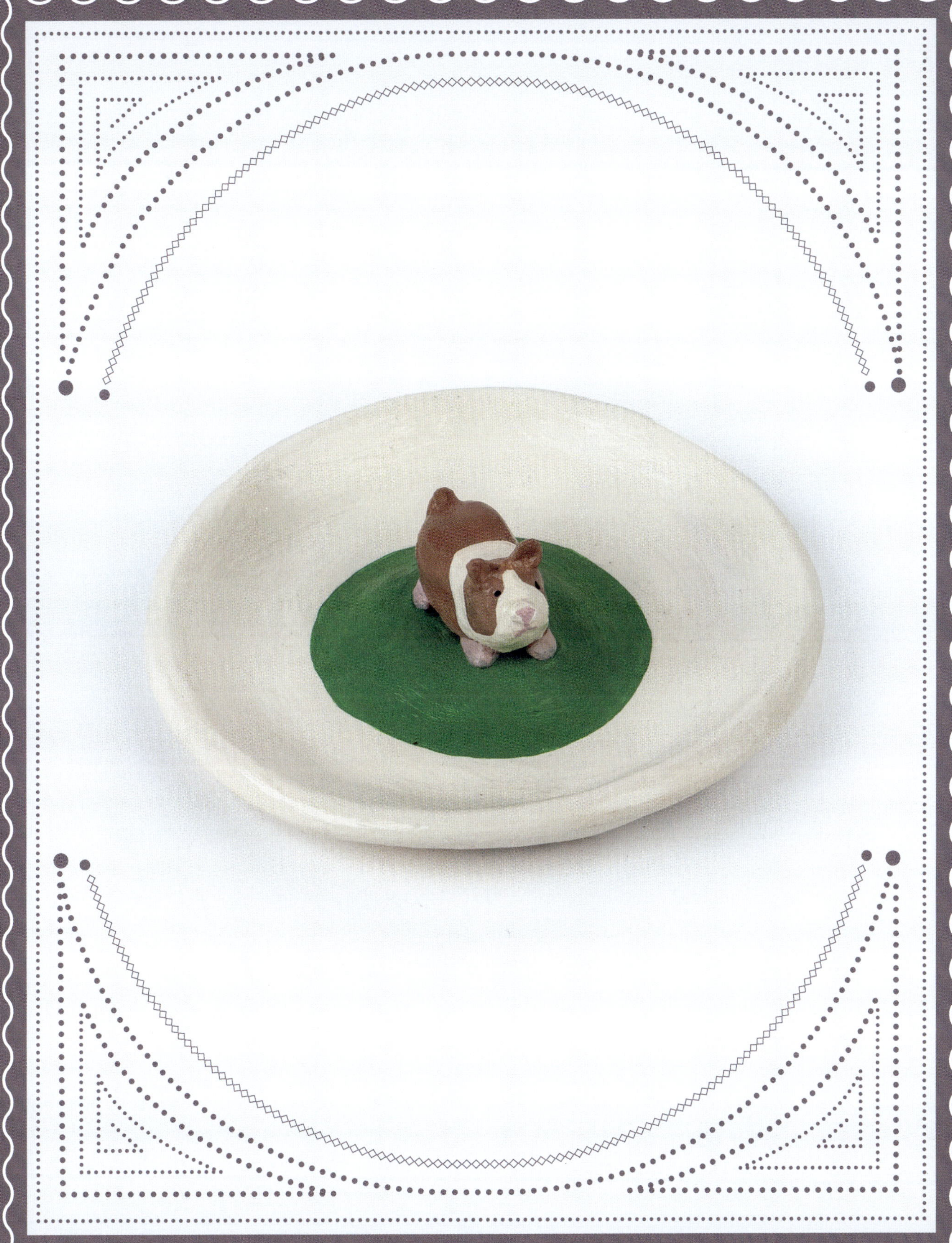

Dinosaur Dish

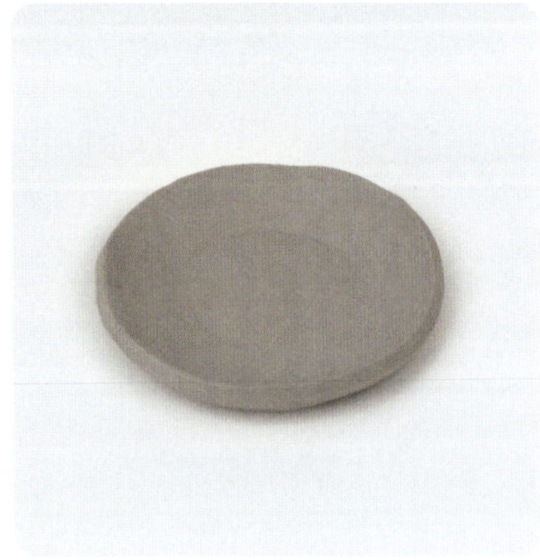

1. Create a dish (see Small Dish Tutorial on page 86).

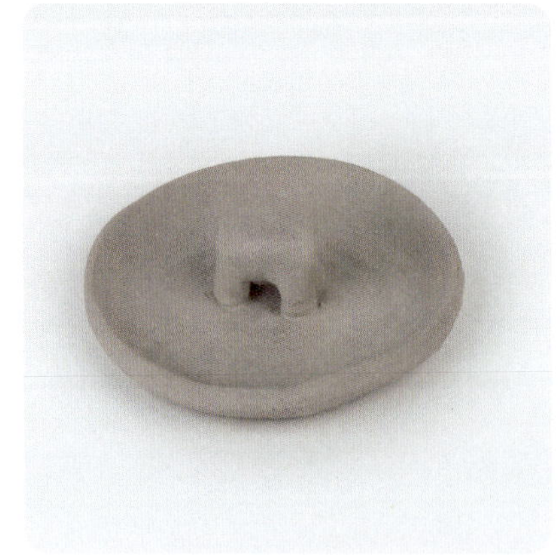

2. Create a log shape for the dinosaur's body and then roll out a coil. Cut the coil into 4 stubs for legs. Connect stubs to the body and attach them to the center of the dish.

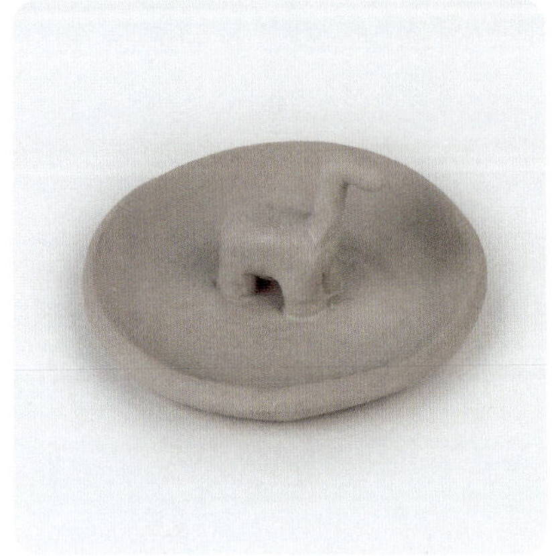

3. Roll a coil and cut one end at a slant. Connect the slanted end to the front of your form to make the neck. Add a bit of clay behind the neck where it meets the body and smooth the components together. Sculpt an oval shape and connect it to the top of the neck for the head.

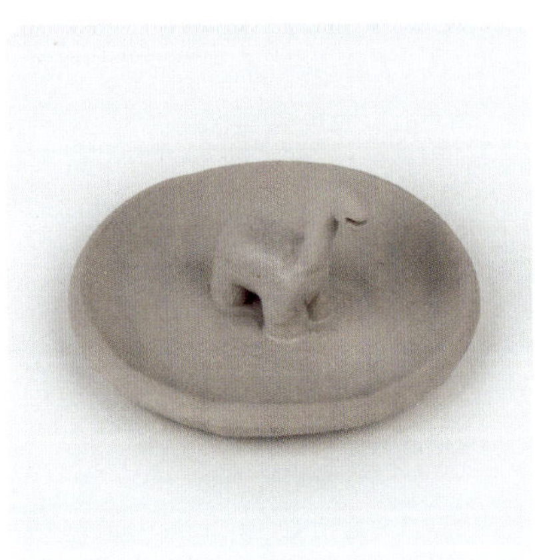

4. Use a cutting tool to make a mouth.

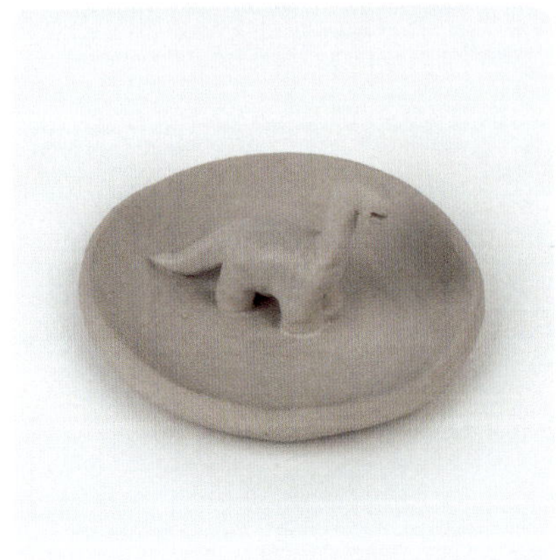

5. Roll out a coil and pinch it into a pointed end. Attach it to the back of the body to create a tail.

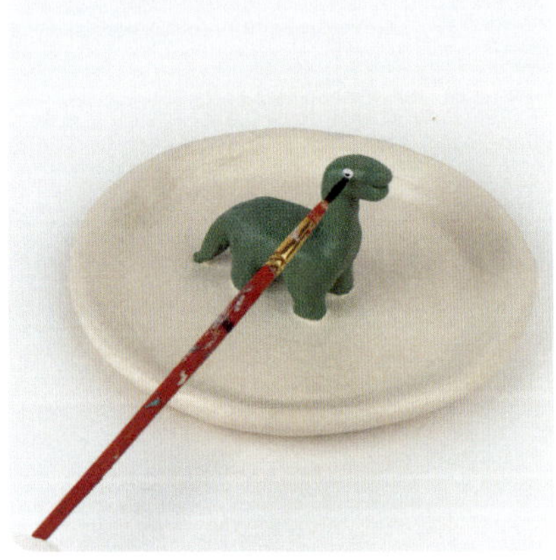

6. Once dry, paint the dish a solid color and paint the dinosaur as you like. When the paint is dry, seal the piece with Mod Podge to finish.

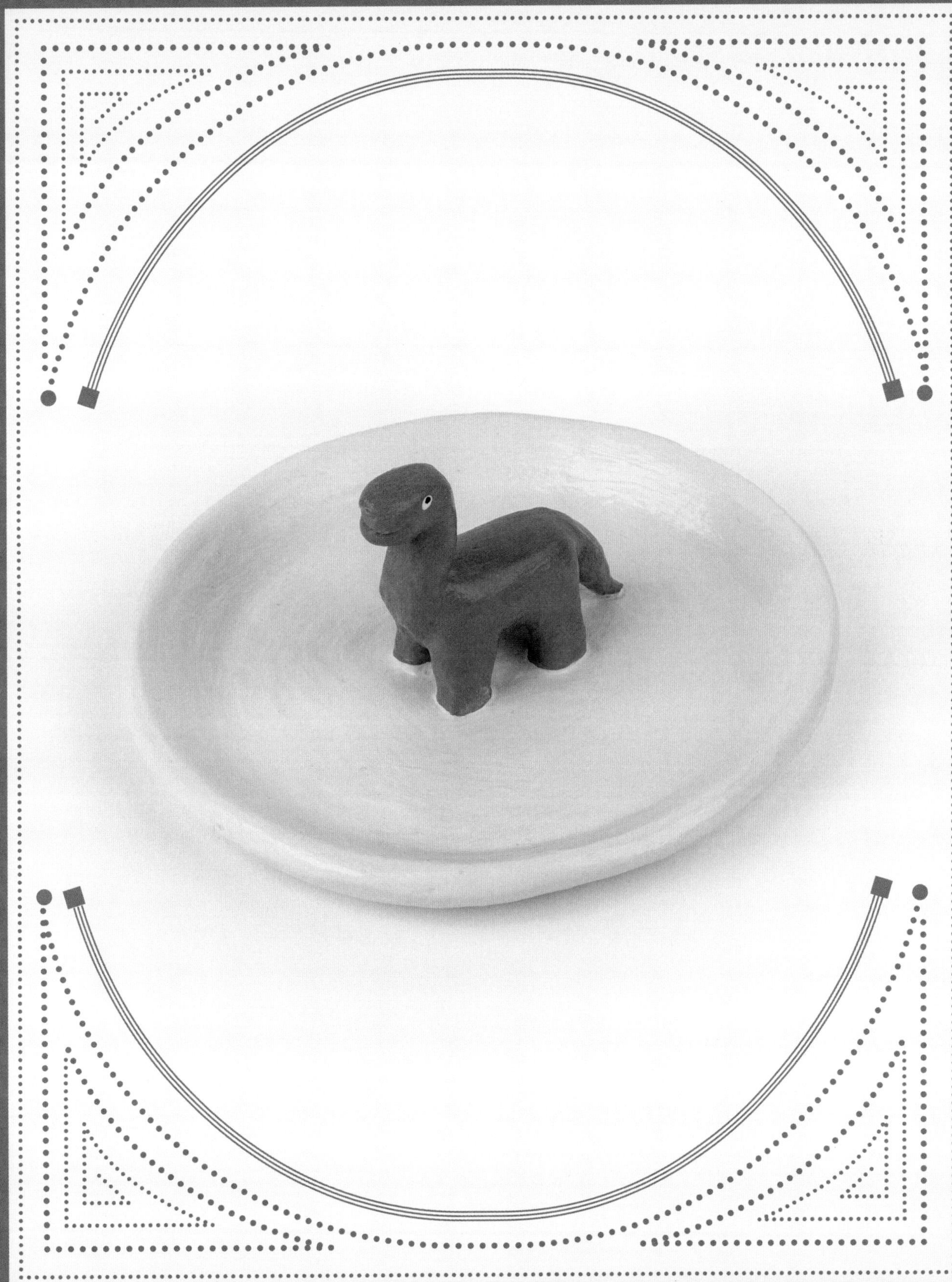

Elephant Dish

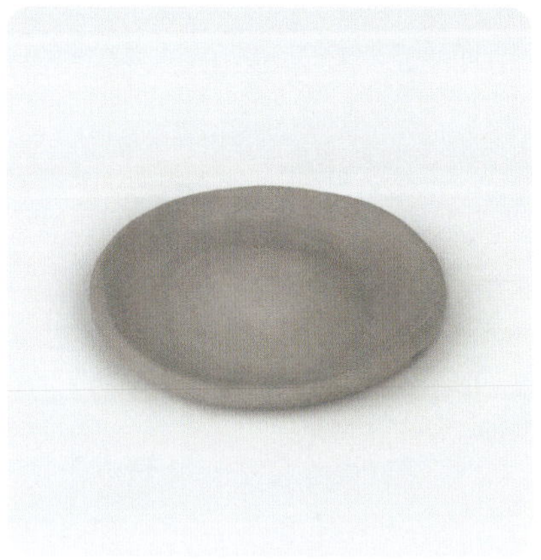

1. Create a dish (see Small Dish Tutorial on page 86). Roll out a ball and flatten it, then connect and smooth it into the middle of your dish to create a mound.

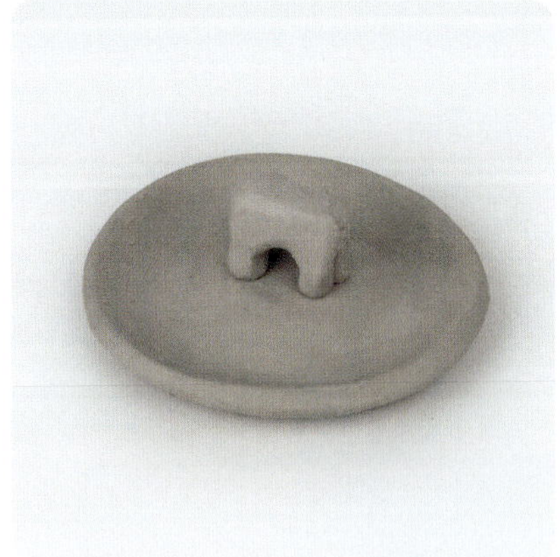

2. Roll out a short log shape for the elephant's body. Roll out a coil and cut it into 4 segments for legs. Attach the body to the legs and then to the center of the mound.

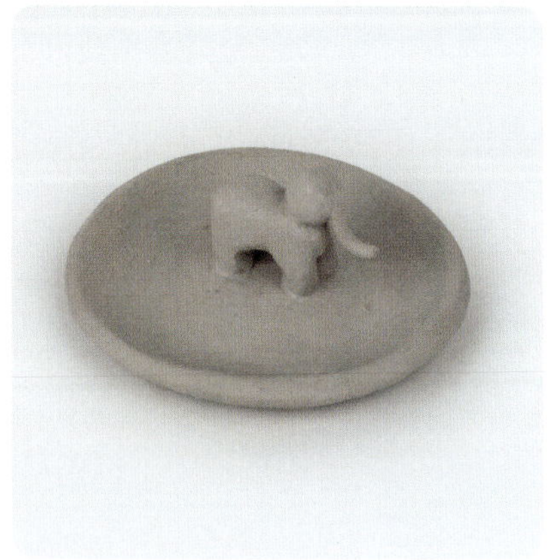

3. Sculpt a ball and connect it to the front of the body for a head. Roll out a coil and cut one edge into a slant. Attach it to the front of the head to form a trunk, then blend and smooth.

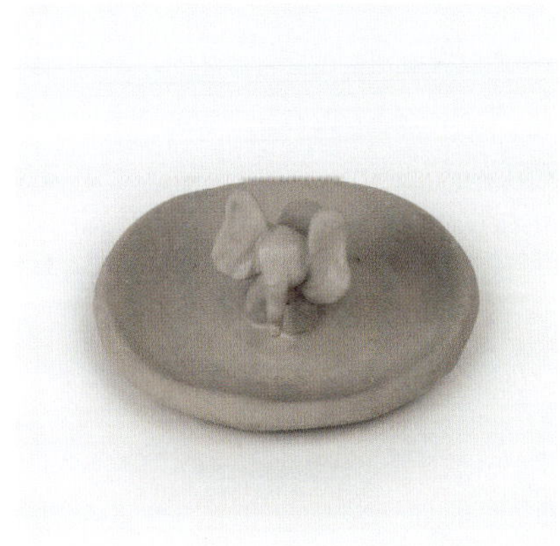

4. For each ear, flatten out an oval of clay and indent one side to make a peanut shape. Connect it to the side and back of the head. Repeat on the other side. Connect a small bit of clay to the back of the body for a tail.

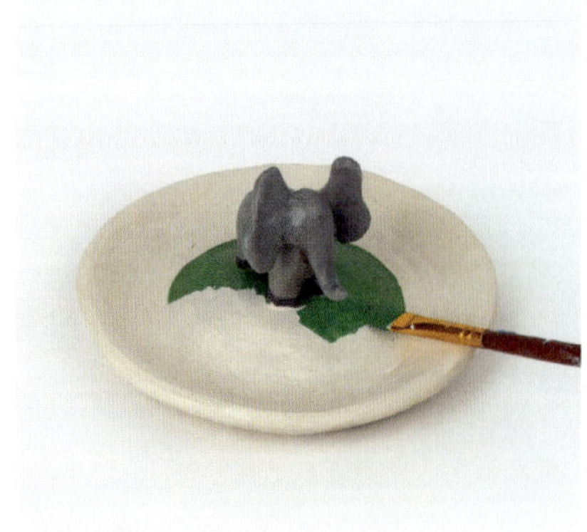

5. Once dry, paint the mound in the center of the dish green and the rest of the dish off-white. Paint details, like eyes, onto the elephant and paint the rest of it gray. When the paint is dry, seal the piece with Mod Podge.

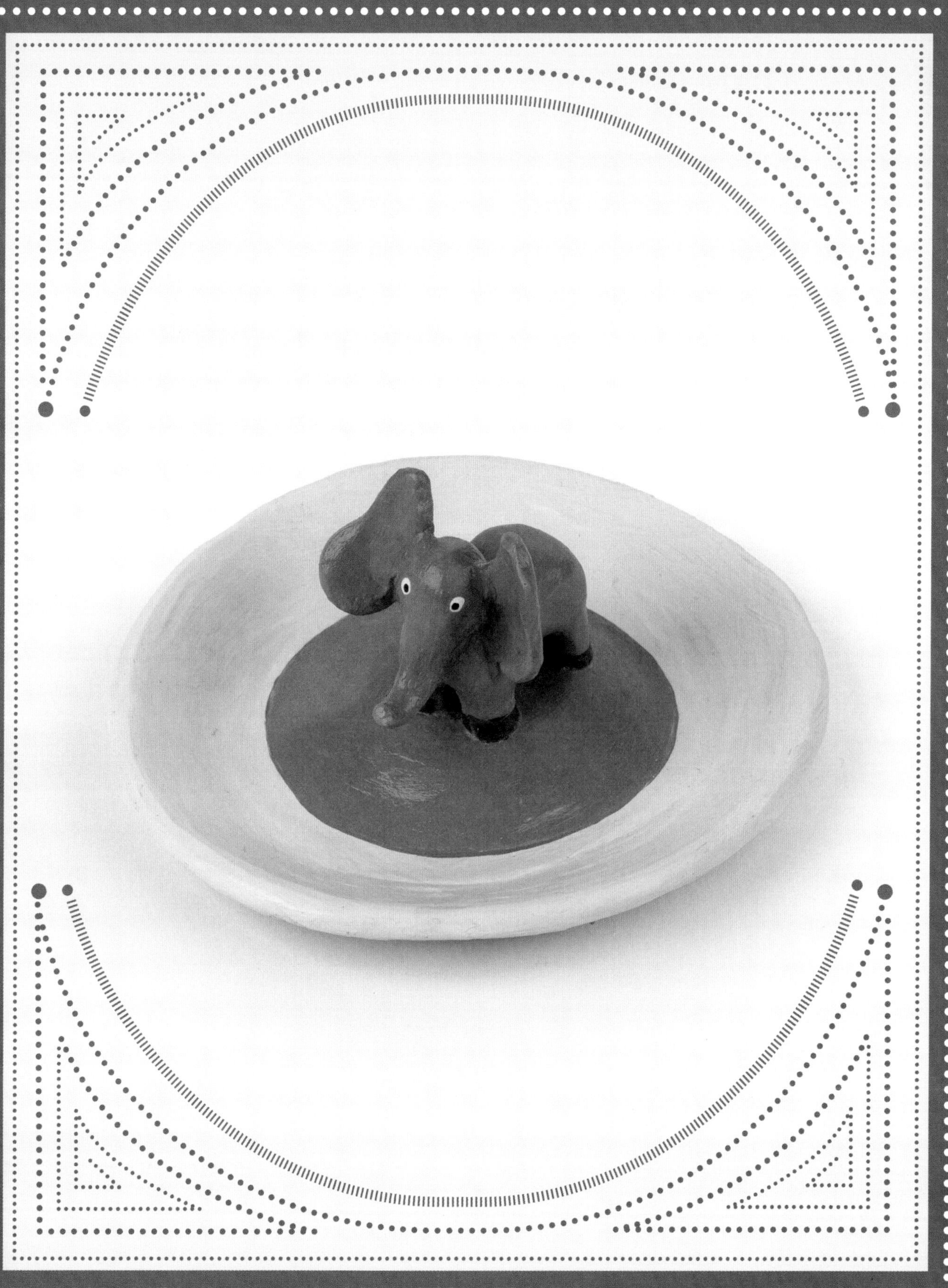

Flower Dish

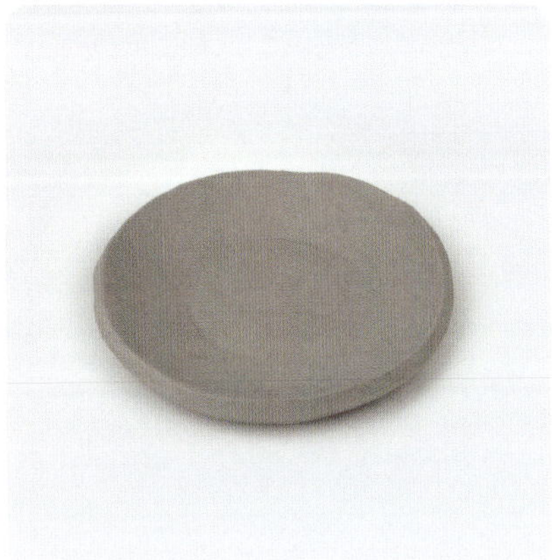

1. Make a dish (see Small Dish Tutorial on page 86).

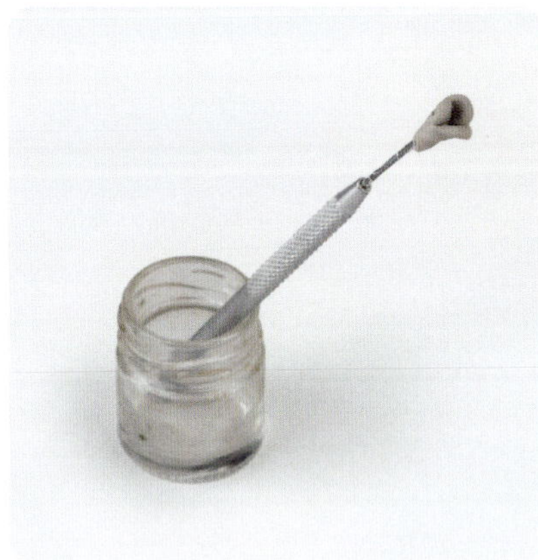

2. Roll and flatten out 3 small balls for petals. Wrap them around the needle tool to create a bud. Rest the needle tool in a small jar or cup to leave your hands free for the clay and to use as a base structure.

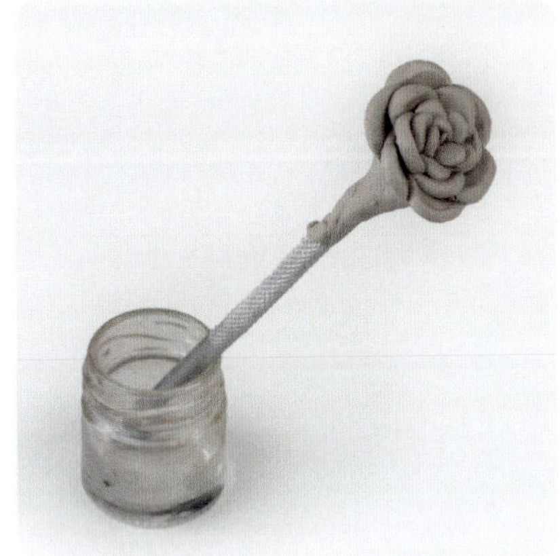

3. Roll out 5 more balls and flatten them into petal shapes. Attach the petals one at a time around the original petals on the needle tool, increasing in size for each layer. Wrap a bit of extra clay to the needle tool handle to keep the flower sturdy.

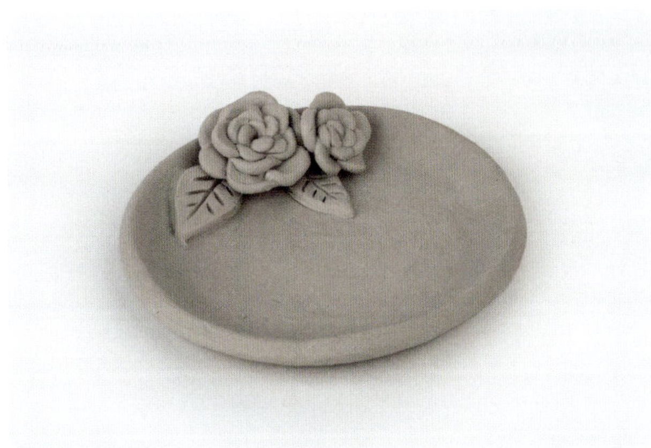

4. Repeat steps 2 and 3 on a slightly smaller scale and attach both flowers to the edge of your dish. Roll out a thin slab and cut out 2 leaf shapes. Attach them to either side of the larger flower and use your needle tool to add textural lines.

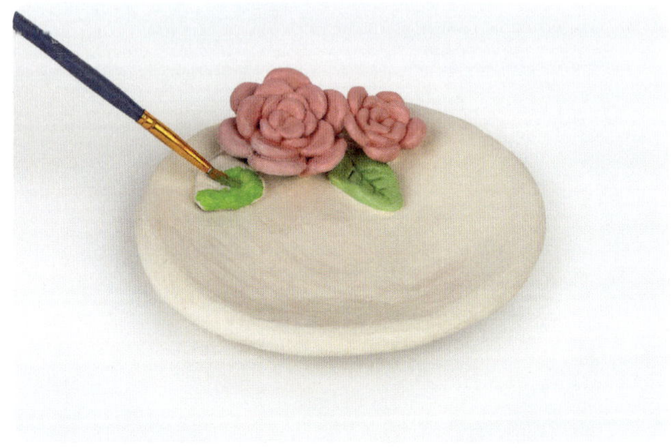

5. Once fully dry, paint the dish a solid color and paint the flowers and leaves as you like. When the paint is dry, seal the piece with Mod Podge to finish.

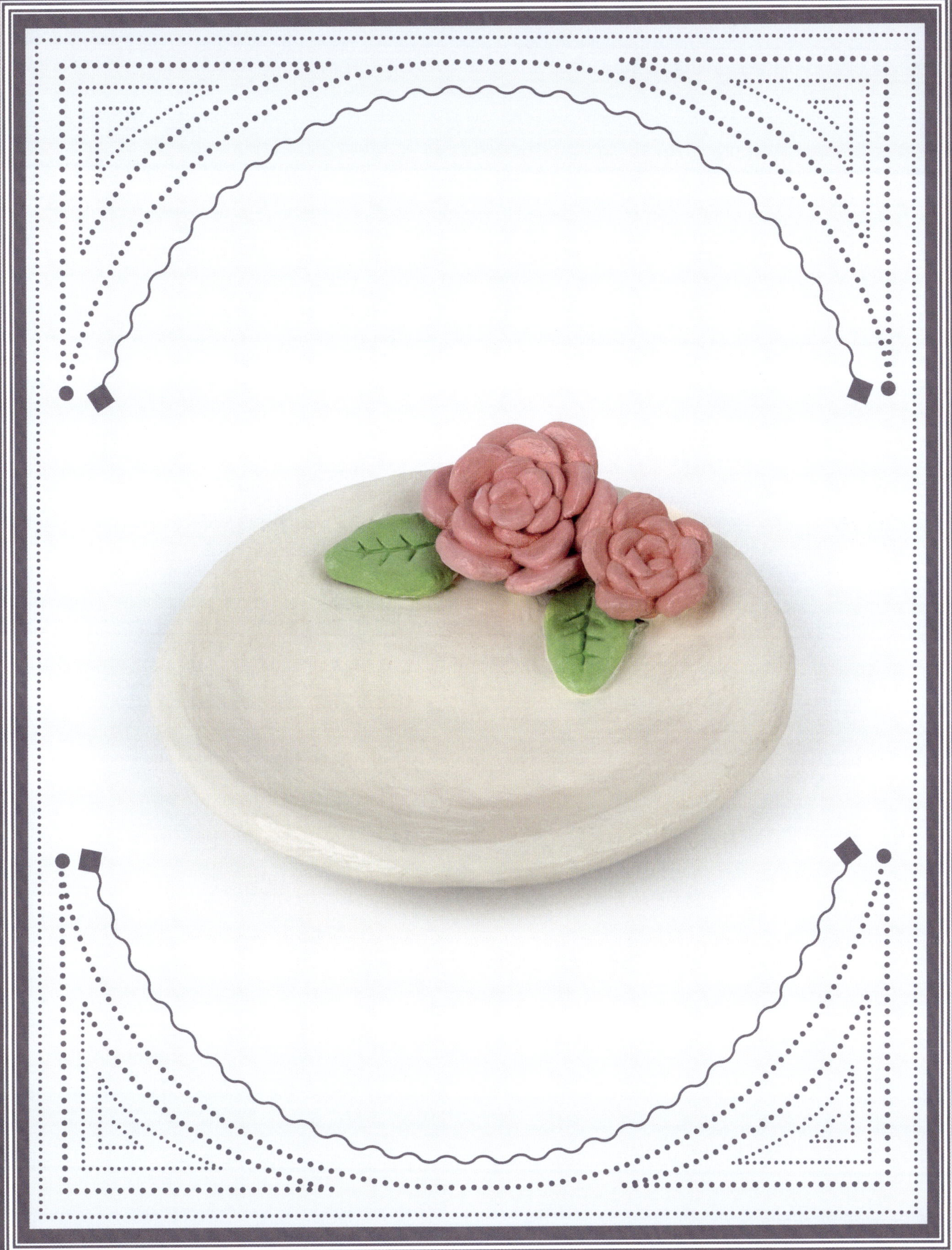

Strawberry Dish

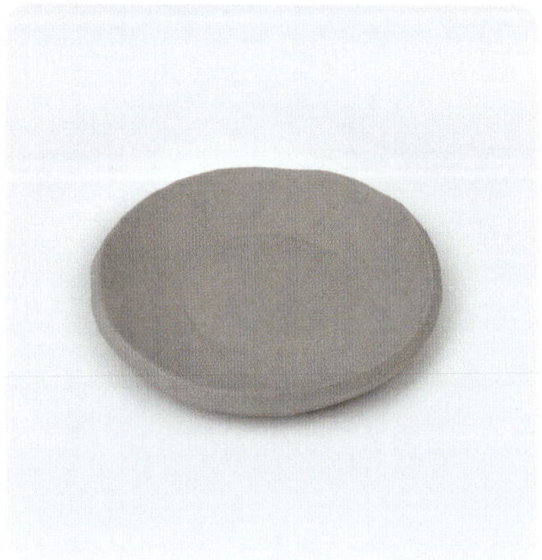

1. Create a dish (see Small Dish Tutorial on page 86).

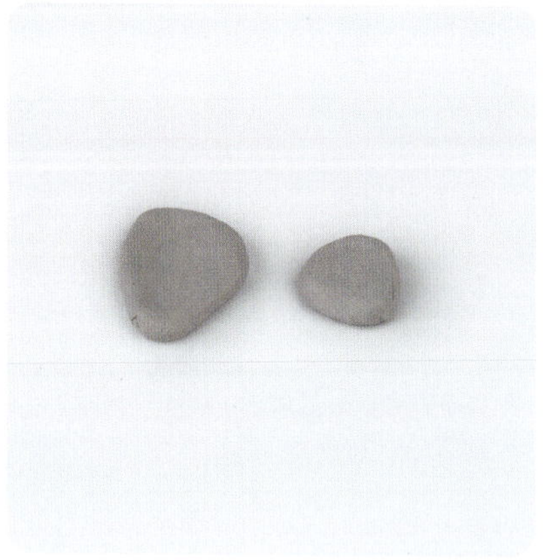

2. To create the strawberries, roll out 2 balls and flatten them into rounded triangles, one slightly smaller than the other.

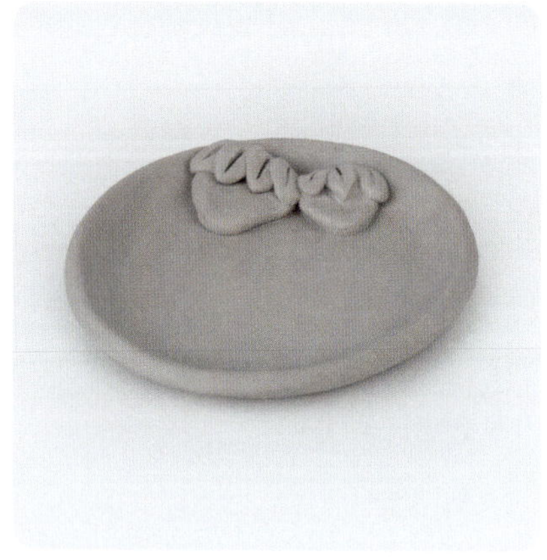

3. Sculpt 3 leaf shapes and attach them to the top of one strawberry. Repeat for the second strawberry and add lines down each leaf.

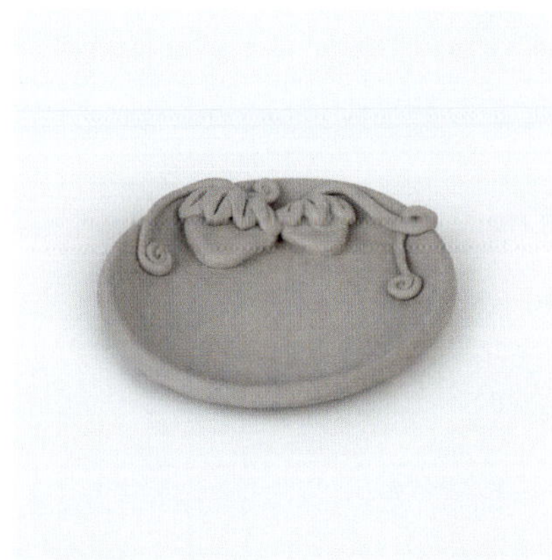

4. For the vines, roll out 2 long thin coils. Place one end of each so that it emerges from each strawberry. Lay the coils along the edge of your dish, adding loops and curls. Sculpt small leaves and attach them along the vines. Use the needle tool to poke shallow holes in the berries.

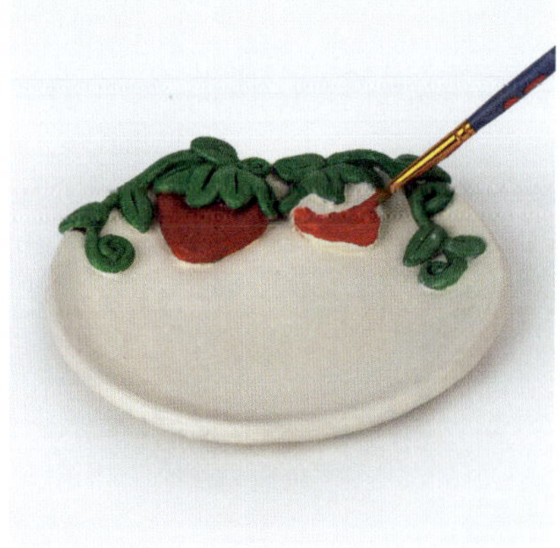

5. Once dry, paint the dish a solid color, such as off-white, the berries red, and the vines green. When the paint is dry, seal the piece with Mod Podge to finish.

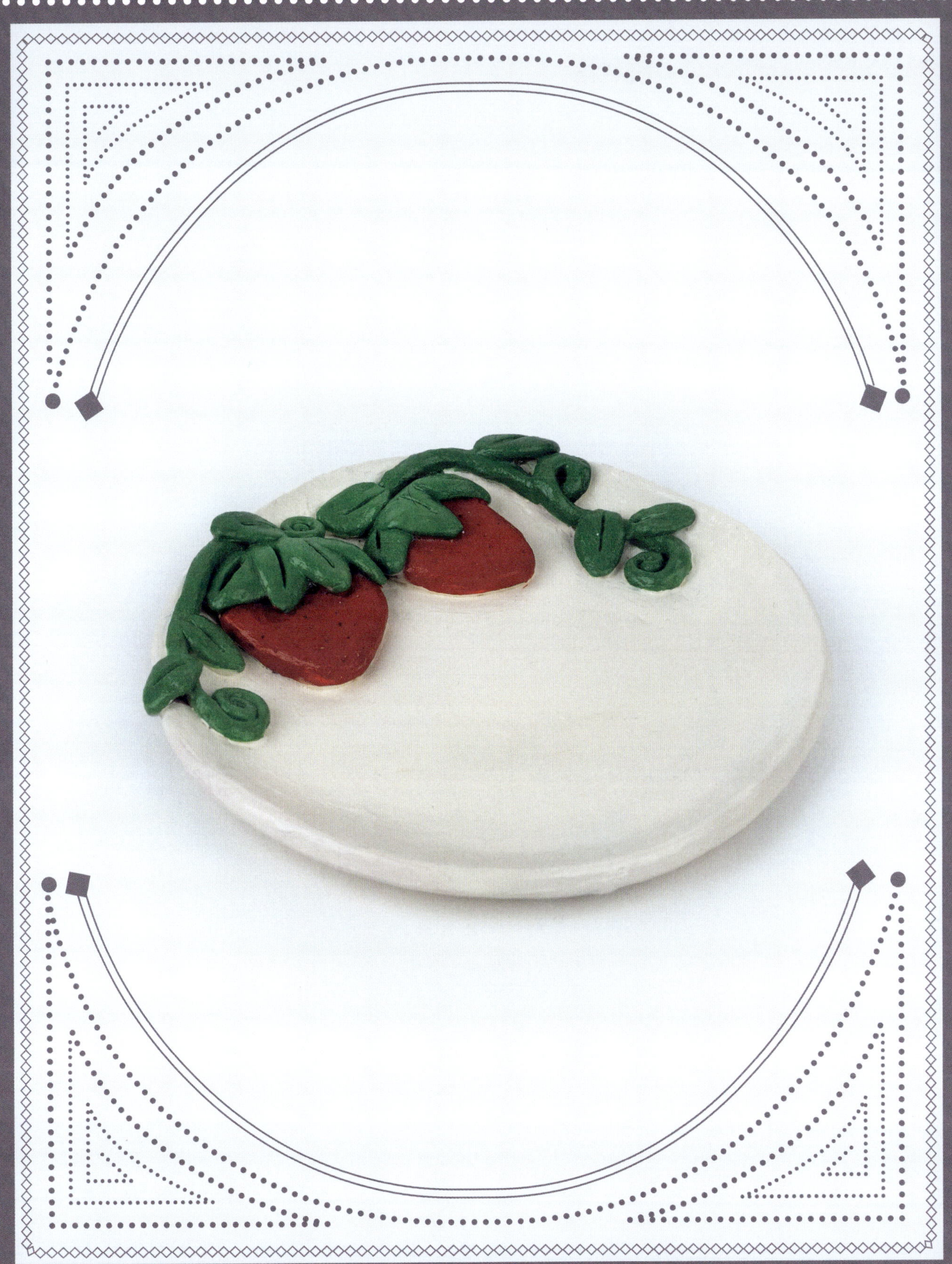

Mushrooms & Snail Dish

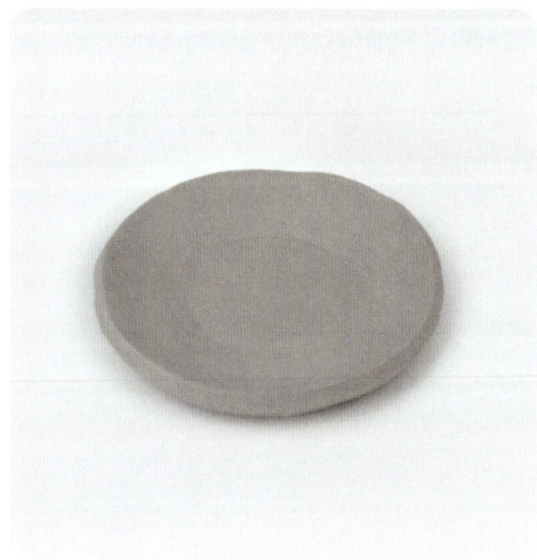

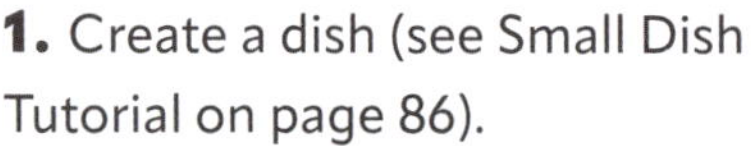

1. Create a dish (see Small Dish Tutorial on page 86).

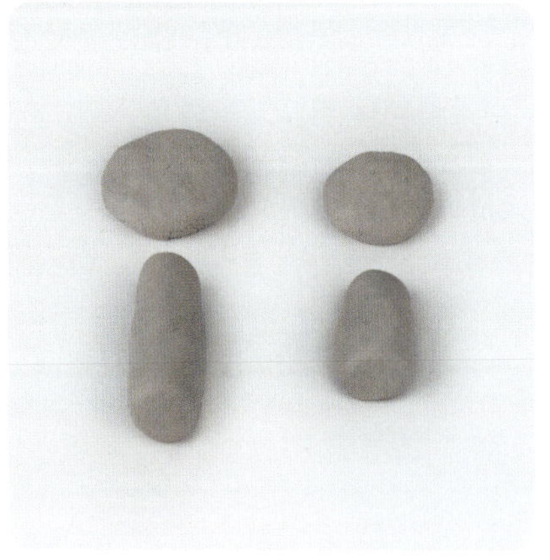

2. For the mushroom stems, roll out 2 coils, one longer than the other. Flatten 2 balls for the mushroom caps and use your thumb to gently press each cap upward, raising the middle.

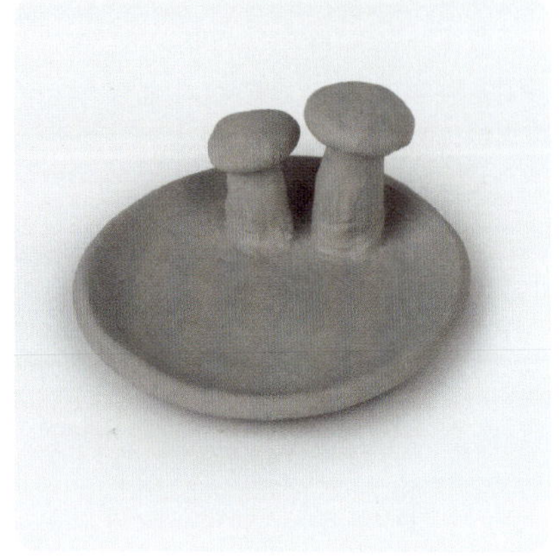

3. Attach the stems to the dish and the caps to the tops of the stems.

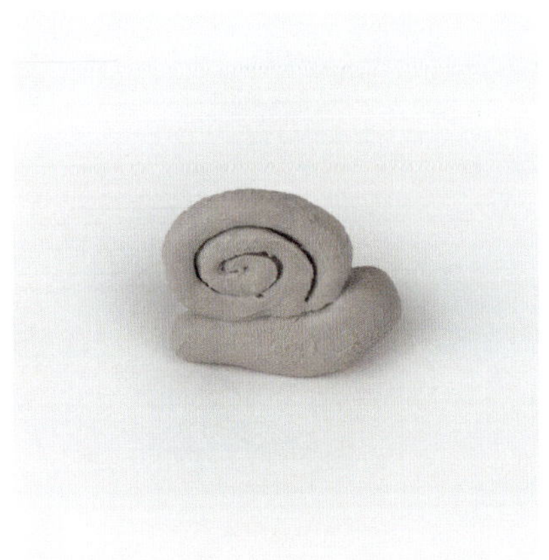

4. For the snail, roll out a long coil and create a spiral. Attach the edge of the coil to another small segment of clay. Lift one end of that segment to make a head.

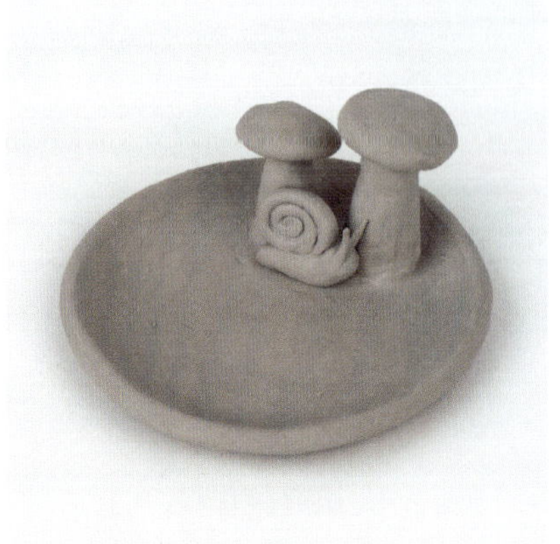

5. Attach the snail to the dish so that it leans against the smaller mushroom stem. Roll tiny coils and carefully attach them to the top of the snail's head. Lean the back coil against the mushroom for support.

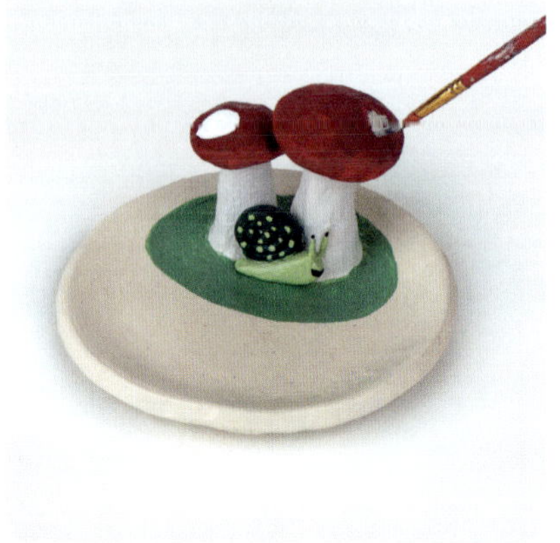

6. Once dry, paint a green circle around the base of the mushrooms and snail and paint the rest of the dish a solid color, such as off-white. Paint the snail and mushrooms as you like. When the paint is dry, seal the piece with Mod Podge to finish.

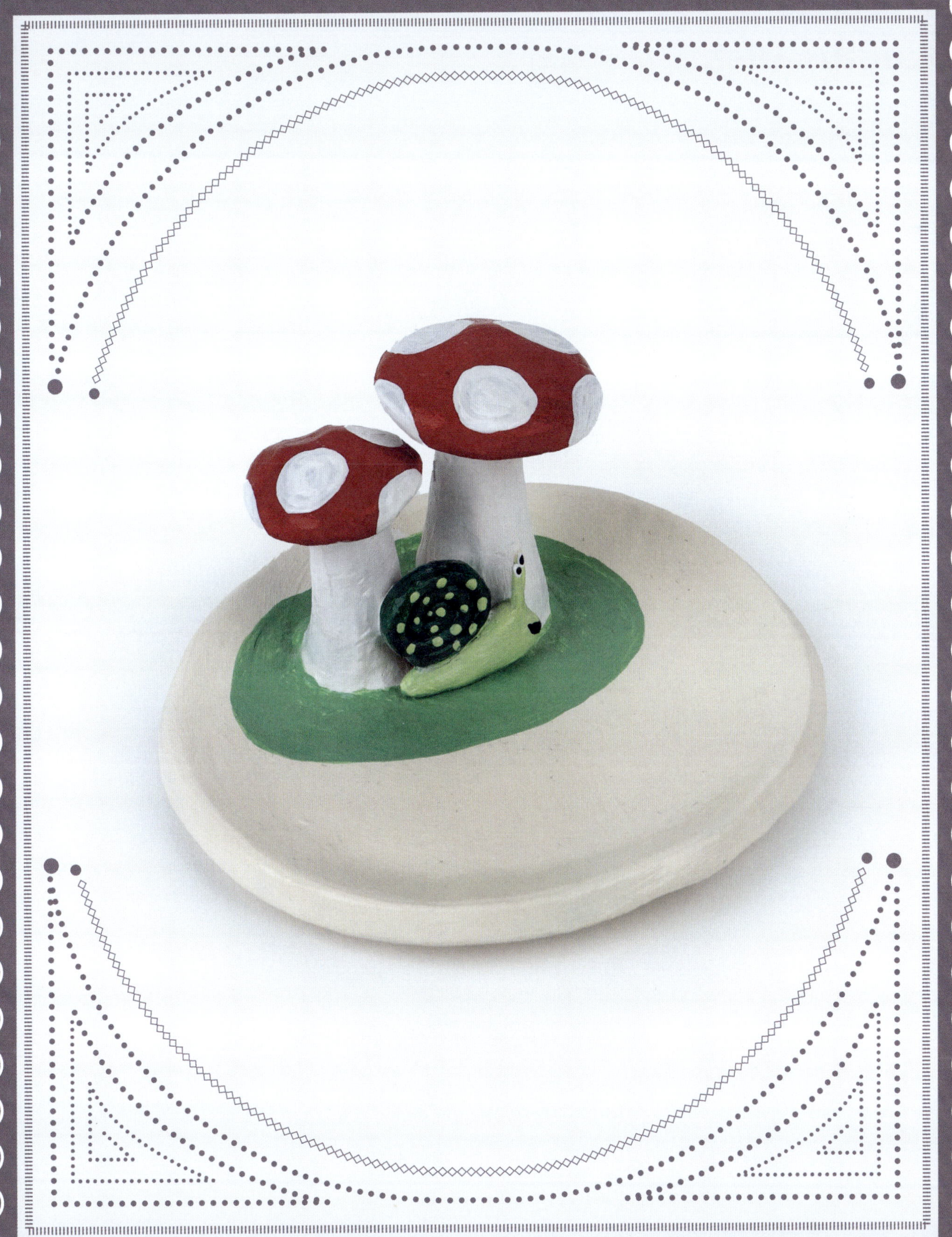

Cactus Dish

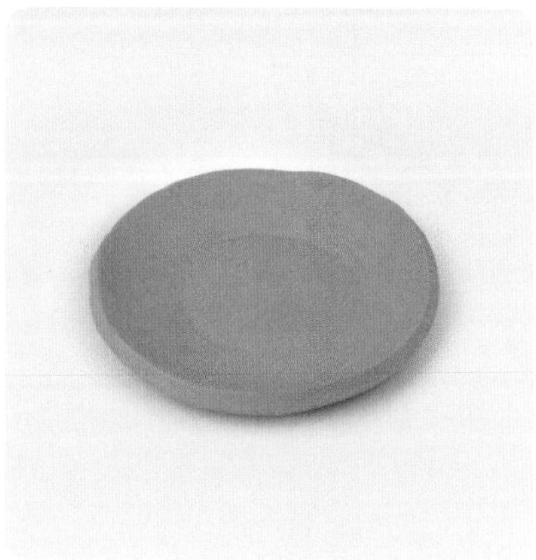

1. Create a dish (see Small Dish Tutorial on page 86).

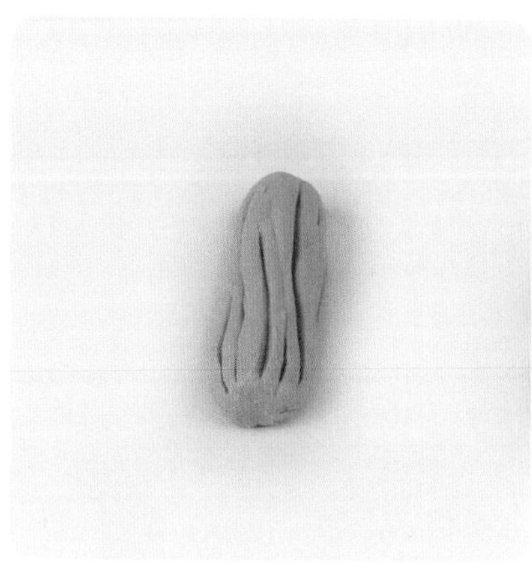

2. Roll out a thick coil. Carve imperfect lines up the sides with a small carving tool. Use a wet paintbrush to smooth.

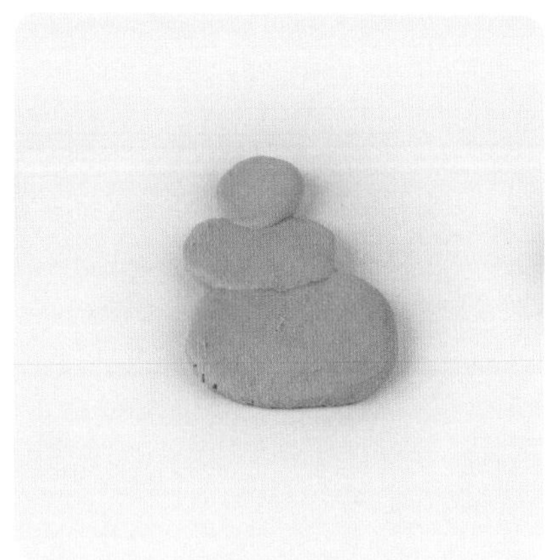

3. Create 3 balls decreasing in size. Flatten the balls and lay them out so they slightly overlap at each connecting point. Score and slip them together (see page 15). If needed, add a bit of clay at the back of the connection points for structural support. Use a needle tool to add dots across the cactus for texture.

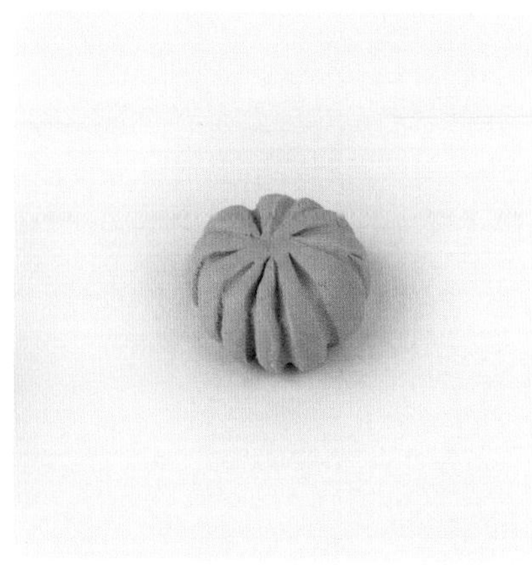

4. Roll out another small ball and slightly flatten it so it's squat. Use a needle tool to carve vertical lines all the way around the ball.

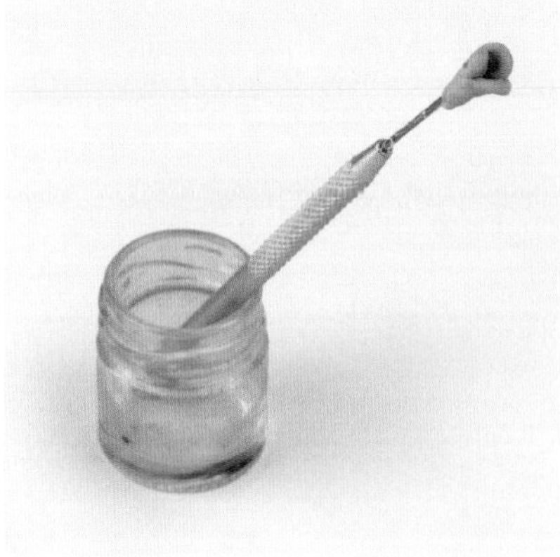

5. Roll and flatten out 3 small balls for petals. Wrap them around the needle tool to create a bud. Rest the needle tool in a small jar or cup to leave your hands free for the clay and to use as a base structure.

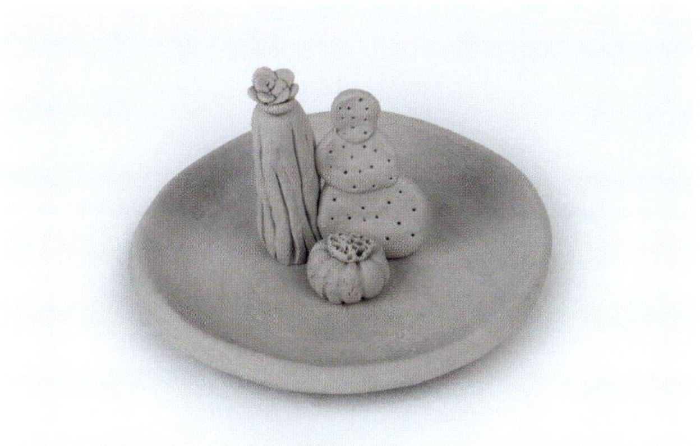

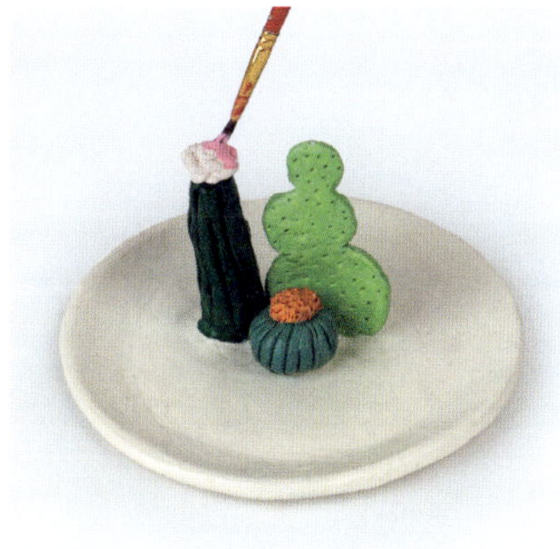

6. Attach each cactus piece to the center of the dish. You may need to add some structural support to the piece from step 3. Do this by rolling out a very thin coil the length of the cactus's back and smoothing it into the base of the dish and the back bottom of the structure. Attach the flower to the top of the tall cactus from step 2. Add a small ball of clay to the top of the squat cactus from step 4 and use your needle tool to add texture to it.

7. Once dry, paint the dish a solid color, such as off-white, and paint the cacti varying shades of green, with different colors for the 2 flowers. When the paint is dry, seal the piece with Mod Podge to finish.

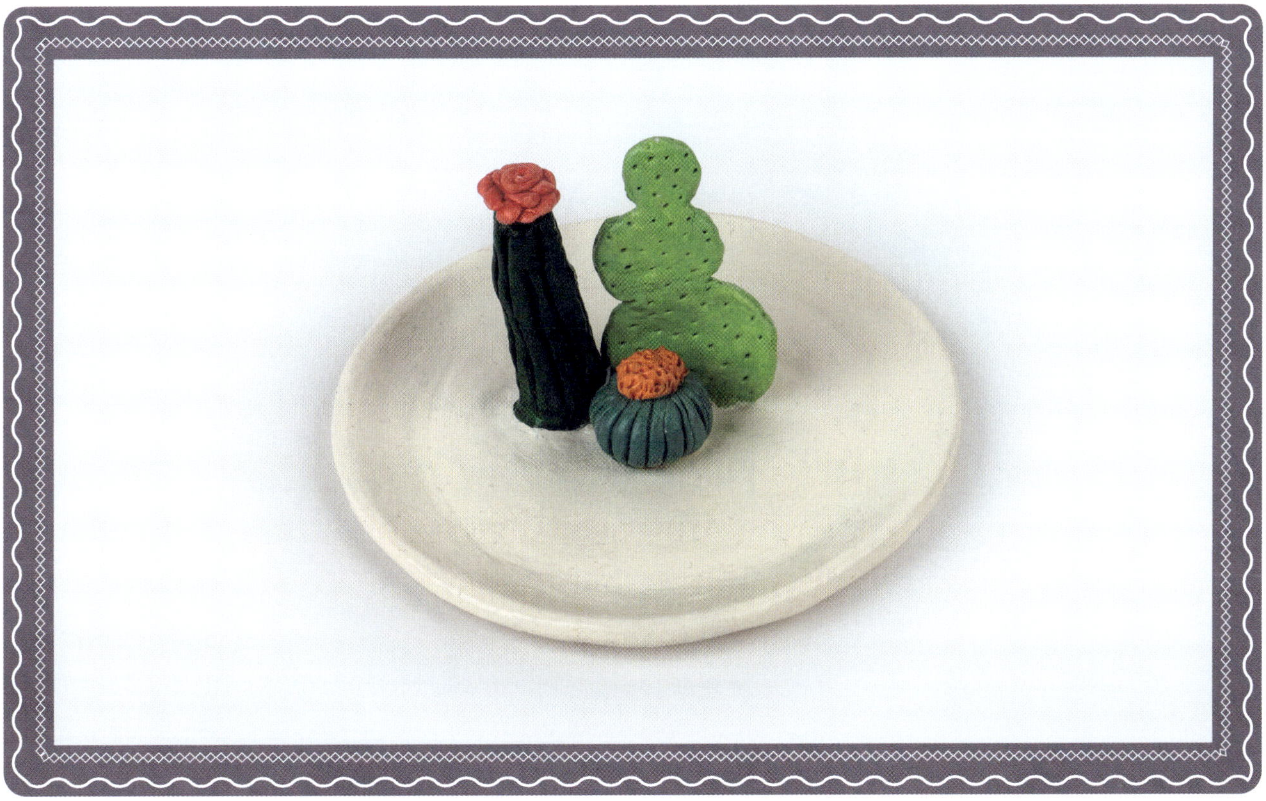

House Dish

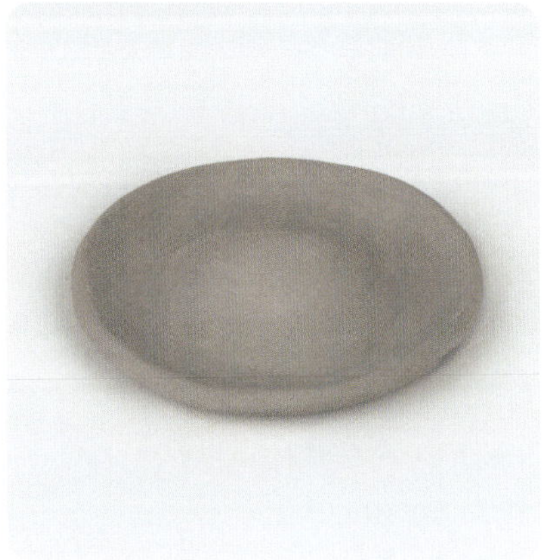

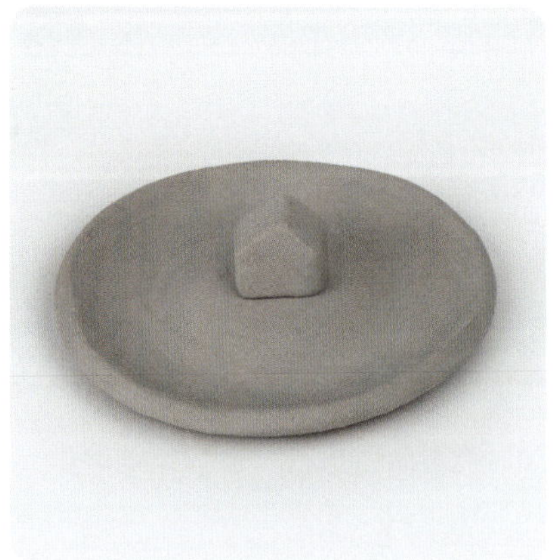

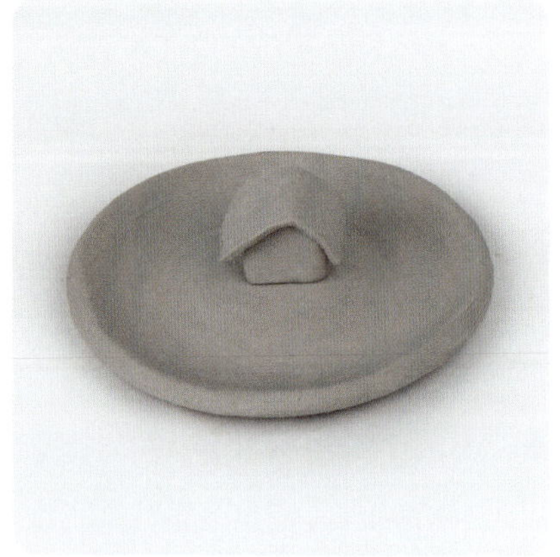

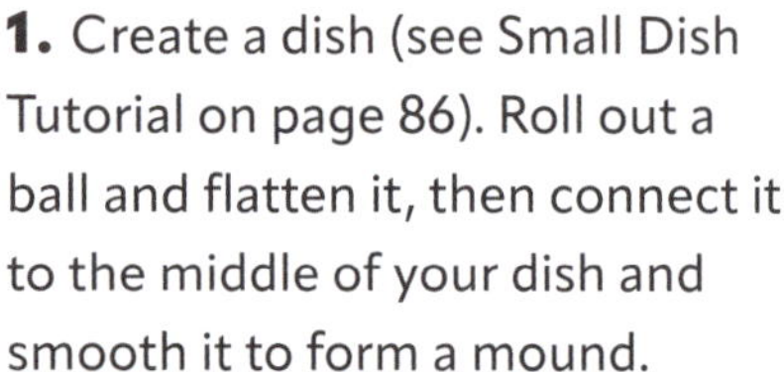

1. Create a dish (see Small Dish Tutorial on page 86). Roll out a ball and flatten it, then connect it to the middle of your dish and smooth it to form a mound.

2. To create the house, sculpt a small cube. Attach it to the middle of the dish on the mound. Use a sharp flat cutting tool to create a slanted roof shape on the top sides of the cube.

3. For the roof, roll out a very thin slab of clay, then cut a rectangle. Score and slip (see page 15) the top of the cube and the underside of the roof piece, then gently fold and press the roof into place.

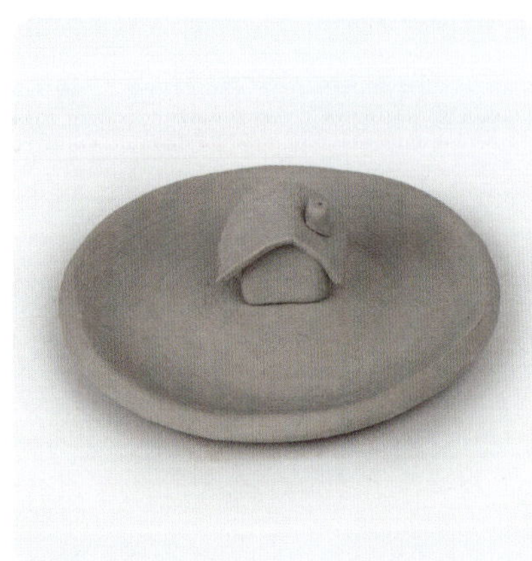

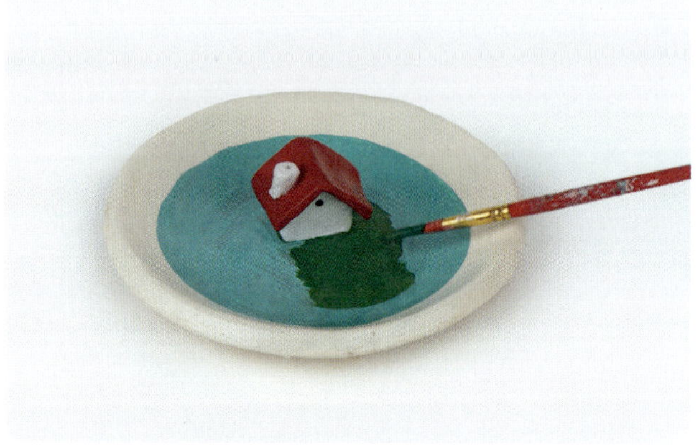

4. To create a chimney, roll out a small coil and cut it into a log shape. Cut one side at the same angle as the roof's slope. Attach it to the side of the roof and poke a small hole in the top with a needle tool.

5. Once dry, paint a dark green circle around the house, then surround that with a circle of lighter green, and paint the rim off-white. Paint details on the house and finish coloring it as you like. When the paint is dry, seal the piece with Mod Podge to finish.

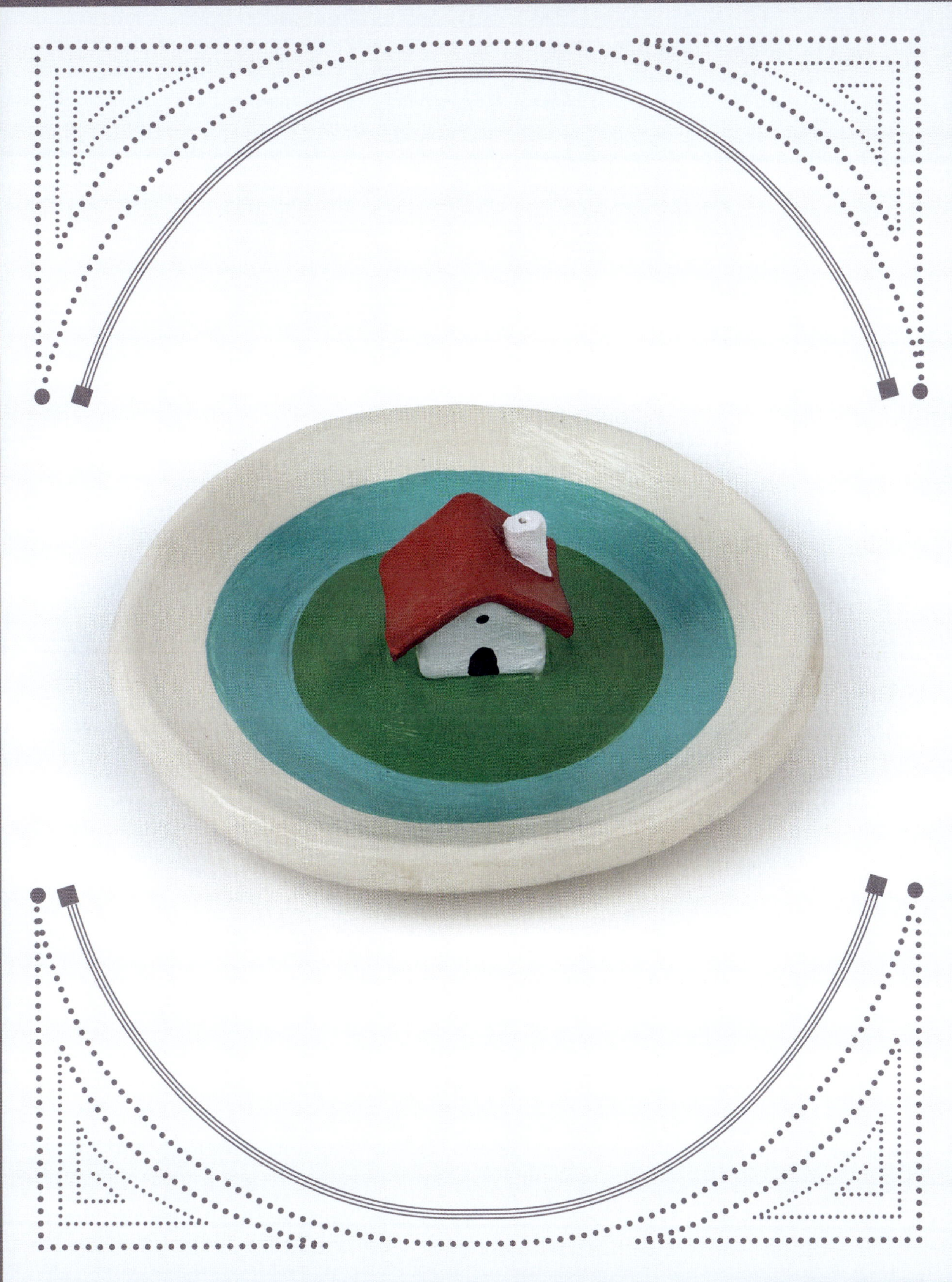

Circular Box Tutorial

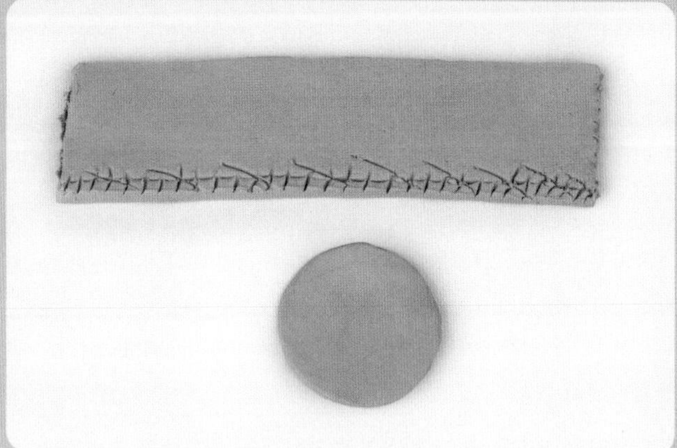

1. Roll out a slab. Cut out a small circle. Use a straight edge to cut a strip long enough to wrap around the circle.

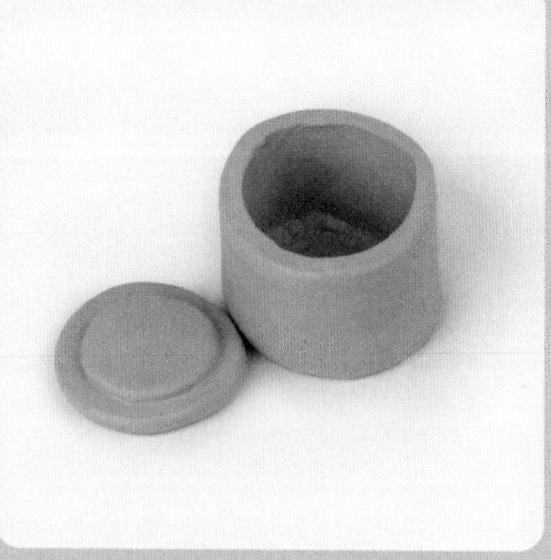

2. Wrap the strip into a cylinder shape around the circle and score and slip the pieces together (see page 15).

To create the lid, cut out another circle the circumference of the top of the box, from outer edge to outer edge. Roll out a slightly thinner slab and cut a circle the size of the inner circumference of the box. Stack and connect the 2 circles. Smooth out any imperfections and allow to dry.

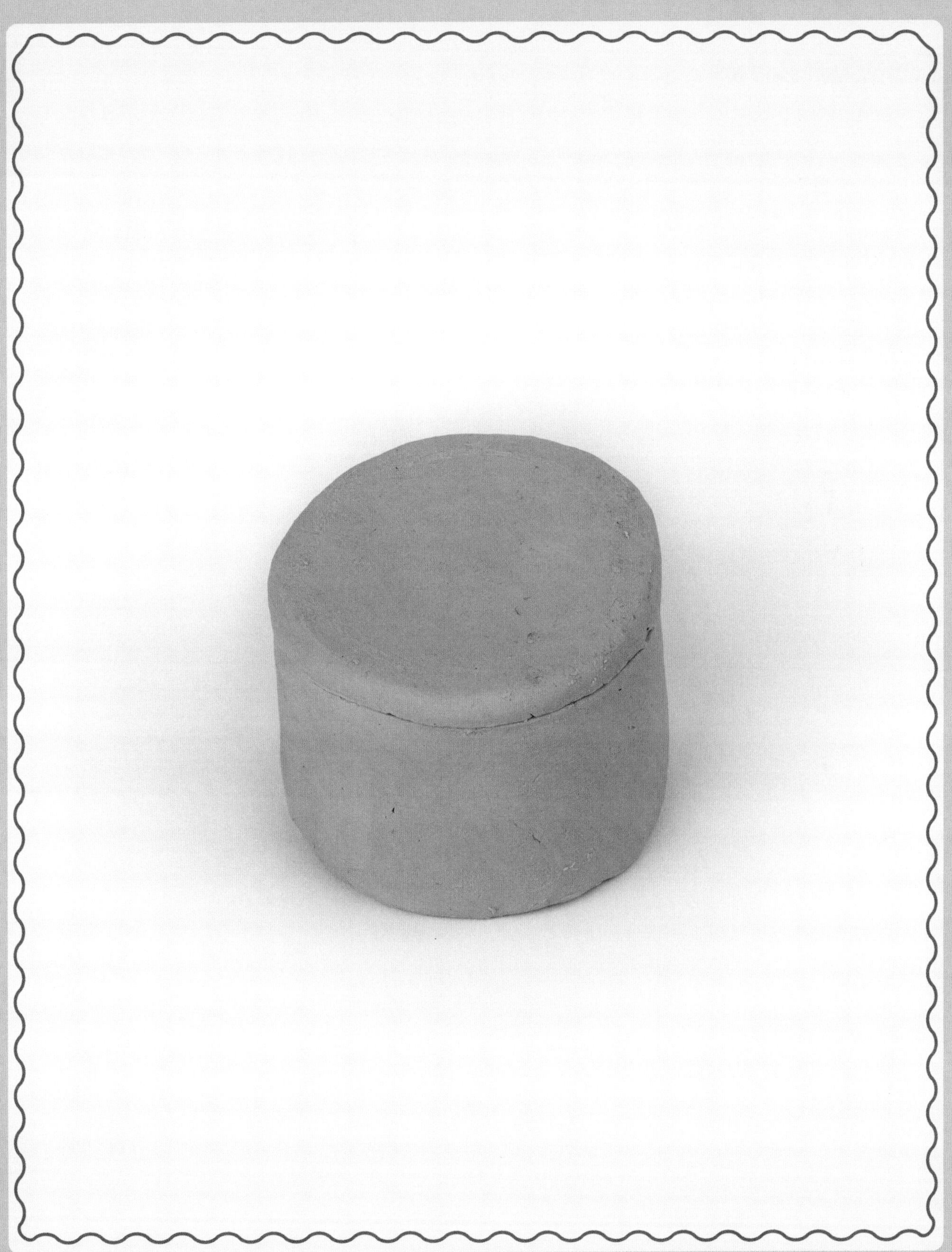

Flower Box

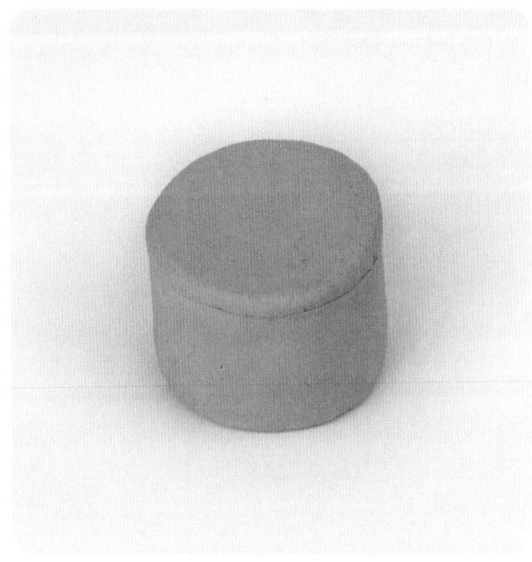

1. Create a box (see Circular Box Tutorial on page 110).

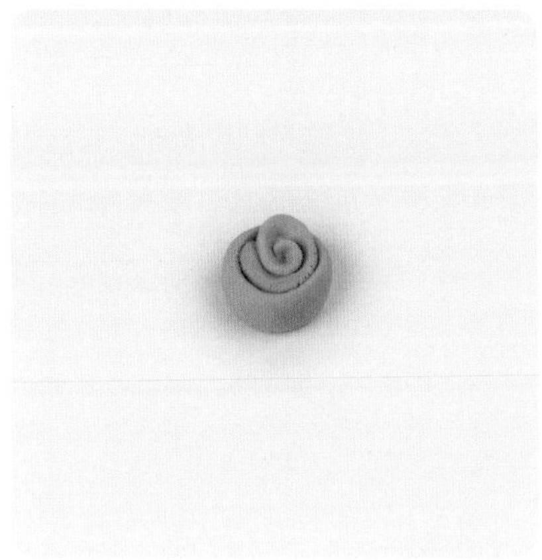

2. Roll out a small coil and flatten it. Wrap the flattened coil around itself to create a bud shape.

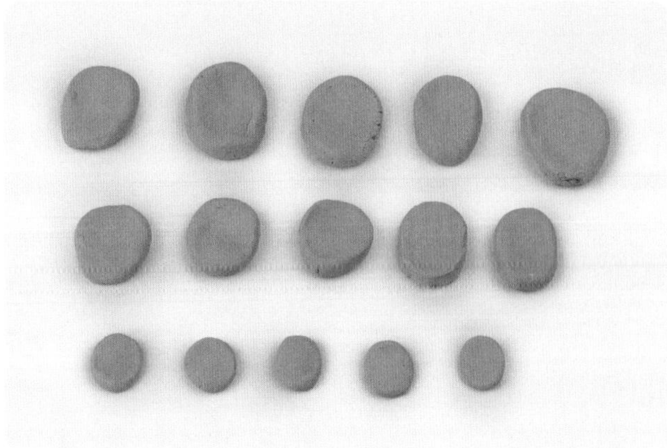

3. Roll out and flatten 15 balls into petals: 3 layers of 5 petals each to wrap around the bud, with each layer increasing in size.

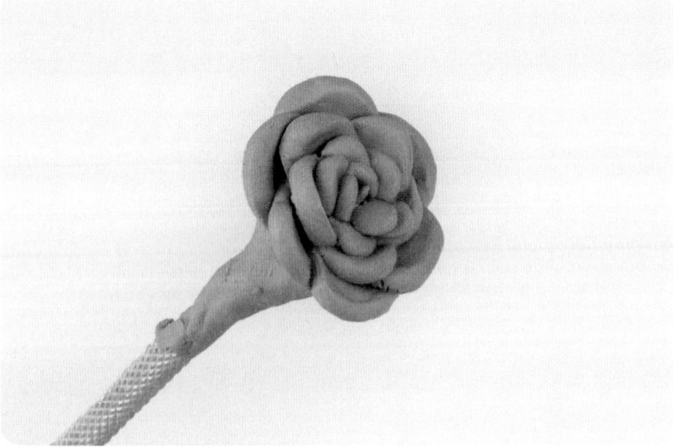

4. Position and attach the petals around the bud.

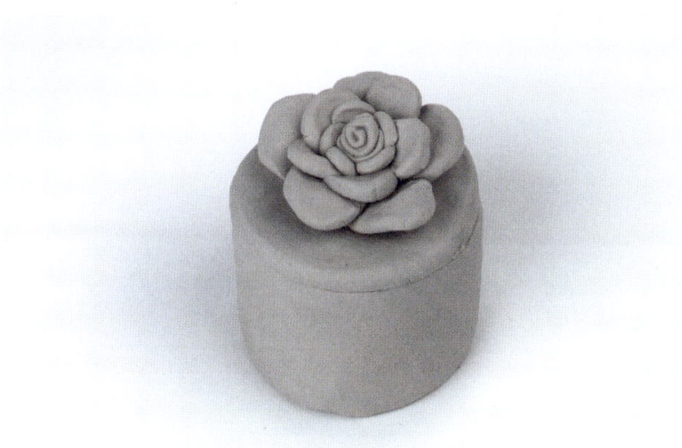

5. Attach the finished flower to the top of your box lid. Use a rib tool to smooth the flower into the top of the lid. Touch up the flower petals gently with a wet brush.

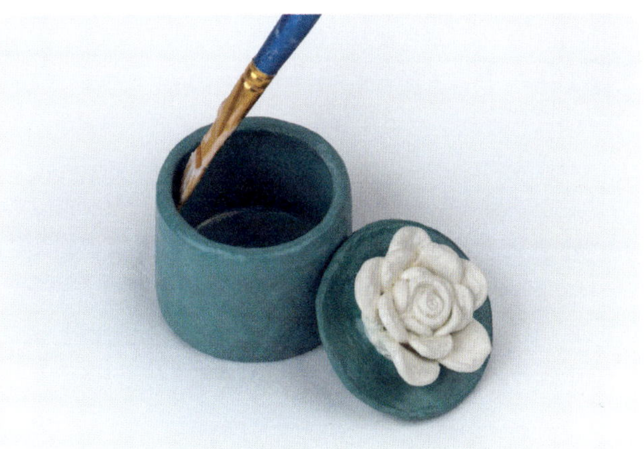

6. Once dry, paint the box and flower colors of your choice. When the paint is dry, seal the piece with Mod Podge to finish.

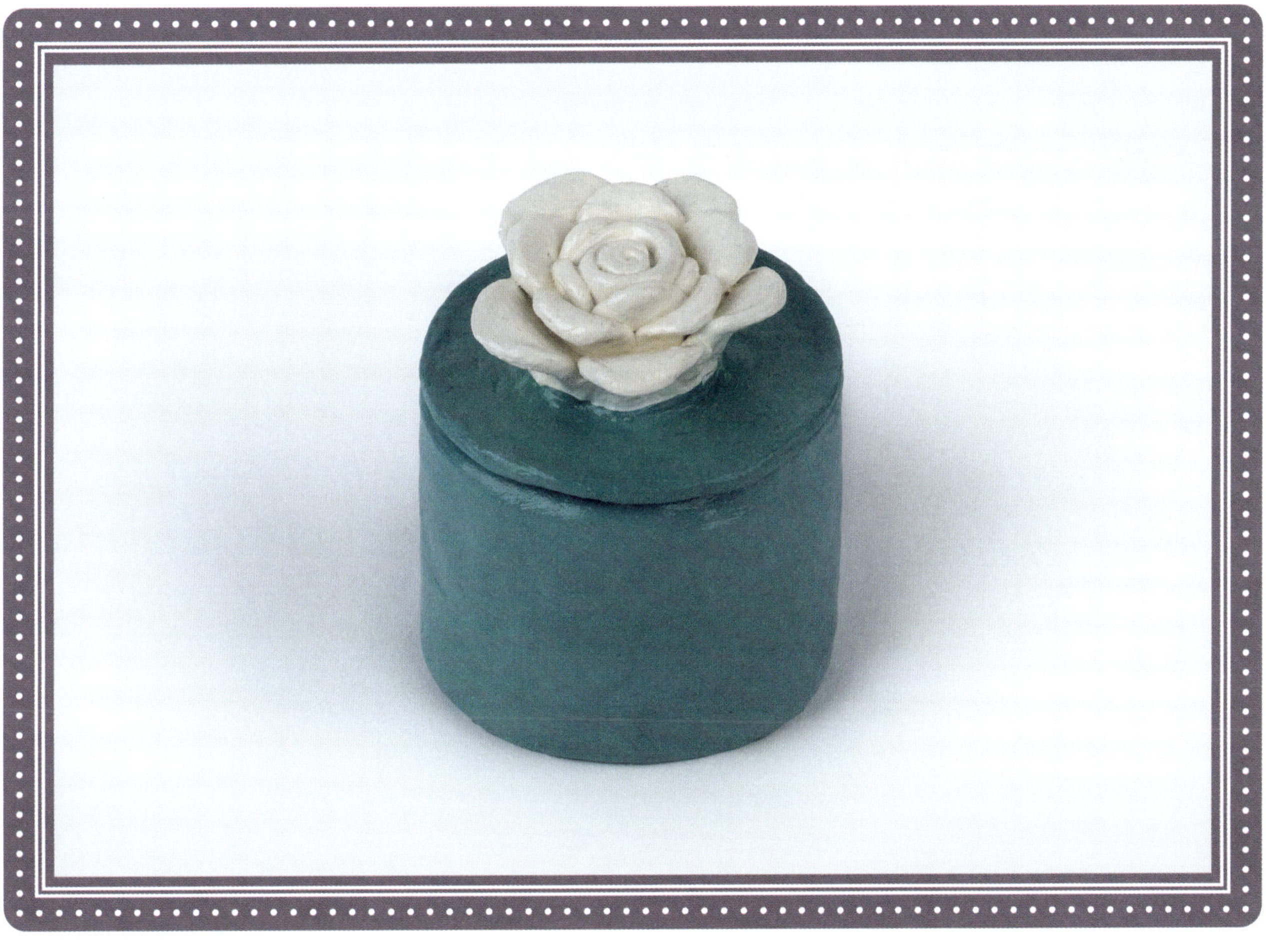

Bow Box

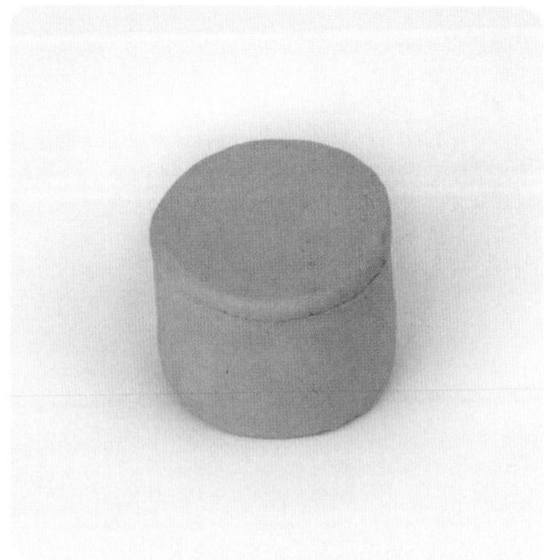

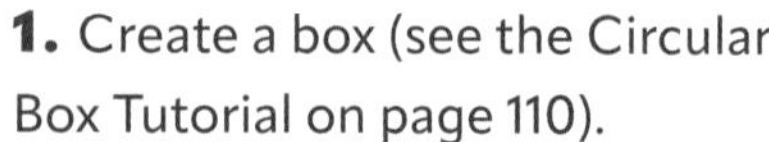

1. Create a box (see the Circular Box Tutorial on page 110).

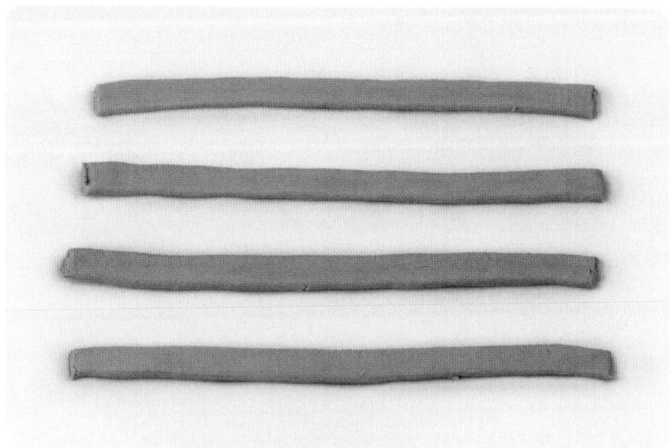

2. Roll out 4 long coils and cut them into segments long enough to wrap vertically around the box like a present. Lightly press to flatten.

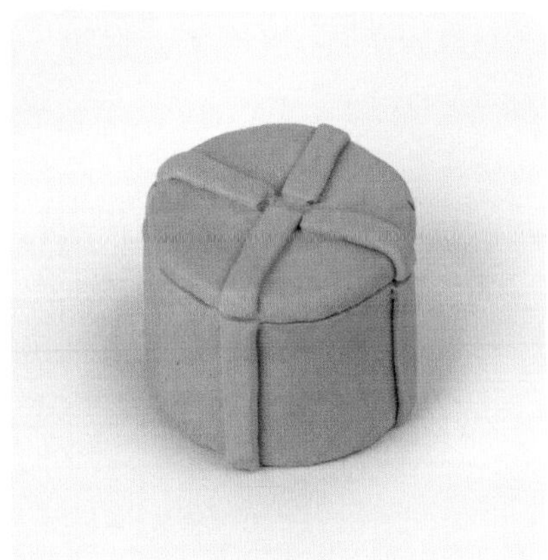

3. Attach the strips in an X shape from the bottom of the box's base to the middle of the lid. Use a cutting tool to slice each strip where the lid and base meet.

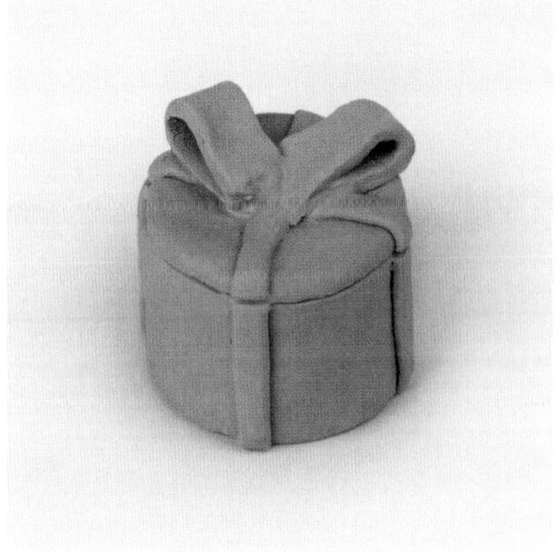

4. Cut out 2 thicker strips about double the length of the box top. Make sure they are very moist and gently fold them over themselves to create a loop effect. Attach them to the center of the box top where the thinner strips meet.

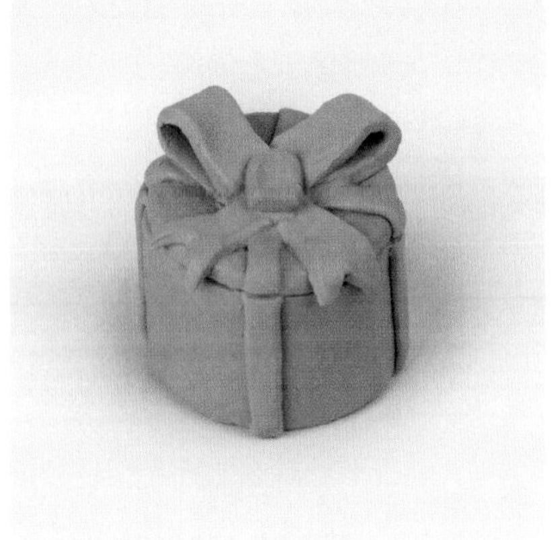

5. To finish the bow, cut out 2 more strips about the same width as the loops. Cut a triangle shape out of one end of each strip and attach them to the top of the box so that they emerge from the bottom of the loops and the ends with the cutouts hang over the side of the box. Sculpt and attach a flattened cube to the middle to hide the joint of the bow. Smooth the components.

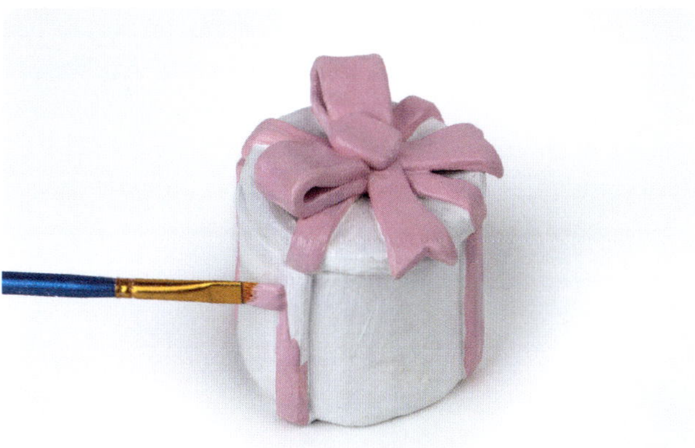

6. Once dry, paint the bow and the inside and outside of the box. When the paint is dry, seal the piece with Mod Podge to finish.

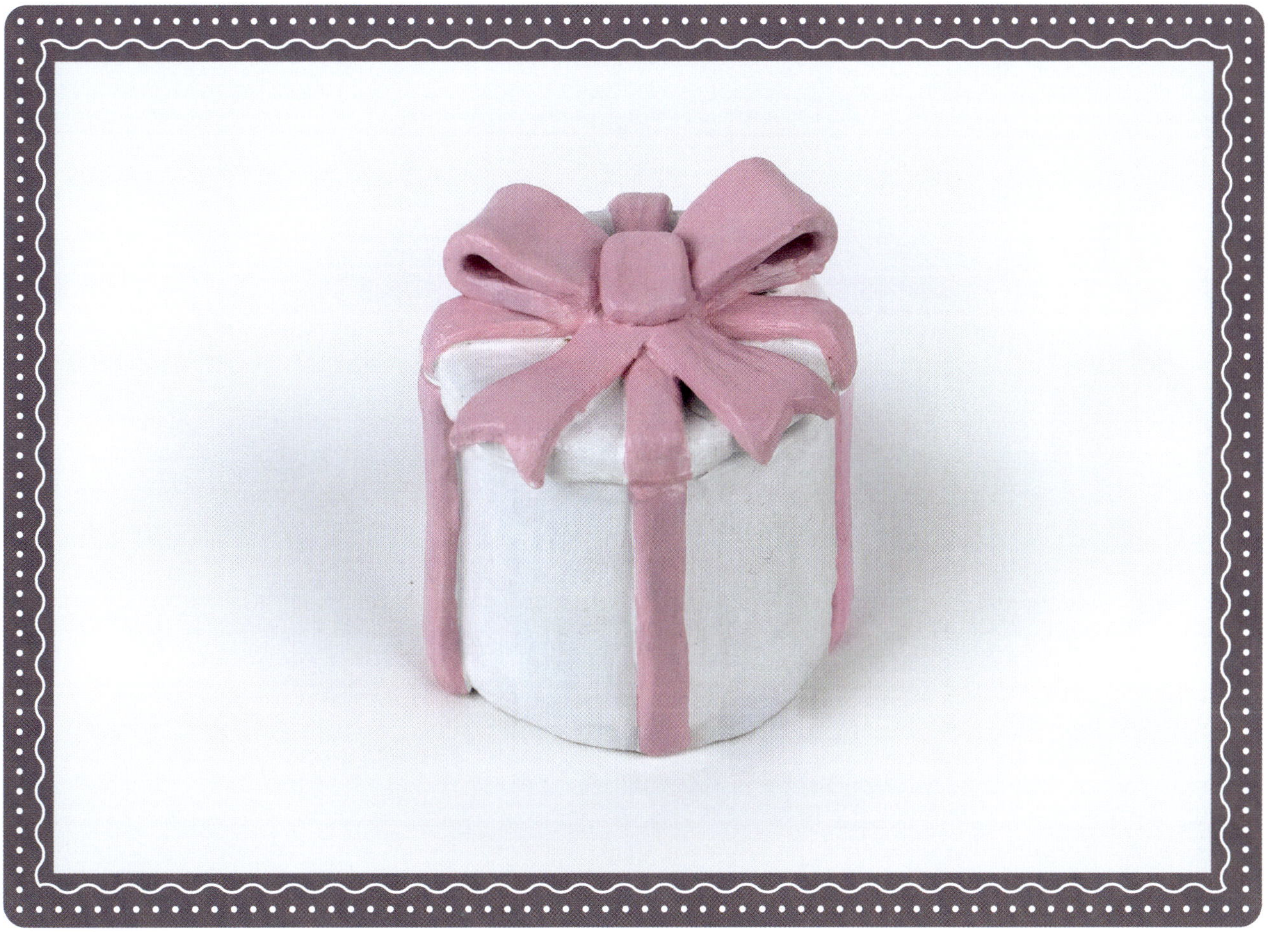

Mushroom Box

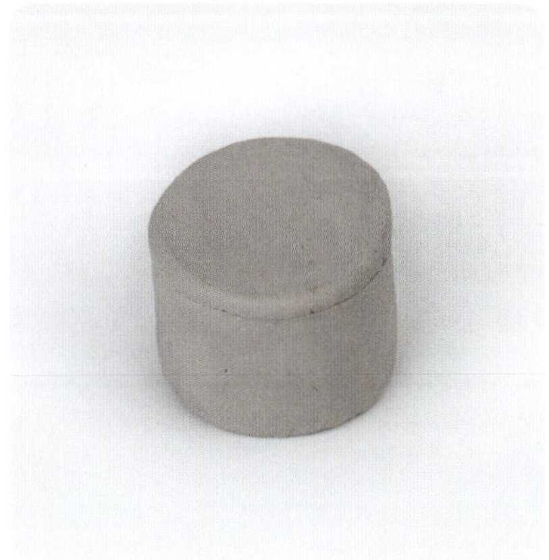

1. Create a box (see Circular Box Tutorial on page 110).

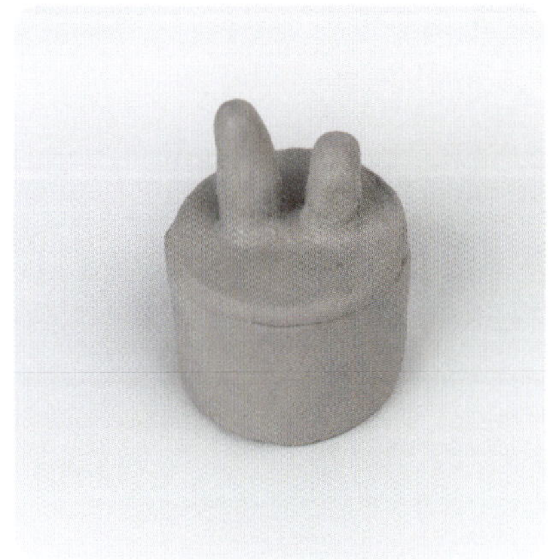

2. For the mushroom stems, roll out 2 thick coils, one slightly longer than the other. Attach them vertically to the center of the lid.

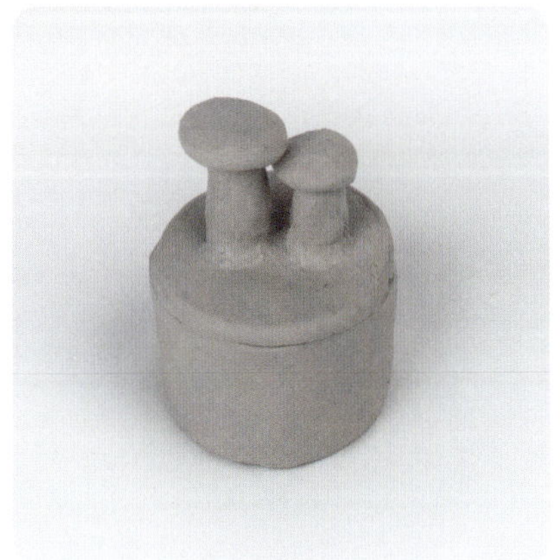

3. Flatten 2 balls into mushroom caps, using your thumb to lightly press the middle upward. Attach them to the tops of the stems.

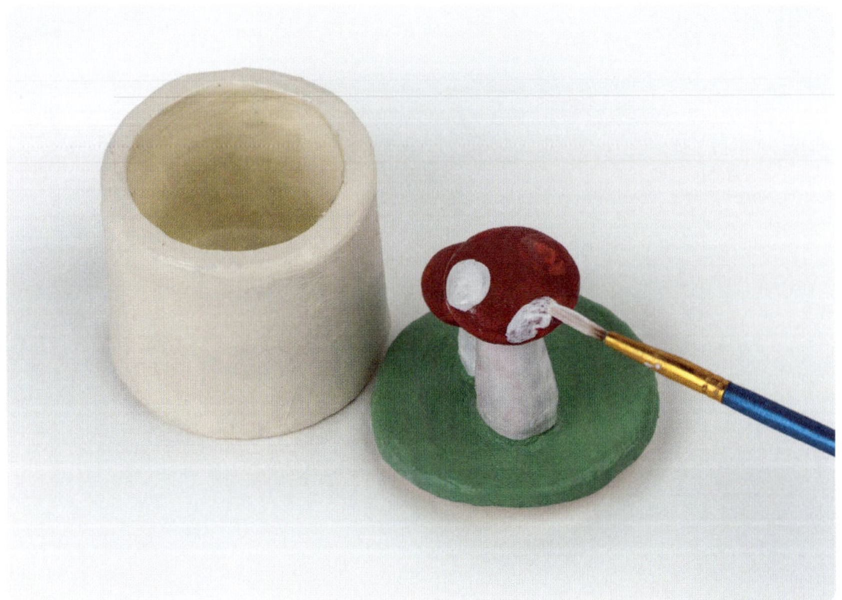

4. Once dry, paint the box inside and out and add whatever details you choose. When the paint is dry, seal the piece with Mod Podge to finish.

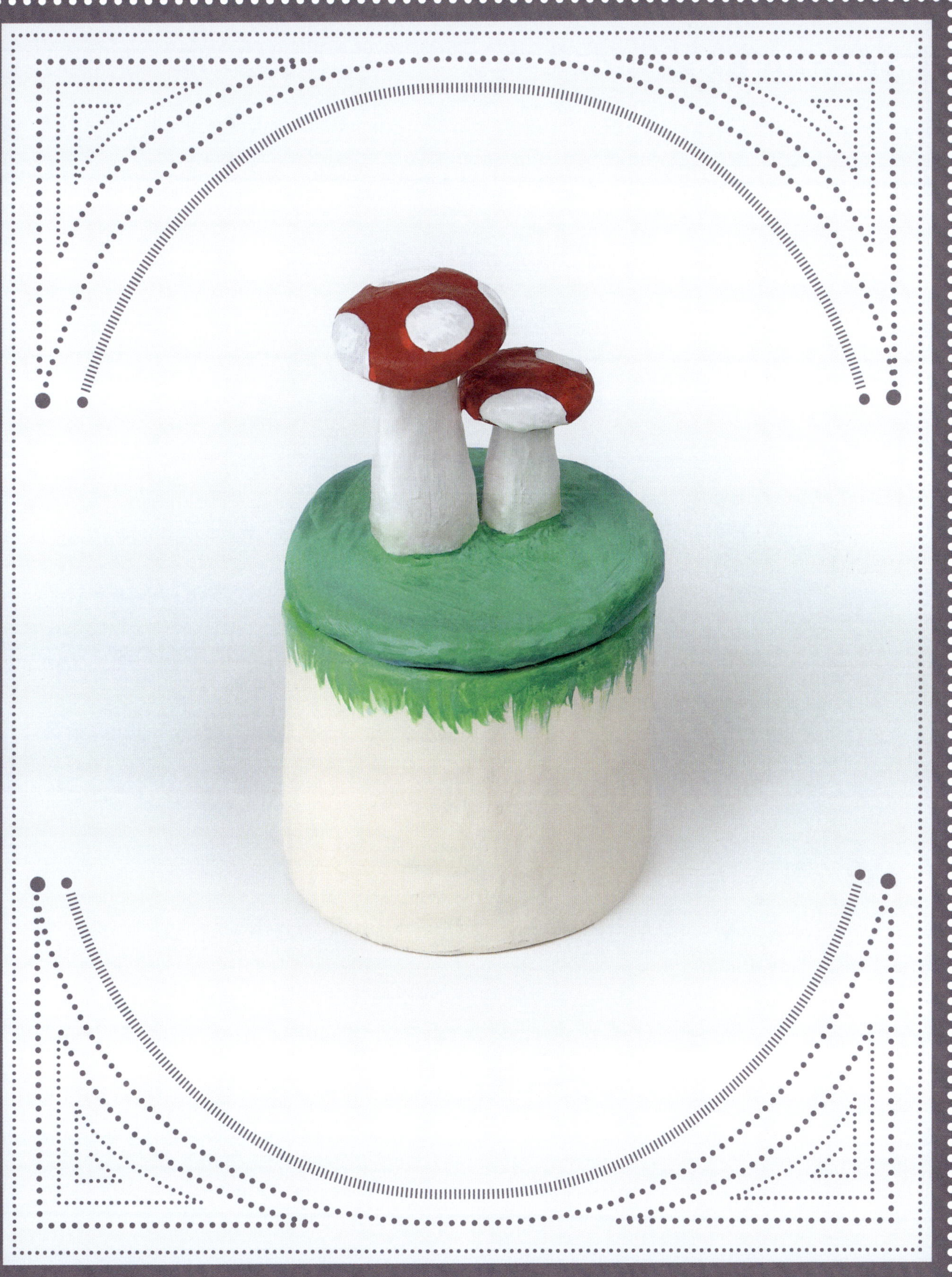

Pancake Box

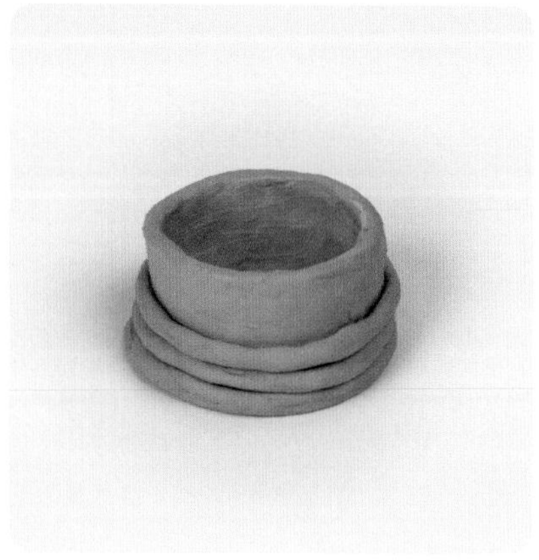

1. Create a box with a lid that is slightly rounded on the sides (see Circular Box Tutorial on page 110). Roll out a coil the thickness of the side of the lid. Score and slip the coil (see page 15) and wrap it around the base of your box, pressing gently as you go to secure it in place.

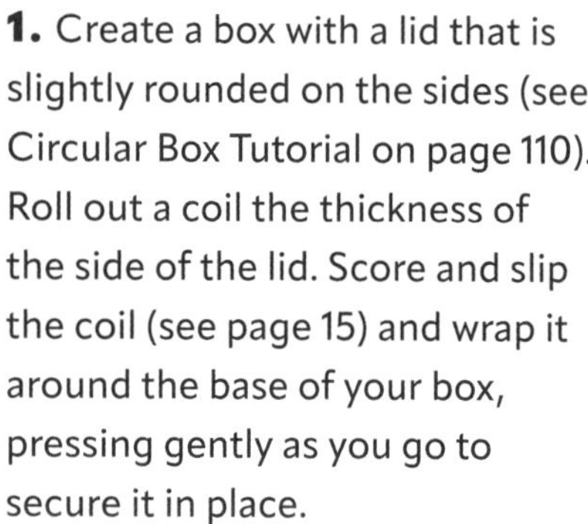

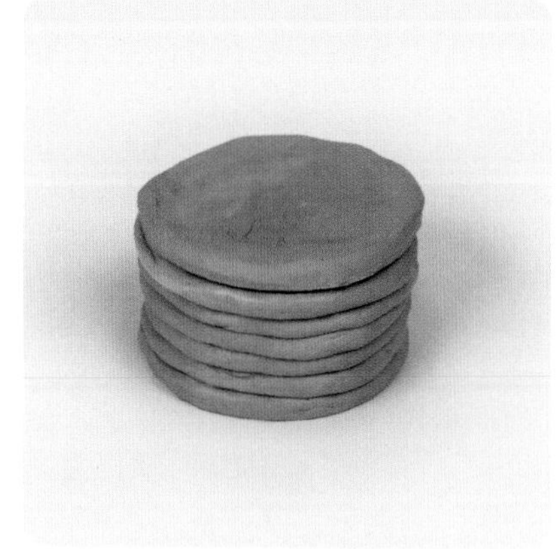

2. Continue to craft and wrap coils all the way up the sides of the box. Blend the last coil into the rim of the box to create a seamless top of the base.

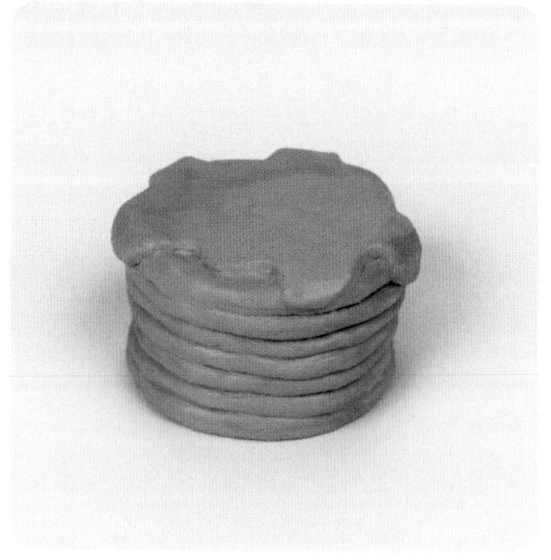

3. Roll out a slab about ¼ inch (6 mm) thick. Use a needle tool to cut out a an imperfect blob shape. Place it on top of the box. Gently press edges downward onto the lid of the box and smooth with a wet brush.

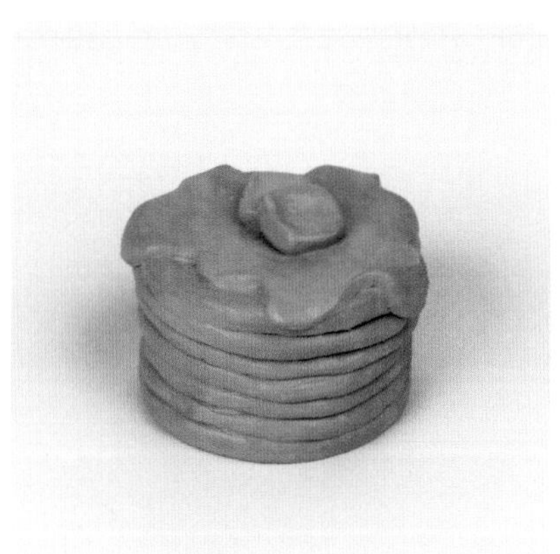

4. Flatten two cubes and attach them to the top of the lid as pats of butter.

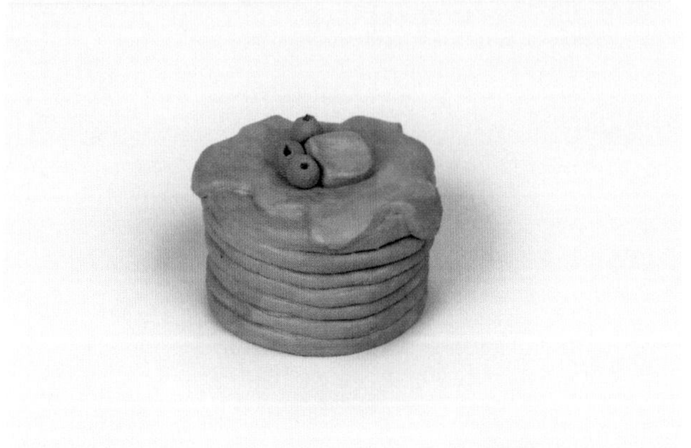

5. Roll out three small balls. Use a needle tool to create a hole in the top of each. Gently pull the clay from the inside to the outside of the holes to create the effect of the top of the blueberries. Add the blueberries to the lid next to the butter.

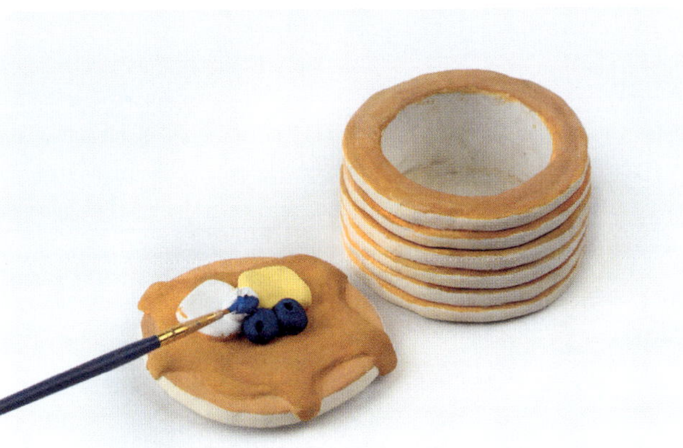

6. Once fully dry, paint the box brown, the blueberries blue, and the squares of butter light yellow. When the paint is dry, seal the piece with Mod Podge to finish.

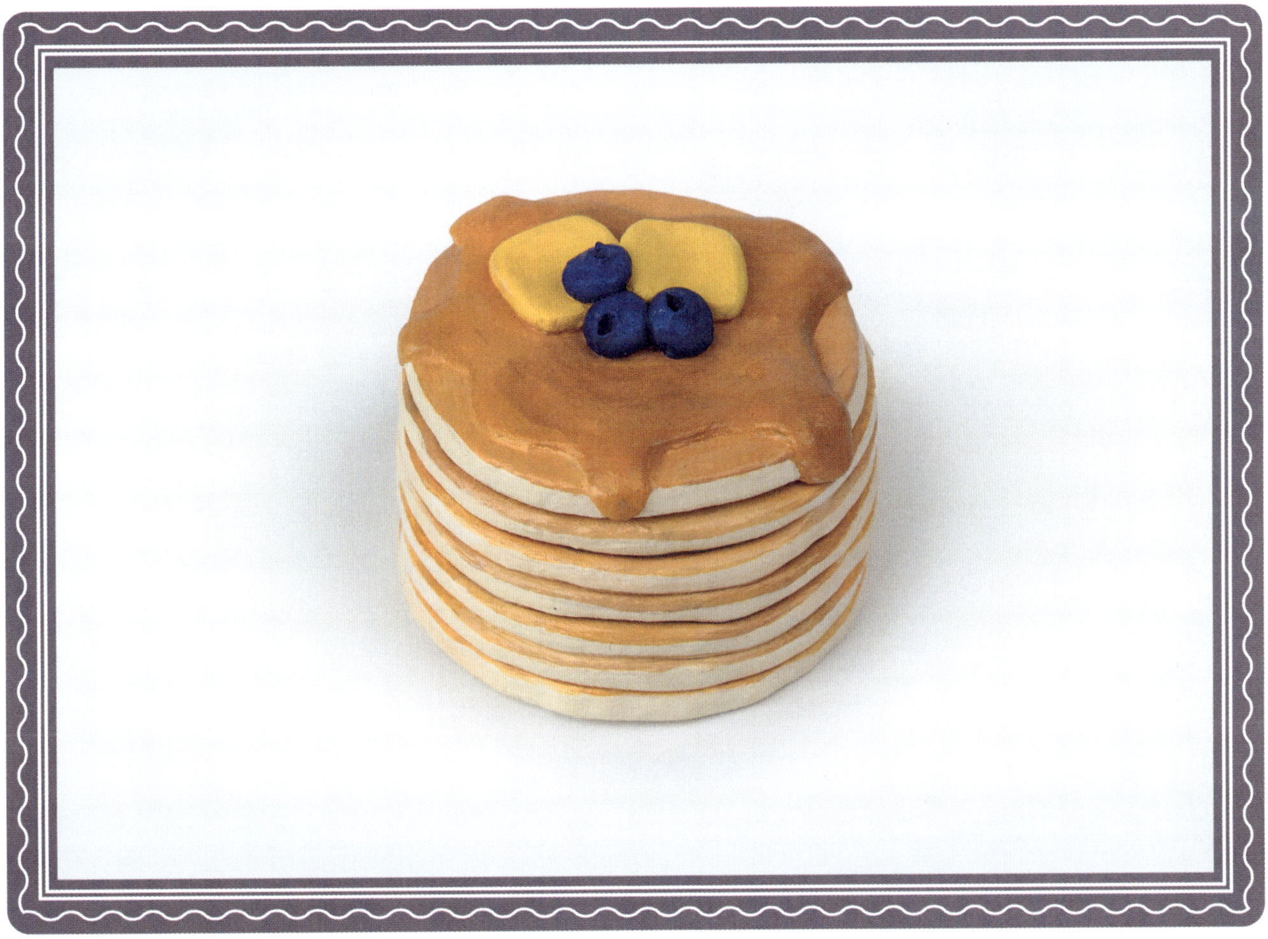

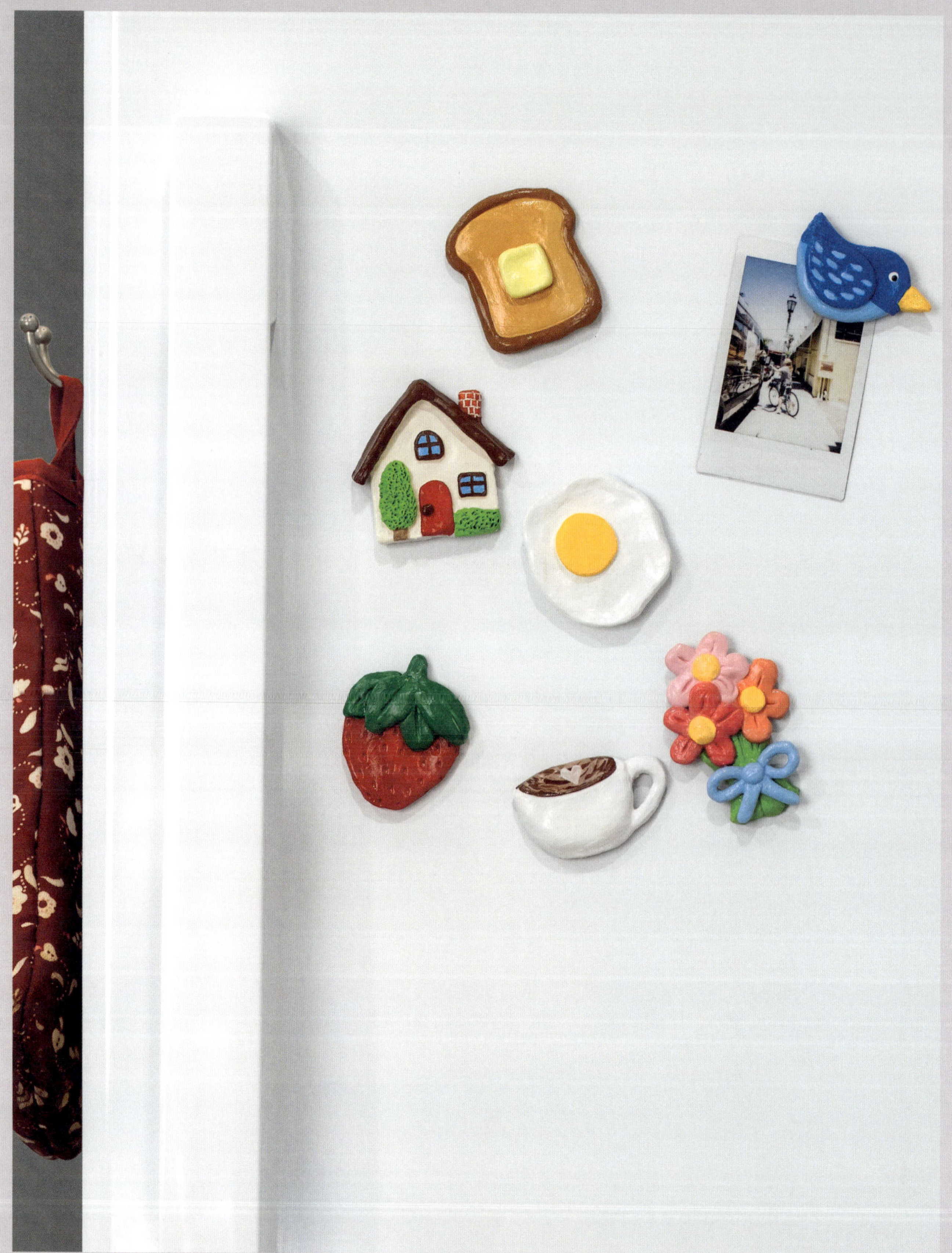

MAGNETS

Pie

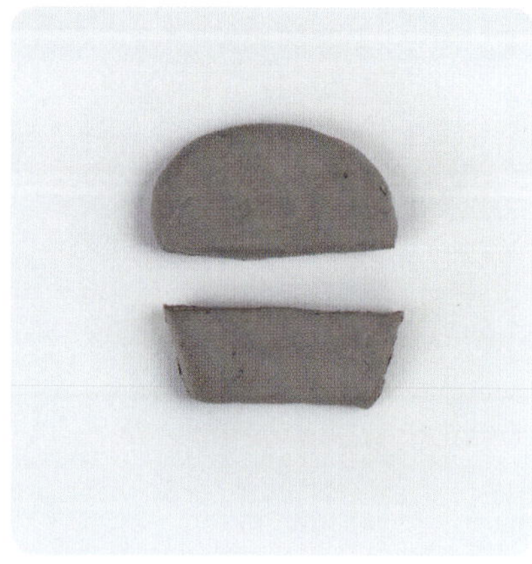

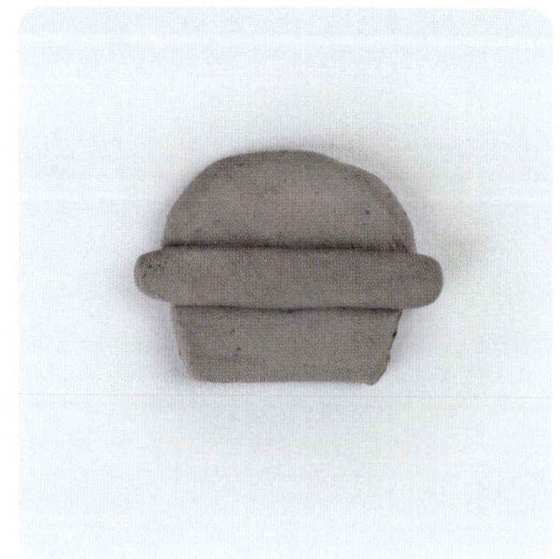

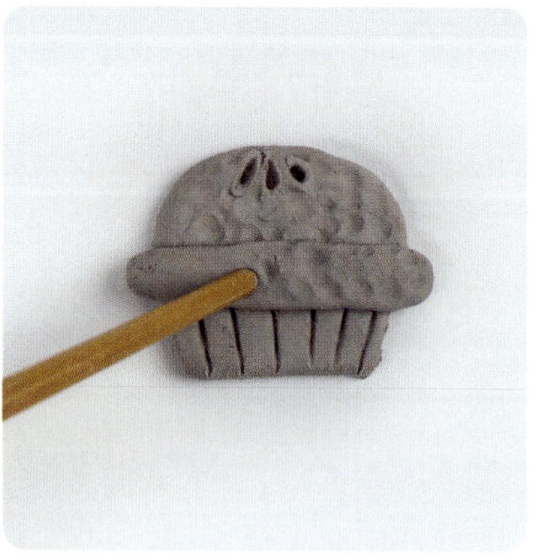

1. Shape a half circle for the pie top and a thin base for the pie pan, both with flat backs. Connect them.

2. Roll out a coil slightly longer than the top of the pan and gently flatten it into the connection point between the pie and the pan with your index finger.

3. Use the back of a paintbrush to create texture on the pie. Use a needle tool to carve lines into the pie pan and three small divots into the top of the pie.

4. Paint the pan a solid color, like gray, and the pie brown. When the paint is dry, seal the piece with Mod Podge.

5. Once fully sealed and dry, use a strong glue (Gorilla Glue or another heavy-duty adhesive) to attach a magnet to the back of the piece.

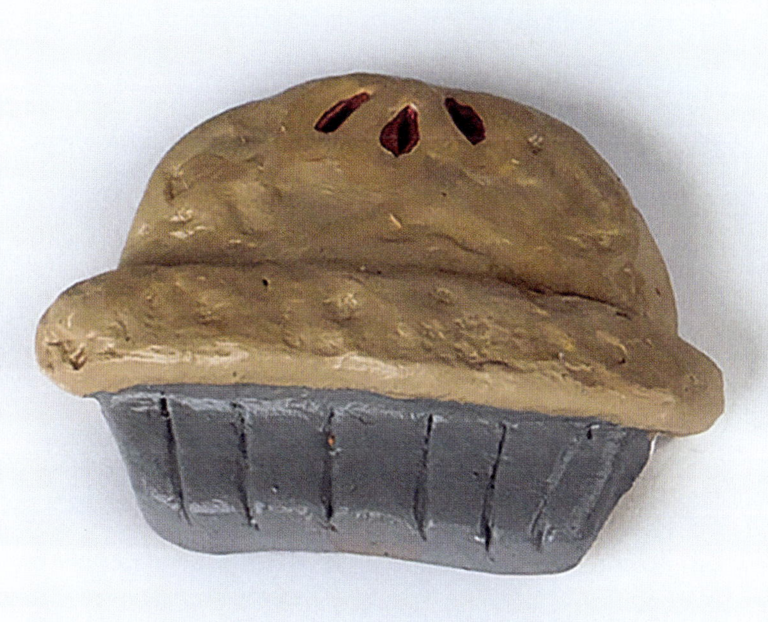

Mushroom

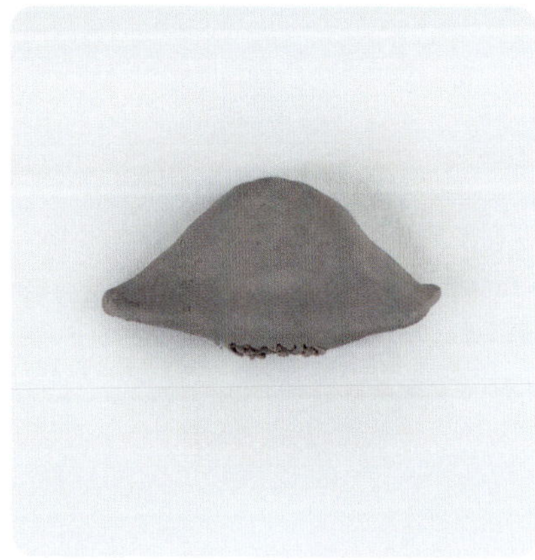

1. Sculpt the mushroom cap out of a small ball of clay. Keep the top rounded and flare the sides outward, flattening the bottom.

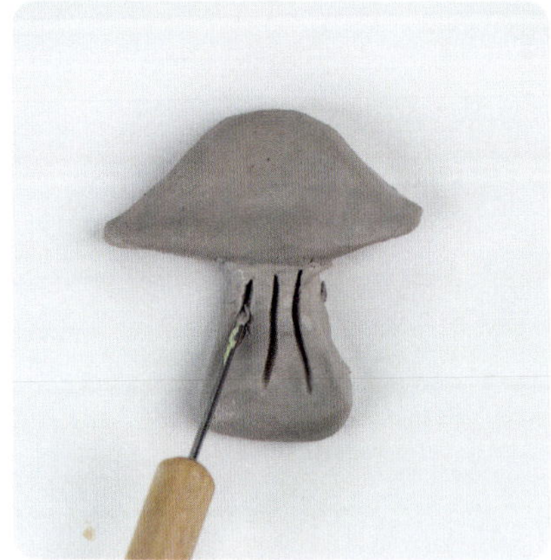

2. Roll out a log of clay and flatten it to form the stem. Connect the cap to the stem and use a needle tool to add lines down the stem.

3. Once fully dry, paint the piece. When the paint is dry, seal the piece with Mod Podge.

4. Once fully dry and sealed, use a strong glue (Gorilla Glue or another heavy-duty adhesive) to attach a magnet to the back of the piece.

TIP!

To mimic a classic toadstool, paint the stem white and the cap red with white polka dots. Or, get creative!

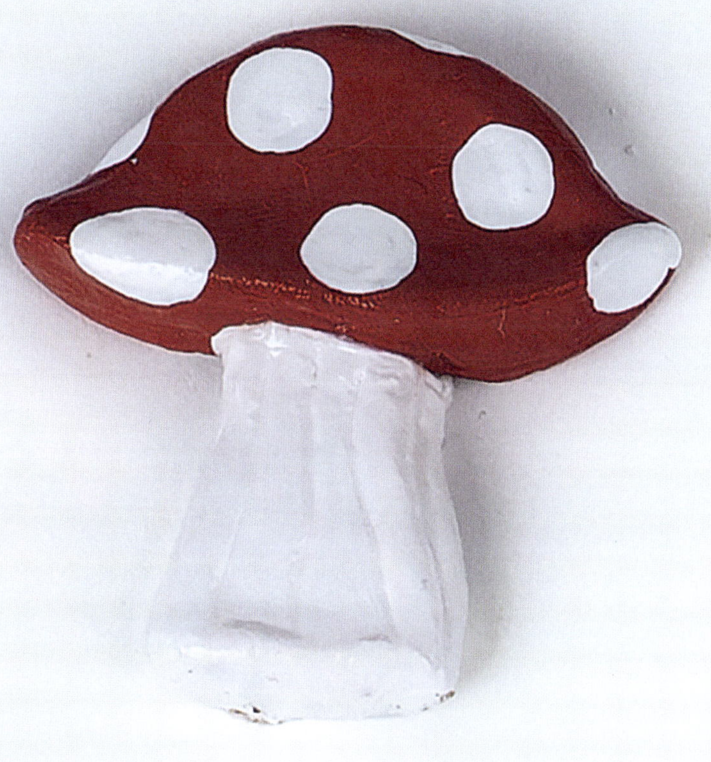

Avocado

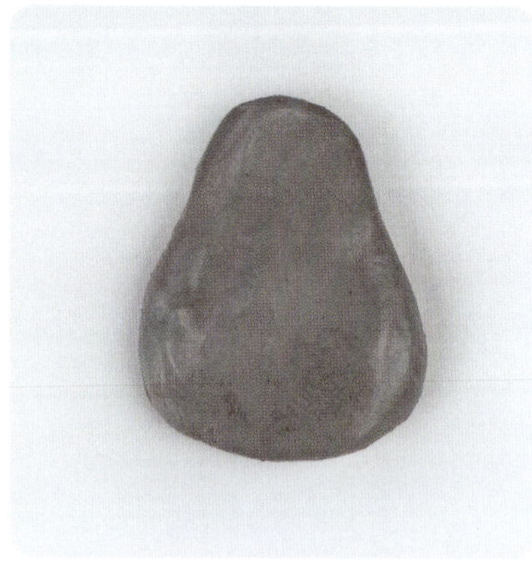

1. Break off a piece of clay and sculpt a pear shape.

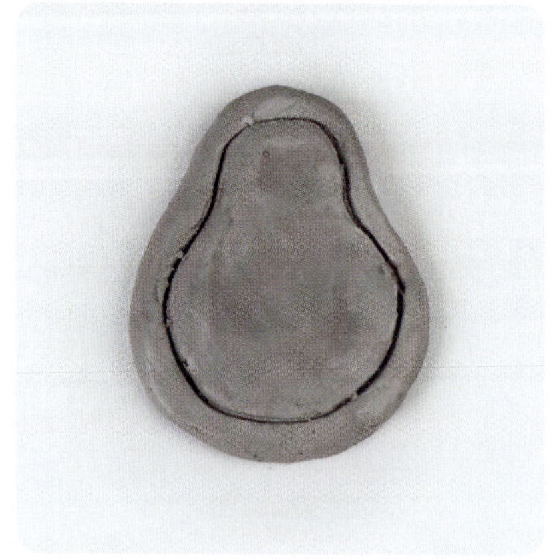

2. Use a needle tool to carve a line along the inner perimeter of the shape.

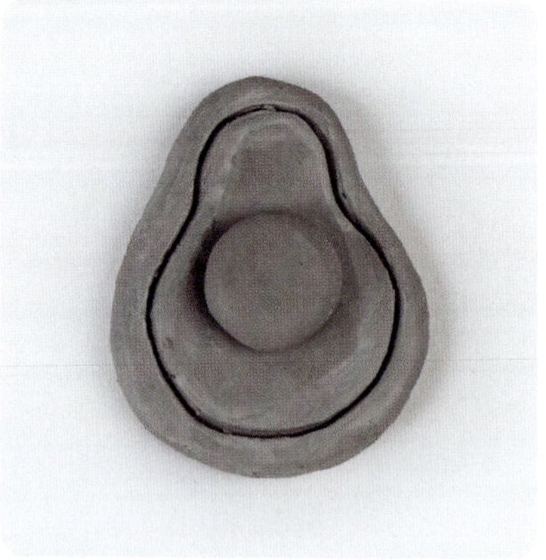

3. Roll out a small ball for the pit. Flatten one side. Attach the flat side to the center of the piece.

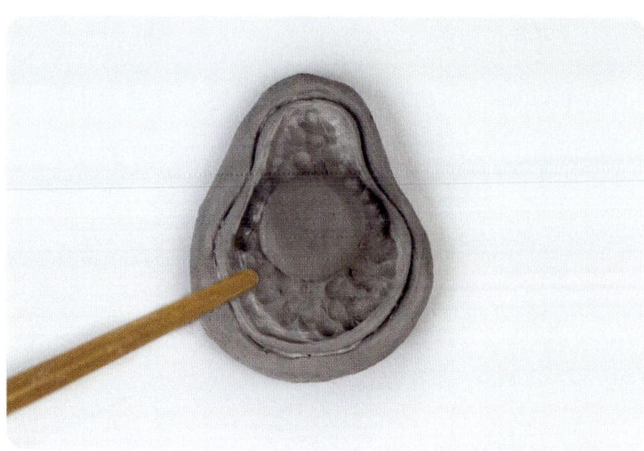

4. Use the back of a paintbrush to add texture to the middle of the avocado, leaving the thin, raised edge untextured.

5. Once fully dry, paint the avocado with gradients of green, with the darkest green on the outer edge and the lightest green around the pit. Paint the pit brown. When the paint is dry, seal the piece with Mod Podge.

6. Once fully dry and sealed, use a strong glue (Gorilla Glue or another heavy-duty adhesive) to attach a magnet to the back of the piece.

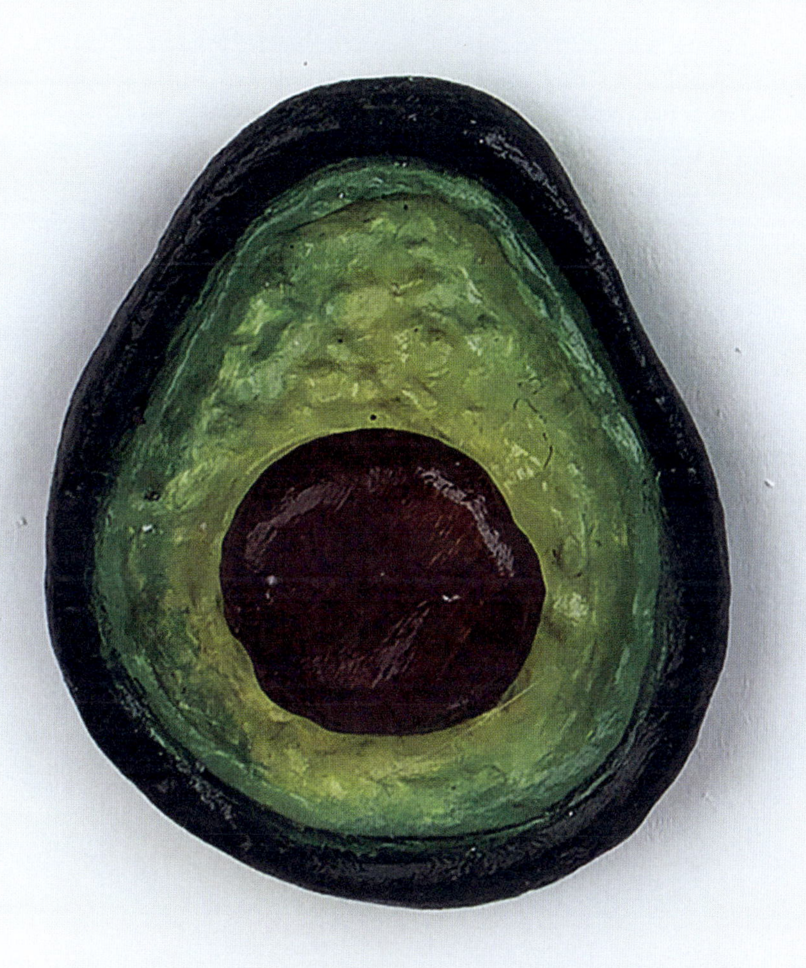

Coffee

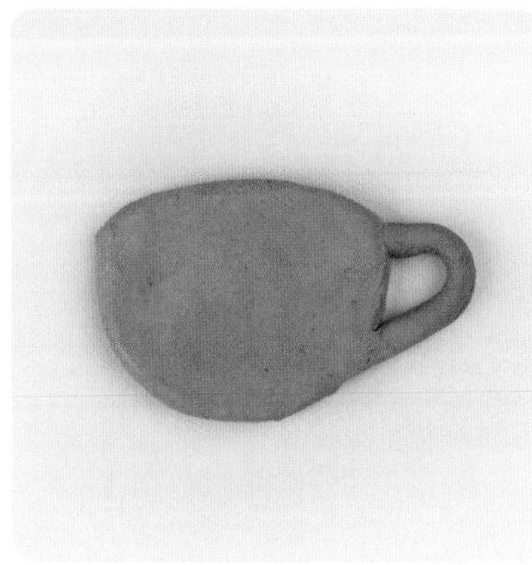

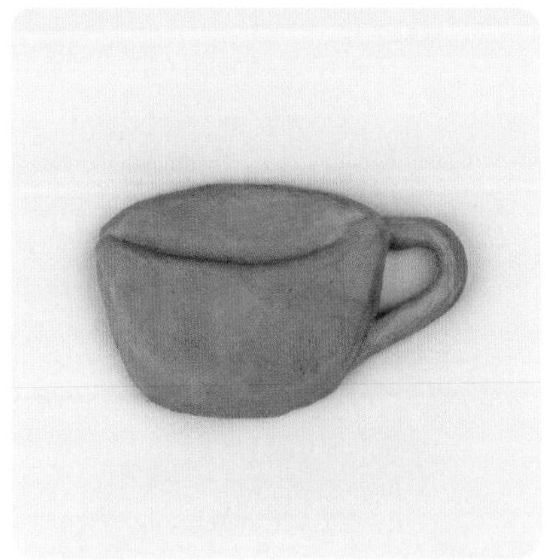

1. Break off a piece of clay and sculpt a shallow cup shape. Add a coil for a handle.

2. Repeat Step 1 with a slightly thinner piece of clay, leaving a small section at the top of the cup open where the "coffee" will go. Attach this piece on top of the first cup shape.

3. Once fully dry, paint the cup a base color, like white, and paint the coffee brown. When the paint is dry, seal the piece with Mod Podge.

4. Once fully dry and sealed, use a strong glue (Gorilla Glue or another heavy-duty adhesive) to attach a magnet to the back of the piece.

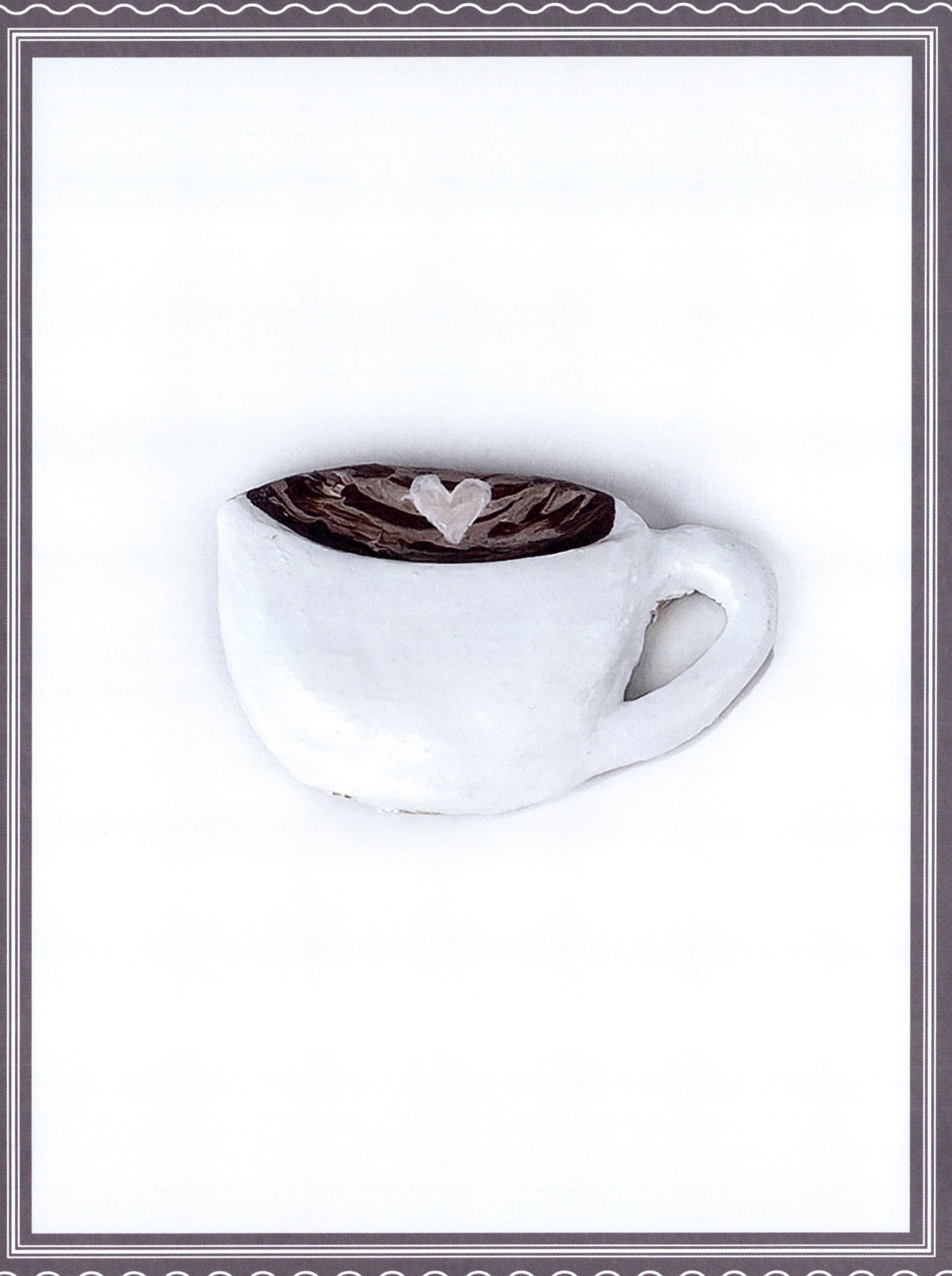

Apple

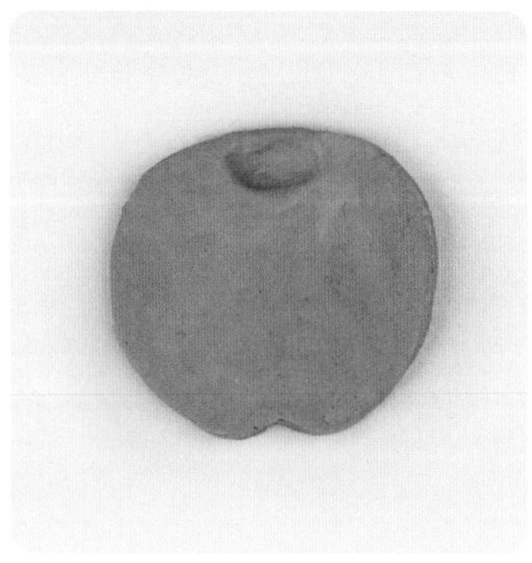

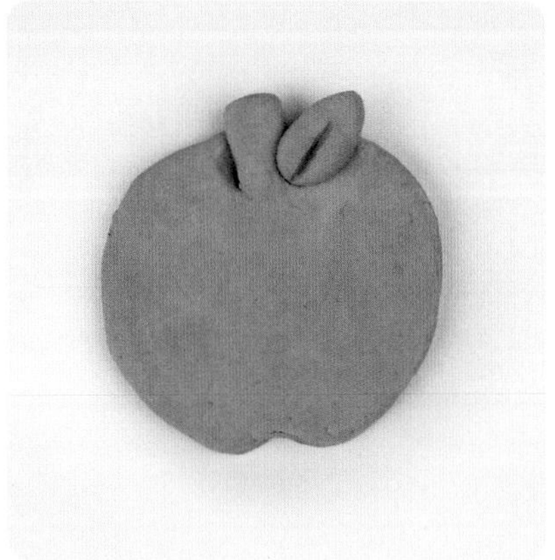

1. Cut a circle out of a slab about ¼ inch (6 mm) thick. Use a needle tool to cut a small portion out of the bottom. Press the opposite, top side of the circle down to create a small divot.

2. Sculpt a stem and leaf and attach into the divot.

3. Once fully dry, paint the stem brown, the leaf green, and the apple the color of your favorite apple variety. When the paint is dry, seal the piece with Mod Podge.

4. Once fully dry and sealed, use a strong glue (Gorilla Glue or another heavy-duty adhesive) to attach a magnet to the back of the piece.

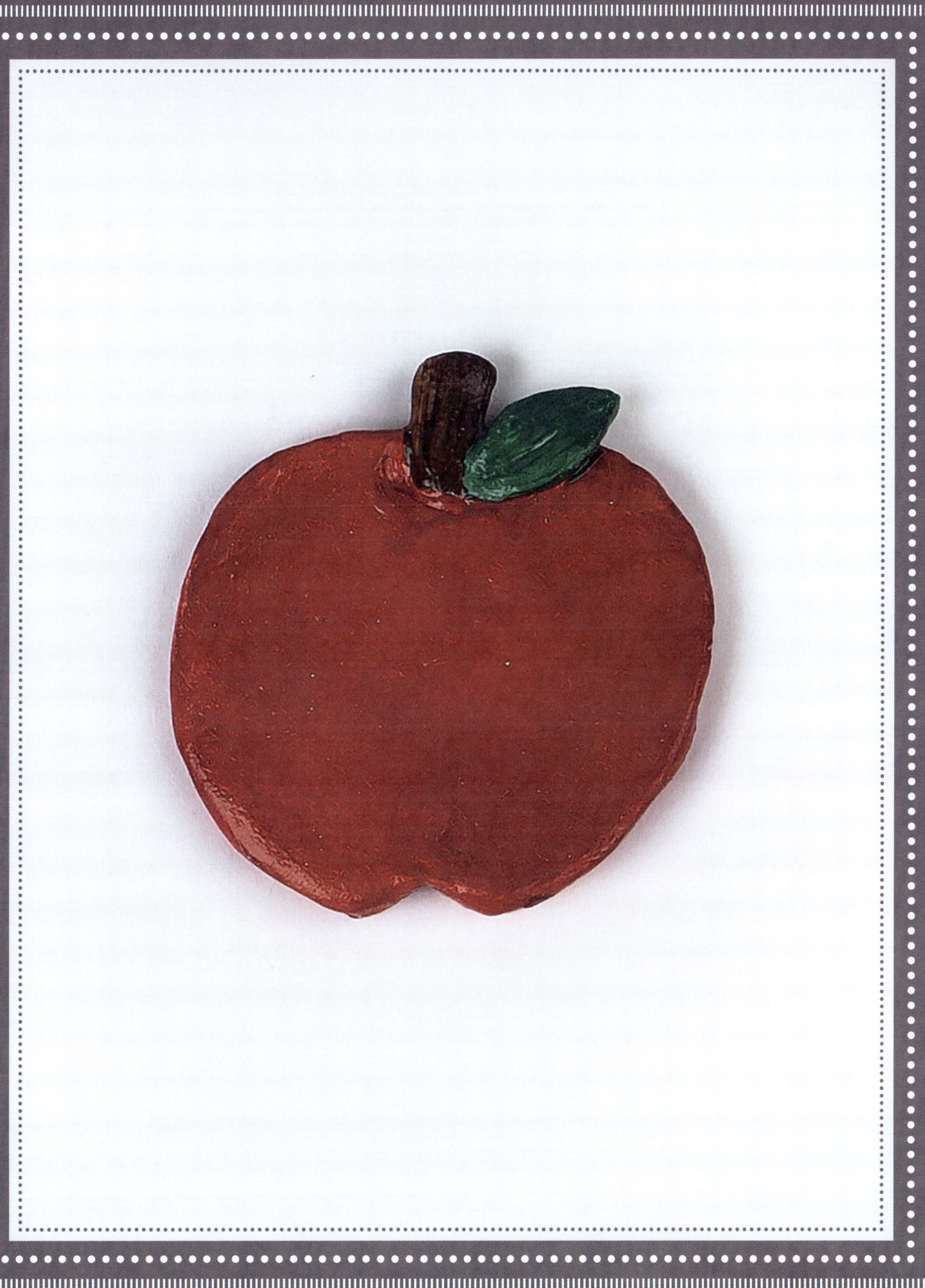

Toast

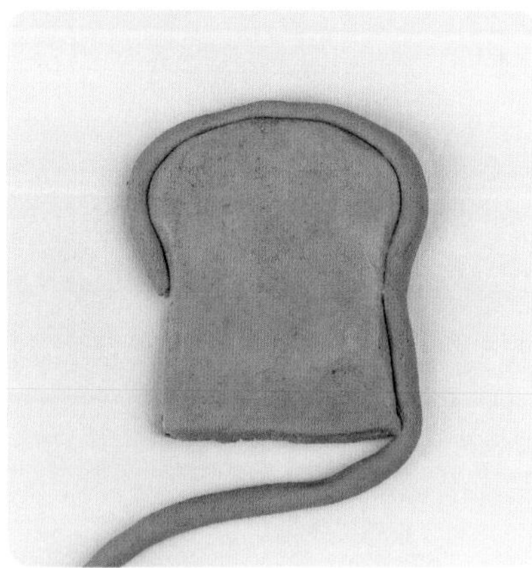

1. Cut a bread shape out of a slab ¼ inch (6 mm) thick and roll a coil long enough to wrap around the shape. Attach and smooth together.

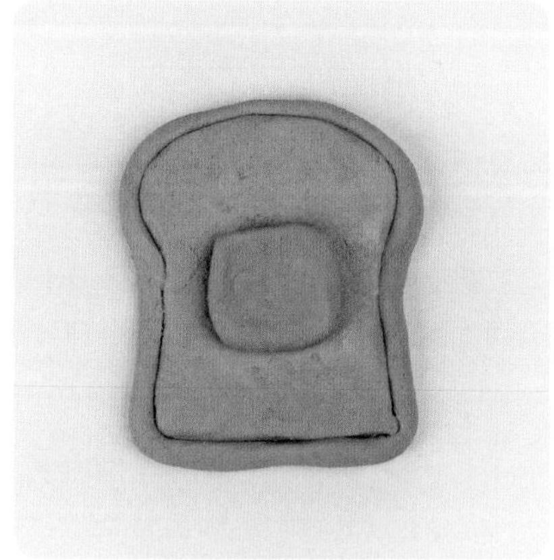

2. For the pat of butter, sculpt a small cube and attach it to the center of the bread.

3. Once fully dry, paint the outer edge of the bread dark brown, the main part of the bread lighter brown, and the butter light yellow. When the paint is dry, seal the piece with Mod Podge.

4. Once fully dry and sealed, use a strong glue (Gorilla Glue or another heavy-duty adhesive) to attach a magnet to the back of the piece.

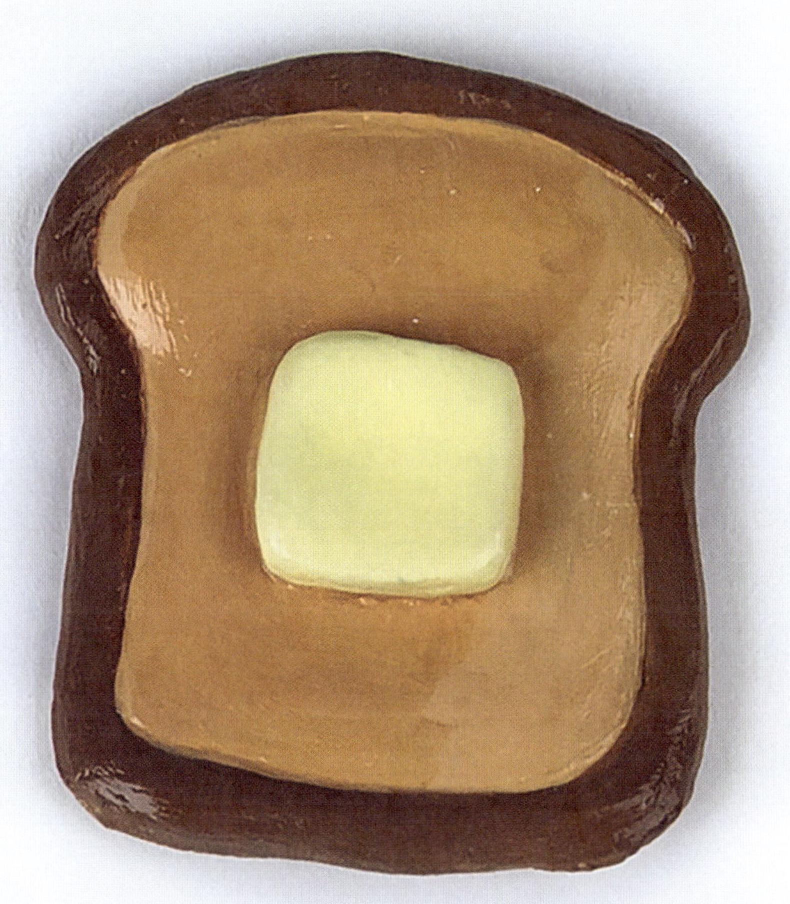

Egg

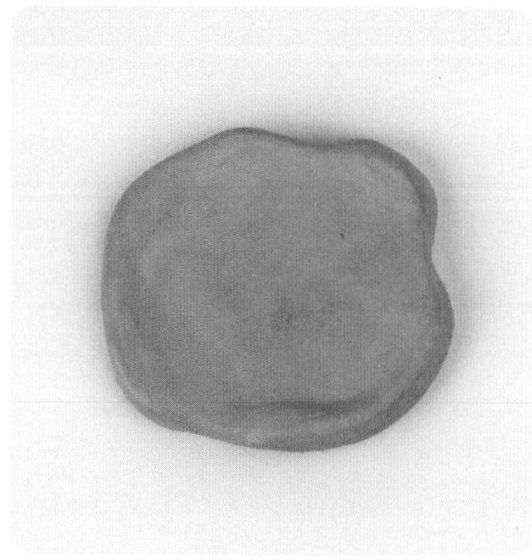

1. Cut a circle out of a slab ¼ inch (6 mm) thick and press the sides to create a waved edge.

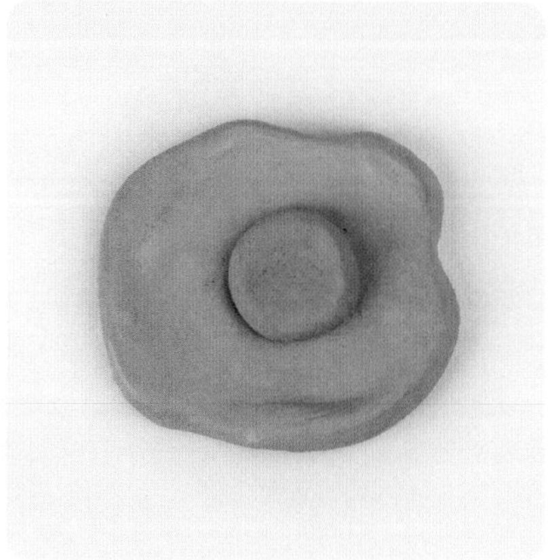

2. For the egg yolk, roll out a small ball and flatten it. Connect the flat side to the center of the egg.

3. Once fully dry, paint the body of the egg white and the yolk yellow. When the paint is dry, seal the piece with Mod Podge.

4. Once fully dry and sealed, use a strong glue (Gorilla Glue or another heavy-duty adhesive) to attach a magnet to the back of the piece.

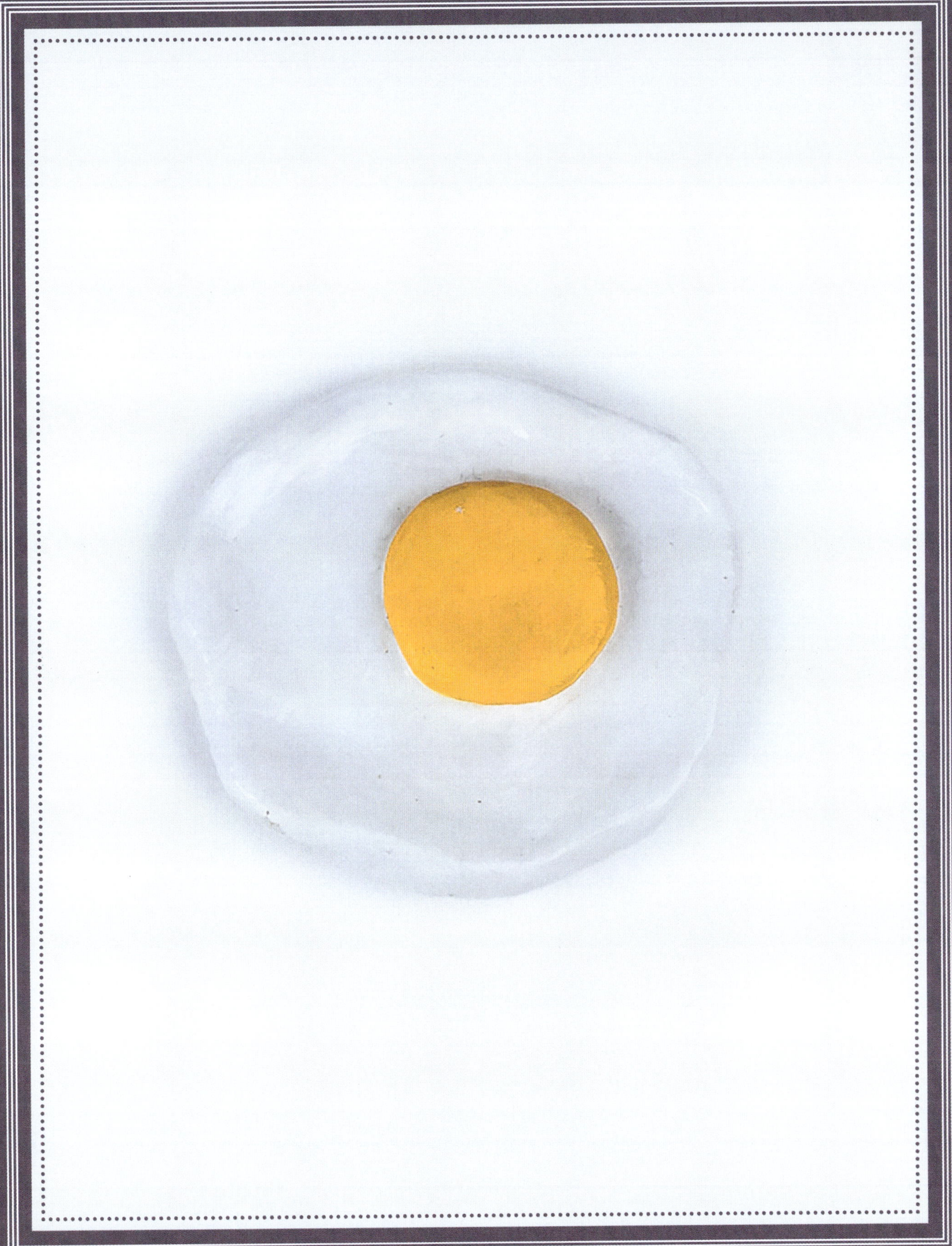

Cake

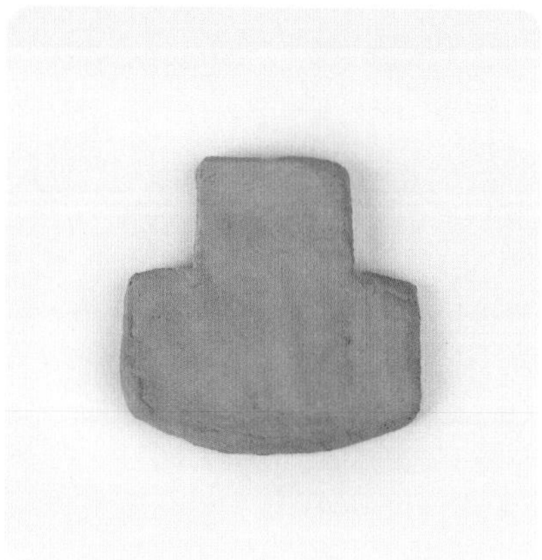

1. From a small slab of clay, cut out a tiered cake shape with a rounded bottom.

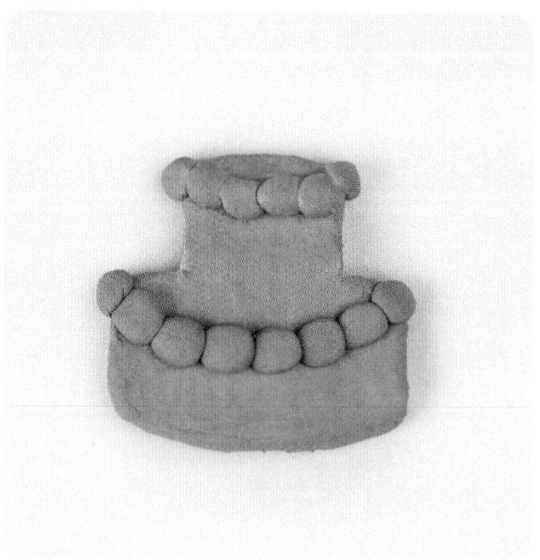

2. Roll out small balls and attach them to the top edge of each tier in a curved line.

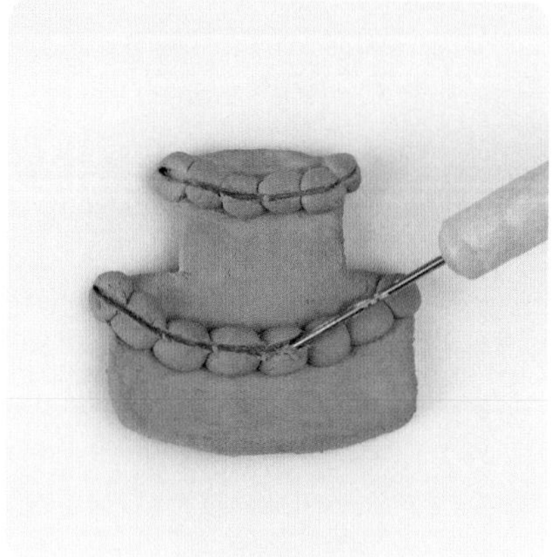

3. Add lines through each ball with a needle tool to create a piping effect.

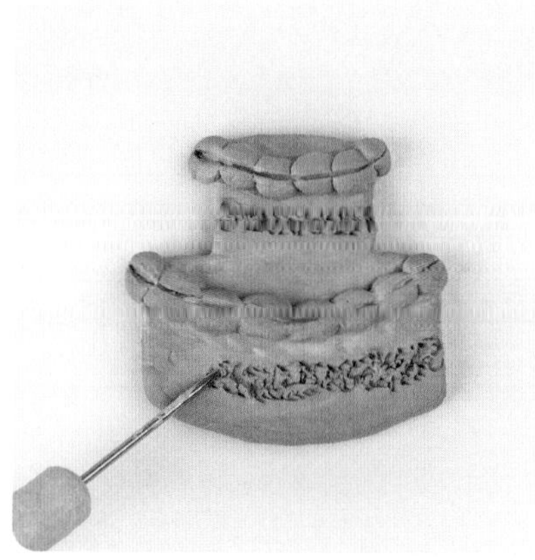

4. Use a needle tool to add textured lines on the exposed sections of cake on each tier.

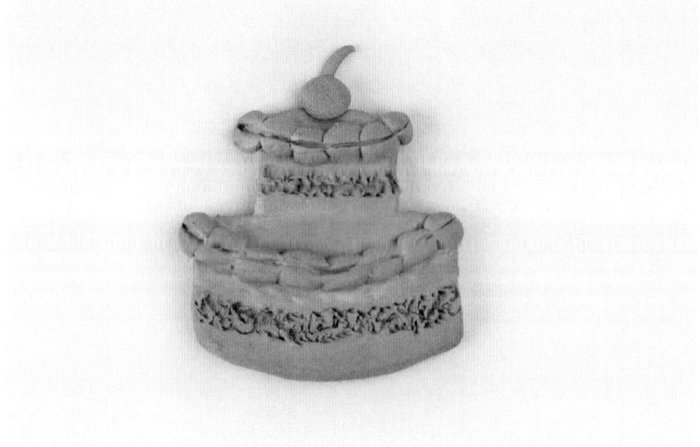

5. Add a small ball with a tiny coil on top for a cherry.

6. Once fully dry, paint with a design of your choice. When the paint is dry, seal the piece with Mod Podge.

7. Once fully dry and sealed, use a strong glue (Gorilla Glue or another heavy-duty adhesive) to attach a magnet to the back of the piece.

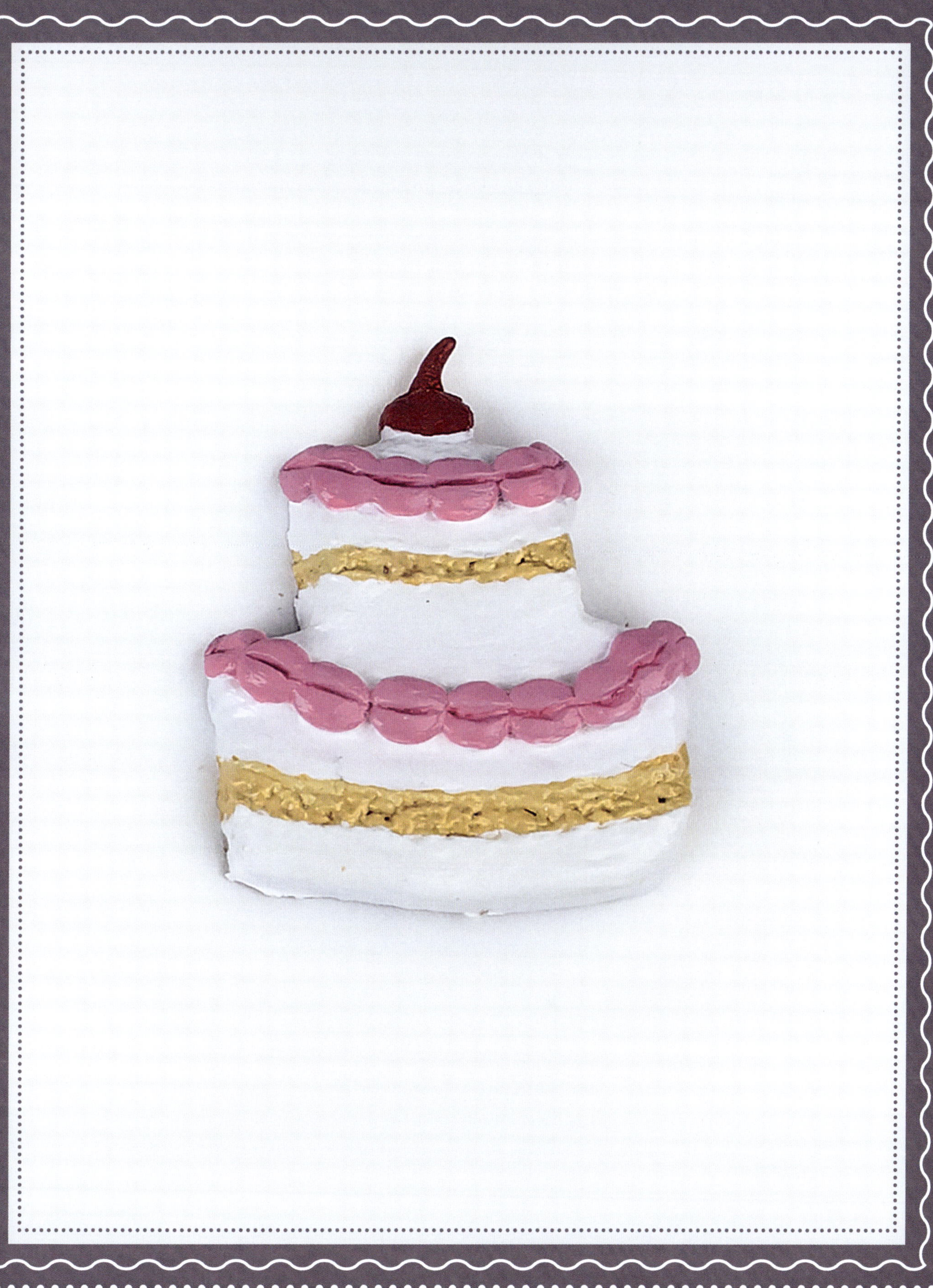

Bananas

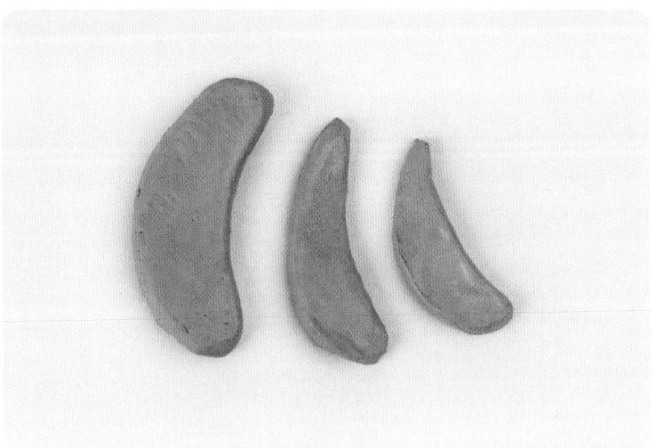

1. From a small slab of clay, cut out three crescent shapes that increase in thickness.

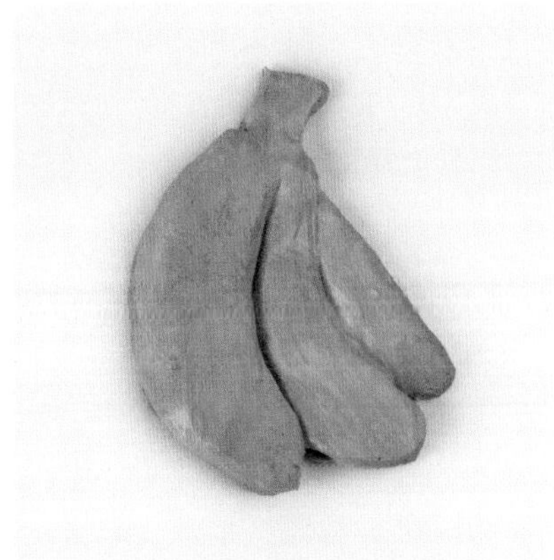

2. Overlap them and attach together. Pinch a small bit of clay into a stem and attach it to the top of the bunch. Use a needle tool to add detail lines down the center of each banana.

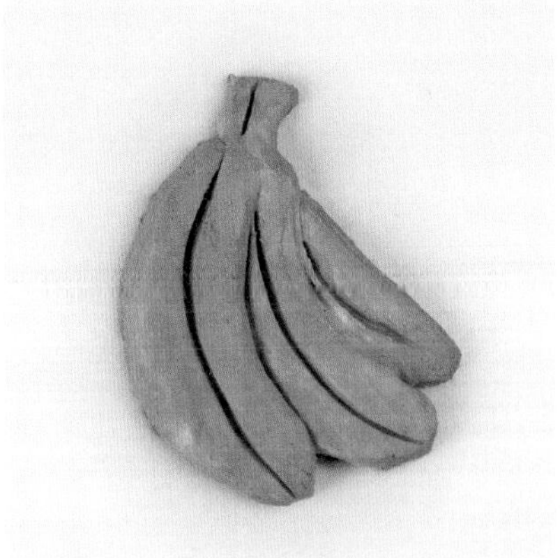

3. Once fully dry, paint the bananas yellow and the stem green. When the paint is dry, seal the piece with Mod Podge.

4. Once fully dry and sealed, use a strong glue (Gorilla Glue or another heavy-duty adhesive) to attach a magnet to the back of the piece.

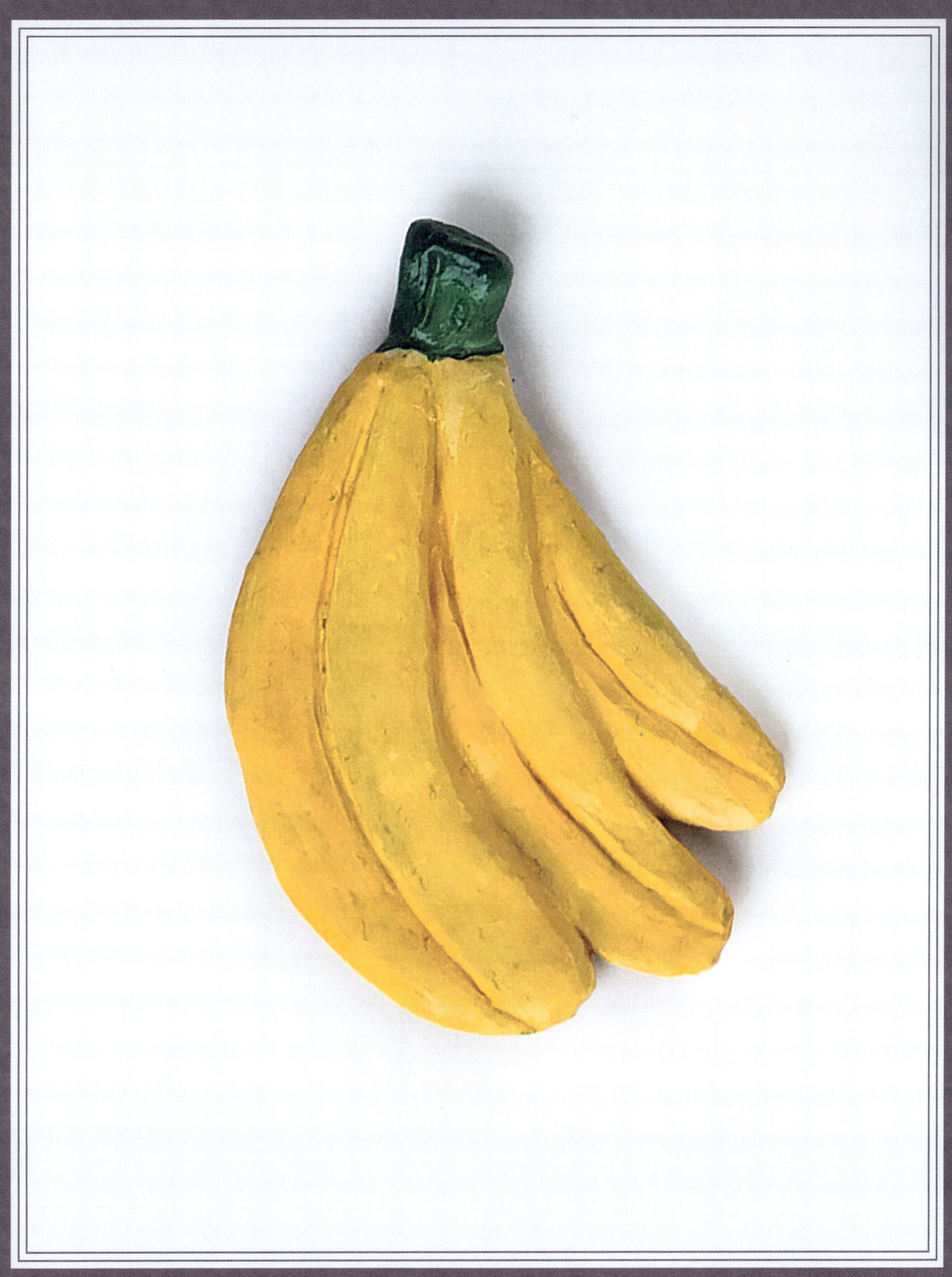

Peach

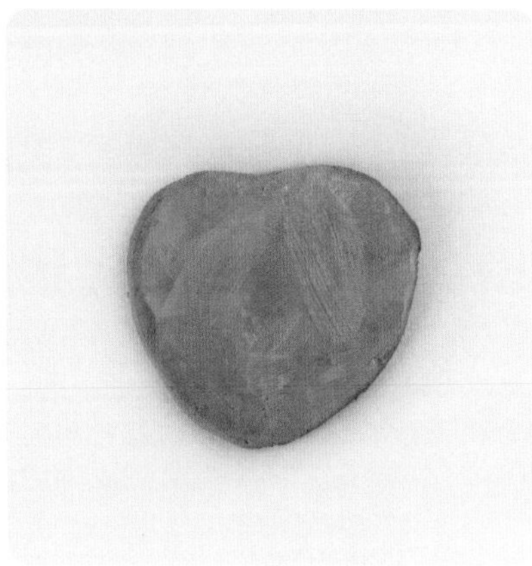

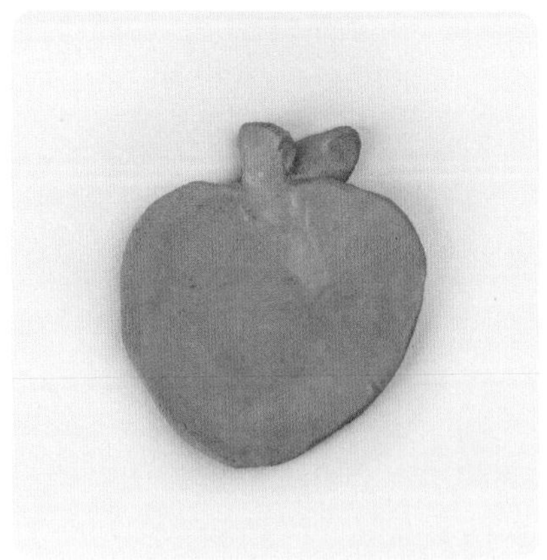

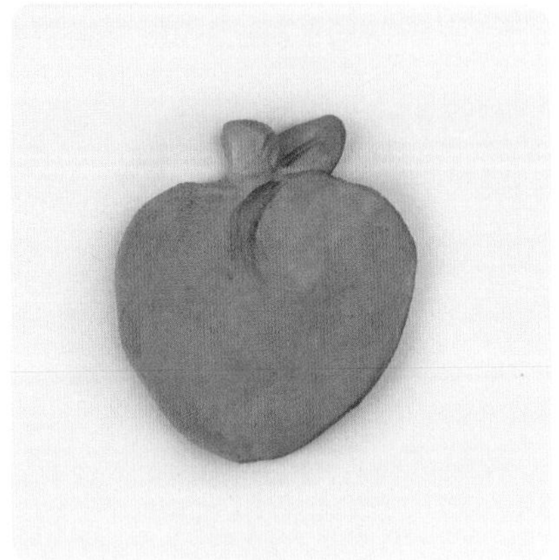

1. Roll out a slab about ¼ inch (6 mm) thick and cut out a circle with a slightly pointed bottom and subtle indentation at the top.

2. Sculpt a stem and leaf and attach to the top of the peach.

3. Add a short, angled, curved line down the top center of the peach and another down the middle of the leaf.

4. Once fully dry, paint the peach pinkish-orange, the stem brown, and the leaf green. When the paint is dry, seal the piece with Mod Podge.

5. Once fully dry and sealed, use a strong glue (Gorilla Glue or another heavy-duty adhesive) to attach a magnet to the back of the piece.

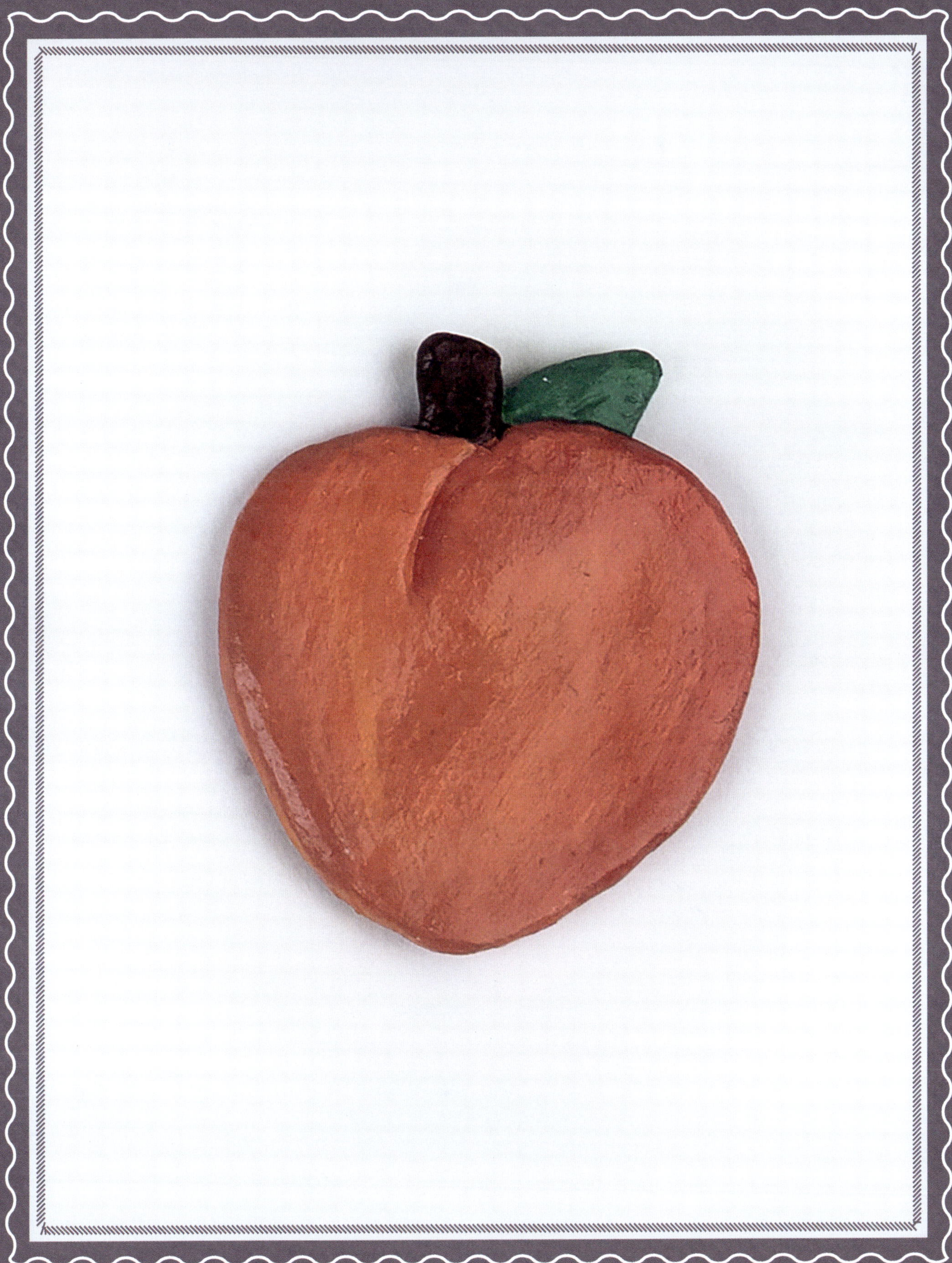

Strawberry

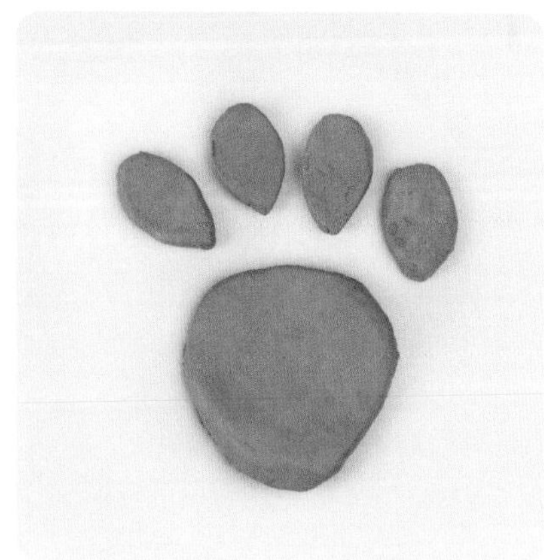

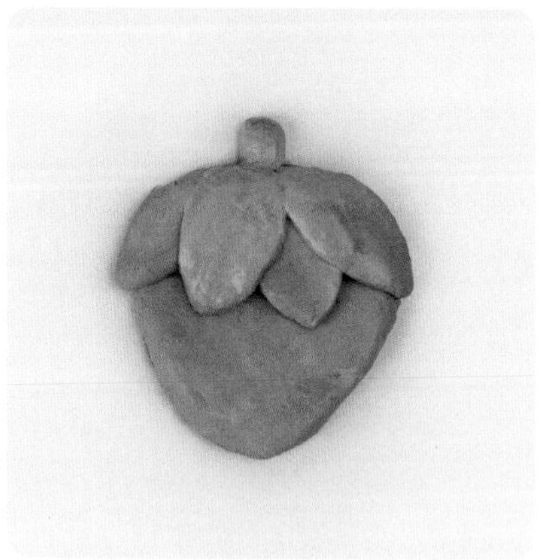

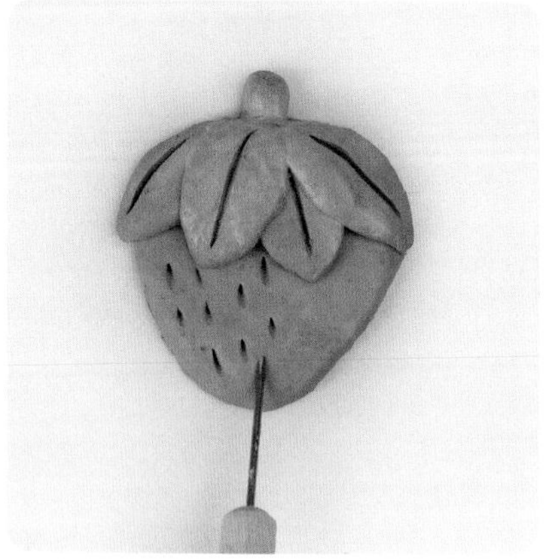

1. Roll out a slab about ¼ inch (6 mm) thick and cut out a rounded triangle shape and 4 leaf shapes.

2. Overlap the leaves and connect them to the top of the strawberry base. Add a small bit of clay for a stem.

3. Use a needle tool to add dots to the strawberry and lines down the middle of each leaf.

4. Once fully dry, paint the strawberry red and the leaves and stem green. When the paint is dry, seal the piece with Mod Podge.

5. Once fully dry and sealed, use a strong glue (Gorilla Glue or another heavy-duty adhesive) to attach a magnet to the back of the piece.

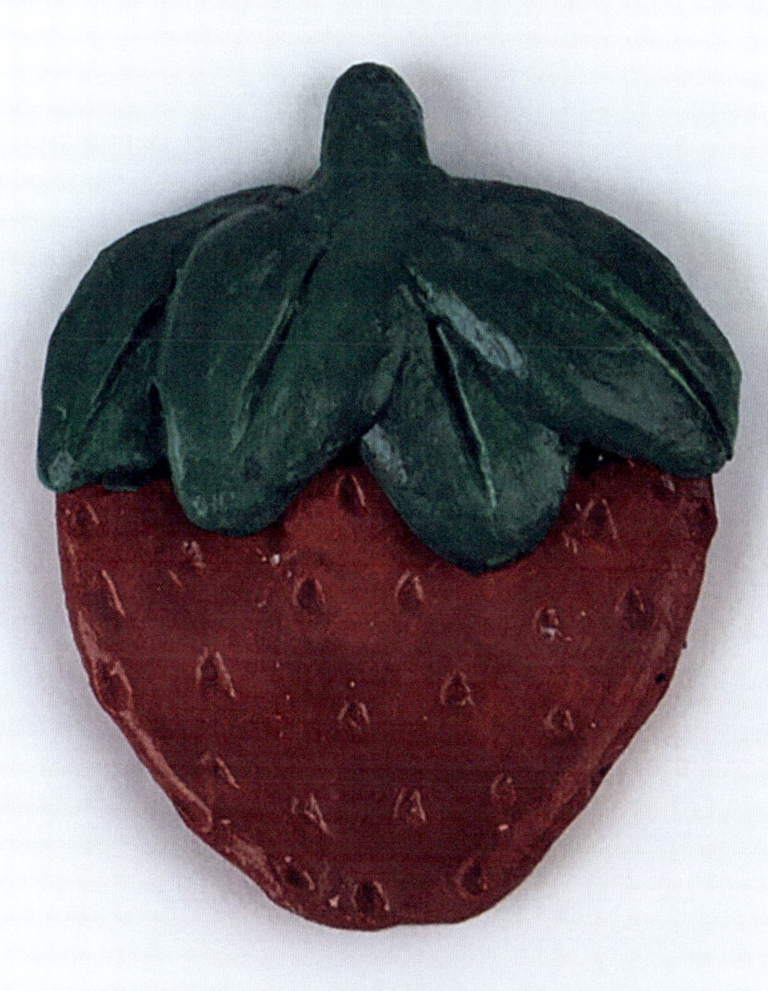

Flowers

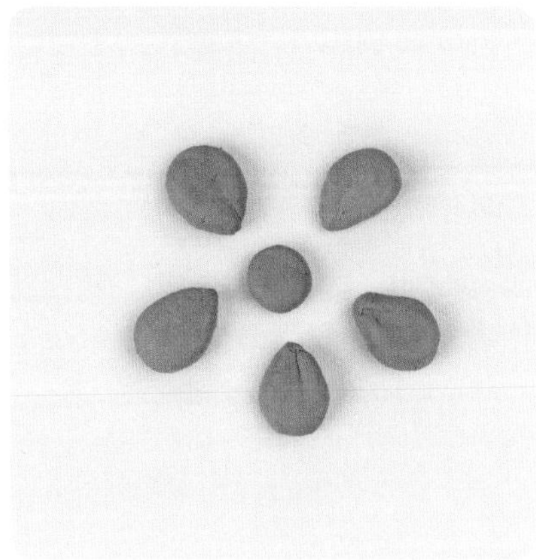

1. Roll out five small ovals and flatten them into petal shapes. Roll out and flatten a circle for the center. Connect the petals to the center.

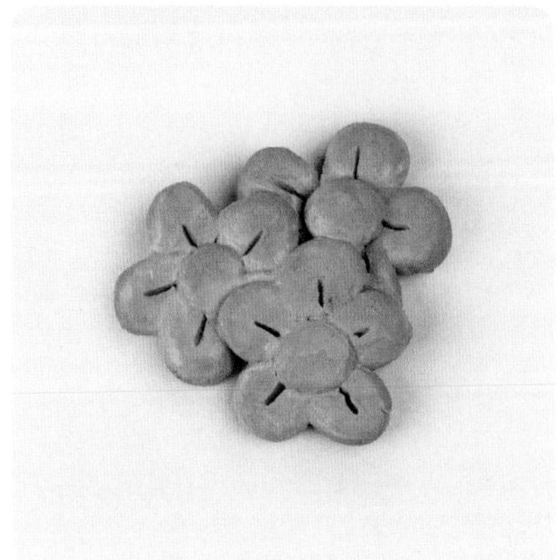

2. Repeat Step 1 two more times. Stack the completed flowers to create a bunch.

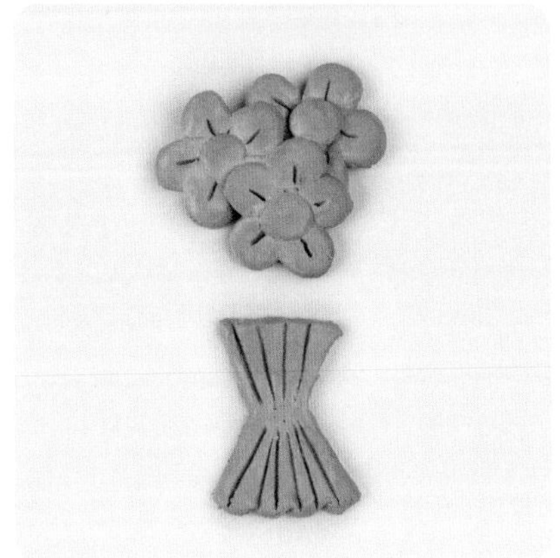

3. To form the stems, add a strip of clay extending from the bottom of the bunch and use your needle tool to add lines to mark the individual stems. Roll out a thin coil and shape into a bow. Attach to the stems.

4. Once fully dry, paint the stems green and the flowers and bow as you like. When the paint is dry, seal the piece with Mod Podge.

5. Once fully dry and sealed, use a strong glue (Gorilla Glue or another heavy-duty adhesive) to attach a magnet to the back of the piece.

TIP!

Dip the coil in water before you shape it to keep it from breaking apart as it bends.

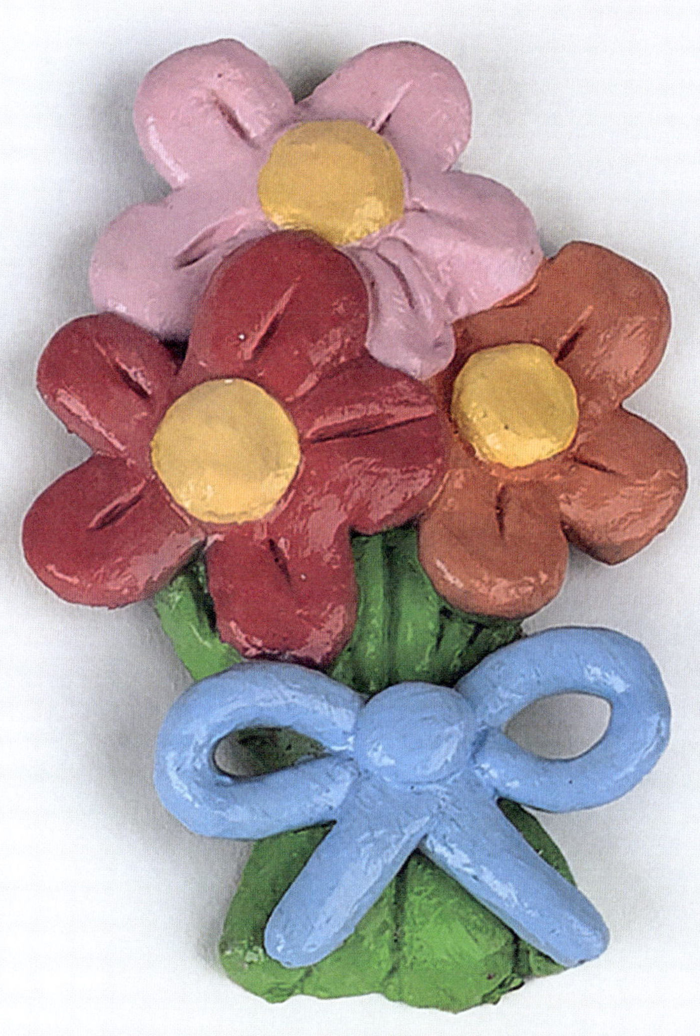

Cactus

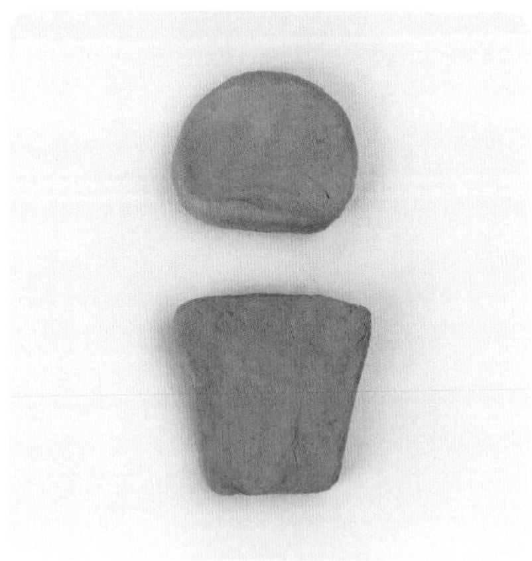

1. Break of a piece of clay and sculpt a small rectangle that widens at one end for the pot and a flattened ball for the cactus.

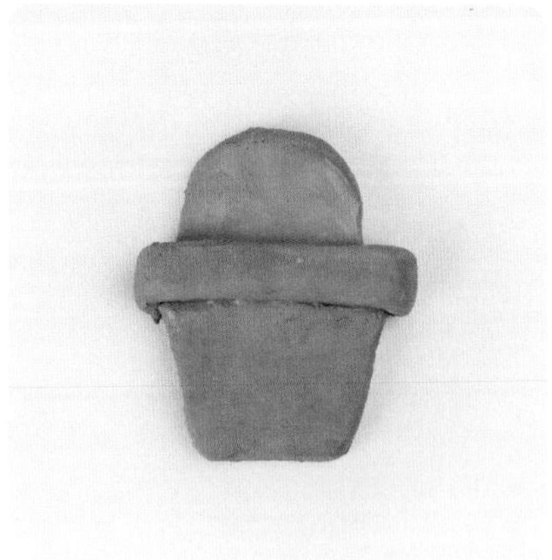

2. Connect them together and add a flattened coil where they meet to create a rim on the pot.

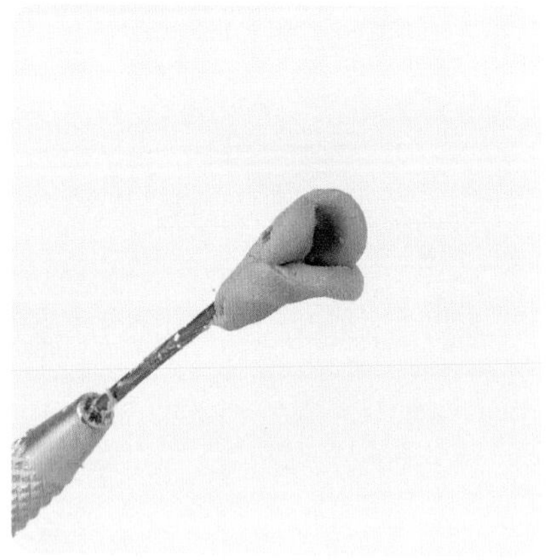

3. Roll out six tiny balls and flatten them into petals. Use the tip of a needle tool to connect the petals together.

4. Attach the flower to the top of the cactus and add a small ball in the center. Use the needle tool to create lines down the cactus body.

5. Once fully dry, paint the pot a base color, like brown, the cactus green, and the flower pink. When the paint is dry, seal the piece with Mod Podge.

6. Once fully dry and sealed, use a strong glue (Gorilla Glue or another heavy-duty adhesive) to attach a magnet to the back of the piece.

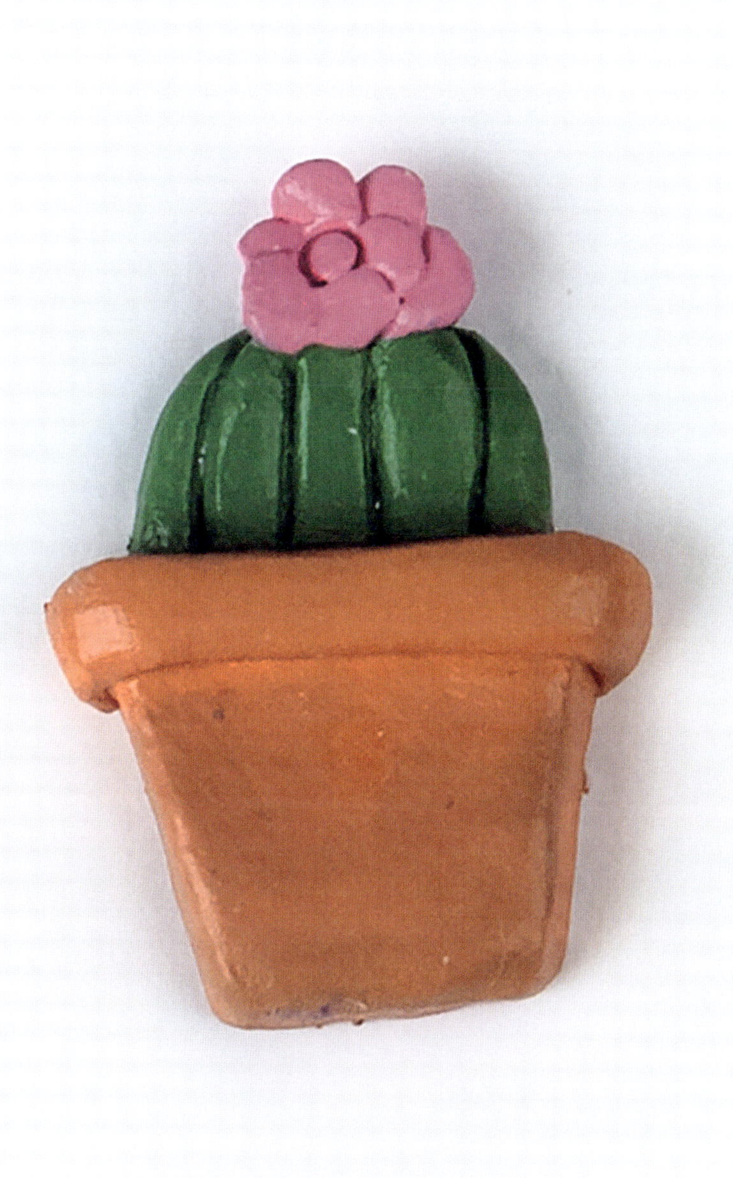

Butterfly

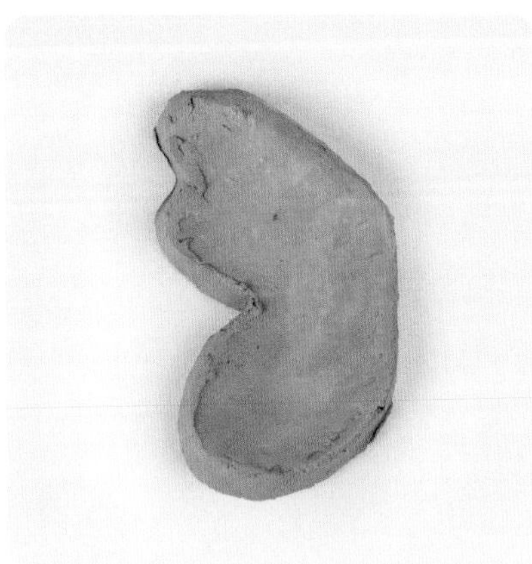

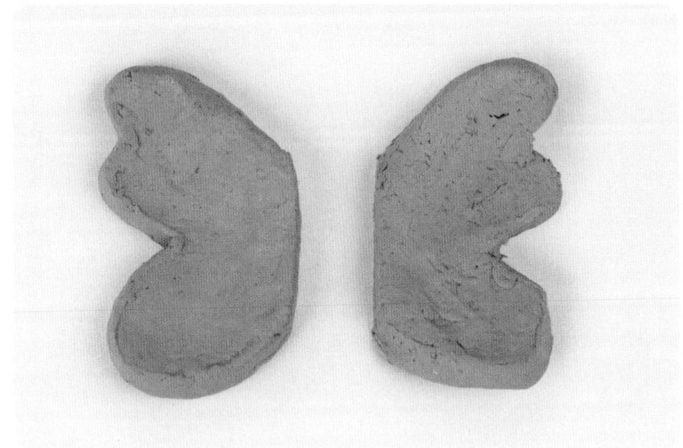

1. Roll out a slab about ¼ inch (6 mm) thick and cut out one wing shape.

2. Use the cut-out wing shape as a stencil to create a second wing.

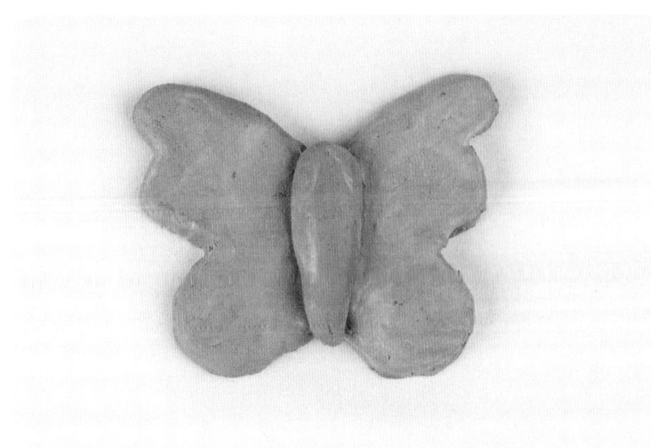

3. Connect the two wings together. Roll out a small coil for the body. Make one end round and the other pointed. Connect to the middle of the butterfly with the pointed end at the bottom.

4. Once fully dry, paint the butterfly as you like. When the paint is dry, seal the piece with Mod Podge.

5. Once fully dry and sealed, use a strong glue (Gorilla Glue or another heavy-duty adhesive) to attach a magnet to the back of the piece.

TIP!

If you need help sculpting the wing shape, use a butterfly-shaped cookie cutter instead!

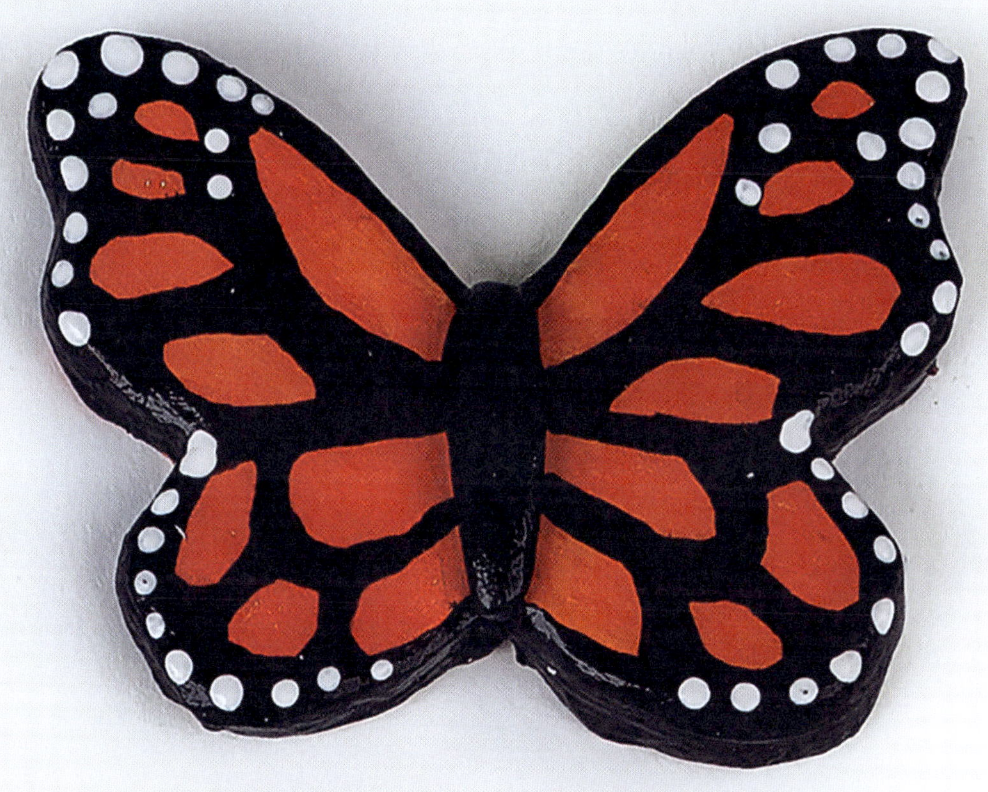

Bird

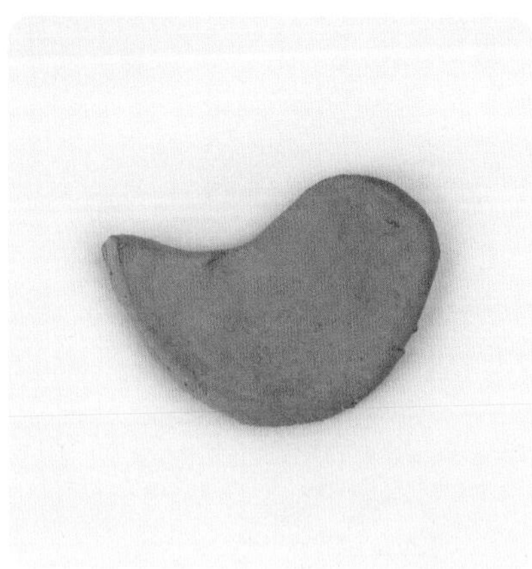

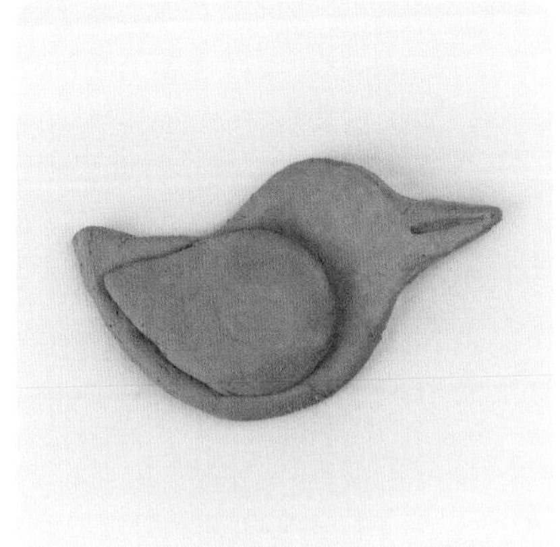

1. Roll out a slab about ¼ inch (6 mm) thick and cut out a bent teardrop shape to form the bird's body and head.

2. For the wing, cut a smaller teardrop shape from the slab.

3. For the beak, sculpt a triangle from a small ball of clay.

4. Attach the wing to the center of the body, with the pointed end facing the bird's tail. Attach the beak to the bird's head. Use a needle tool to add a horizontal line through the center of the beak.

5. Once fully dry, paint an eye onto the bird's head and paint the rest of the bird as you like. When the paint is dry, seal the piece with Mod Podge.

6. Once fully dry and sealed, use a strong glue (Gorilla Glue or another heavy-duty adhesive) to attach a magnet to the back of the piece.

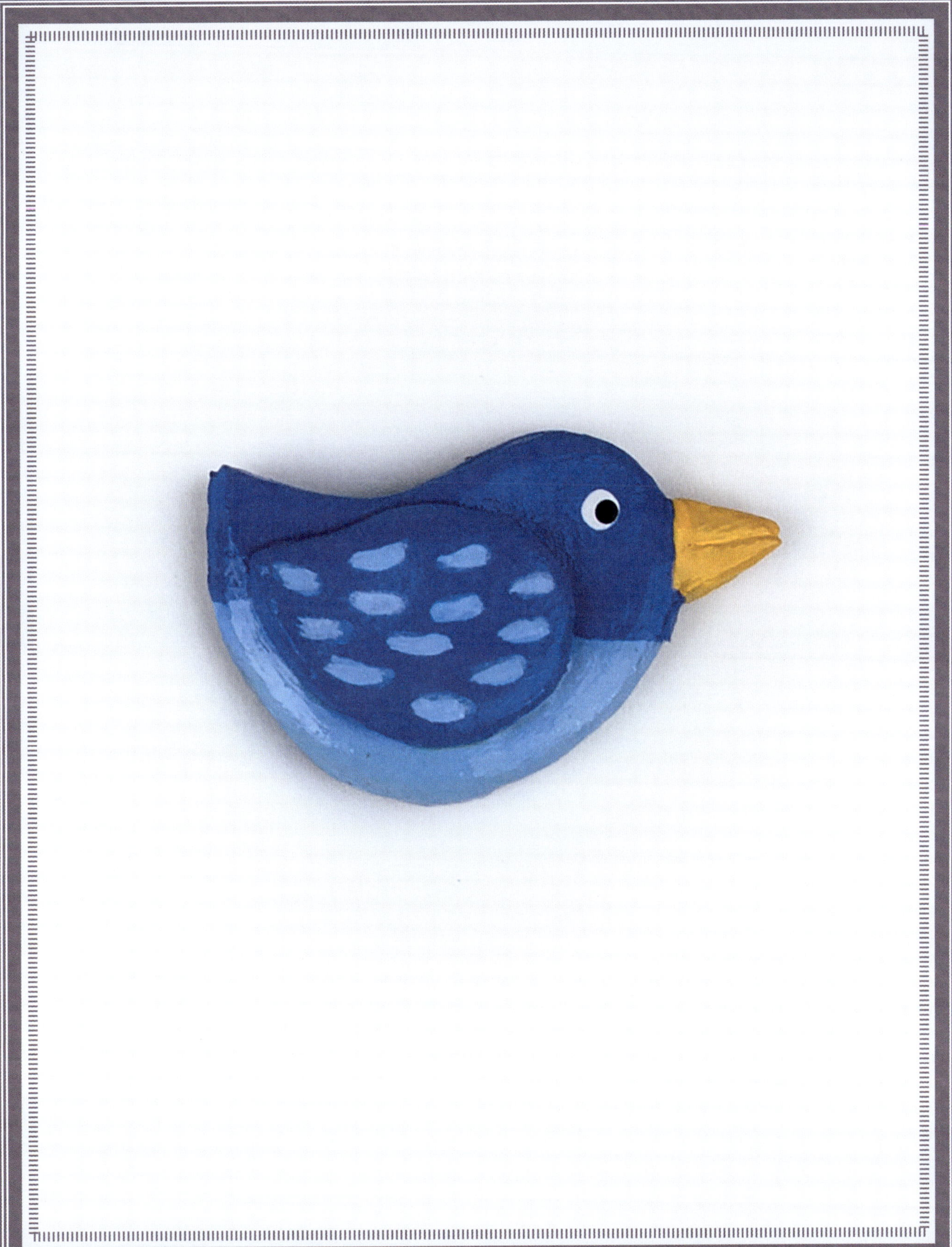

House

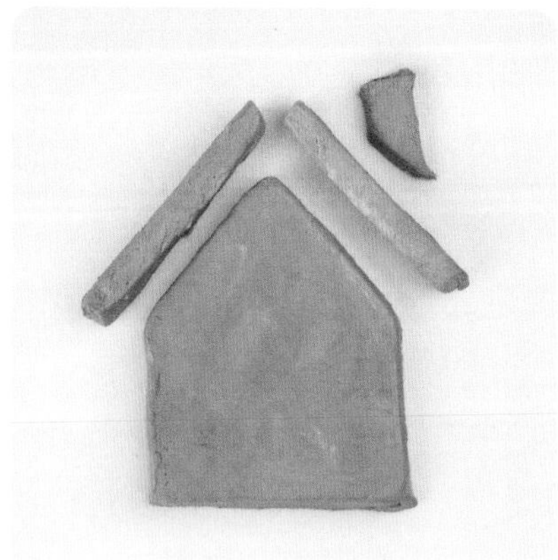

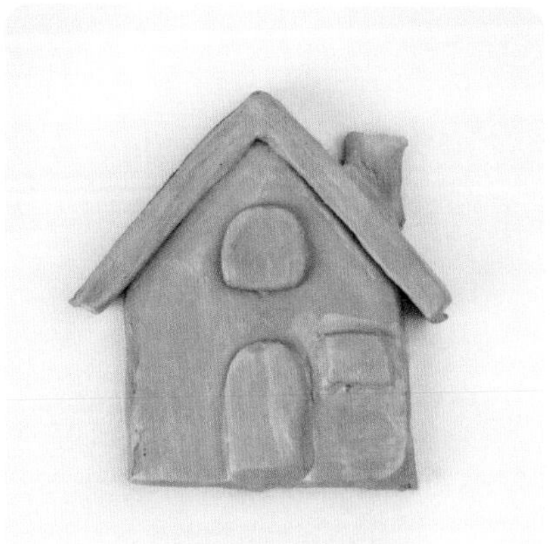

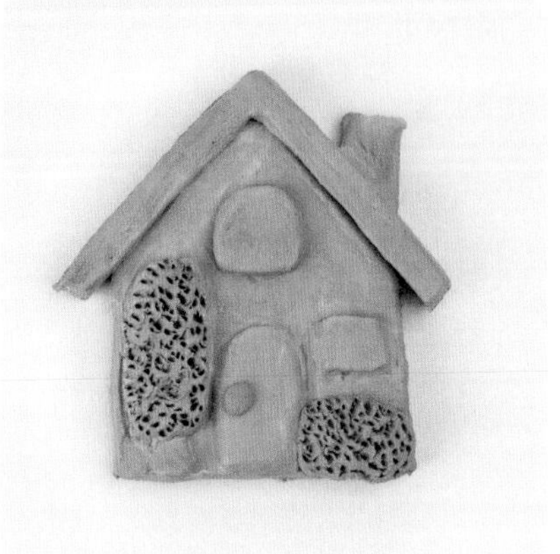

1. Roll out a slab about ¼ inch (6 mm) thick. Cut out a house shape, two strips long enough to extend just a bit over the walls as a slanted roof, and a small piece for the chimney. Cut the chimney end at a slant to match the angle of the roof.

2. Sculpt a door and two windows. Attach them to the front of the house.

3. Add two bits of clay for a tree and bush on either side of the door.

4. Use a needle tool to create leafy texture on the tree and bush.

5. Once fully dry, decorate and add painted details as you like. When the paint is dry, seal the piece with Mod Podge.

6. Once fully dry and sealed, use a strong glue (Gorilla Glue or another heavy-duty adhesive) to attach a magnet to the back of the piece.

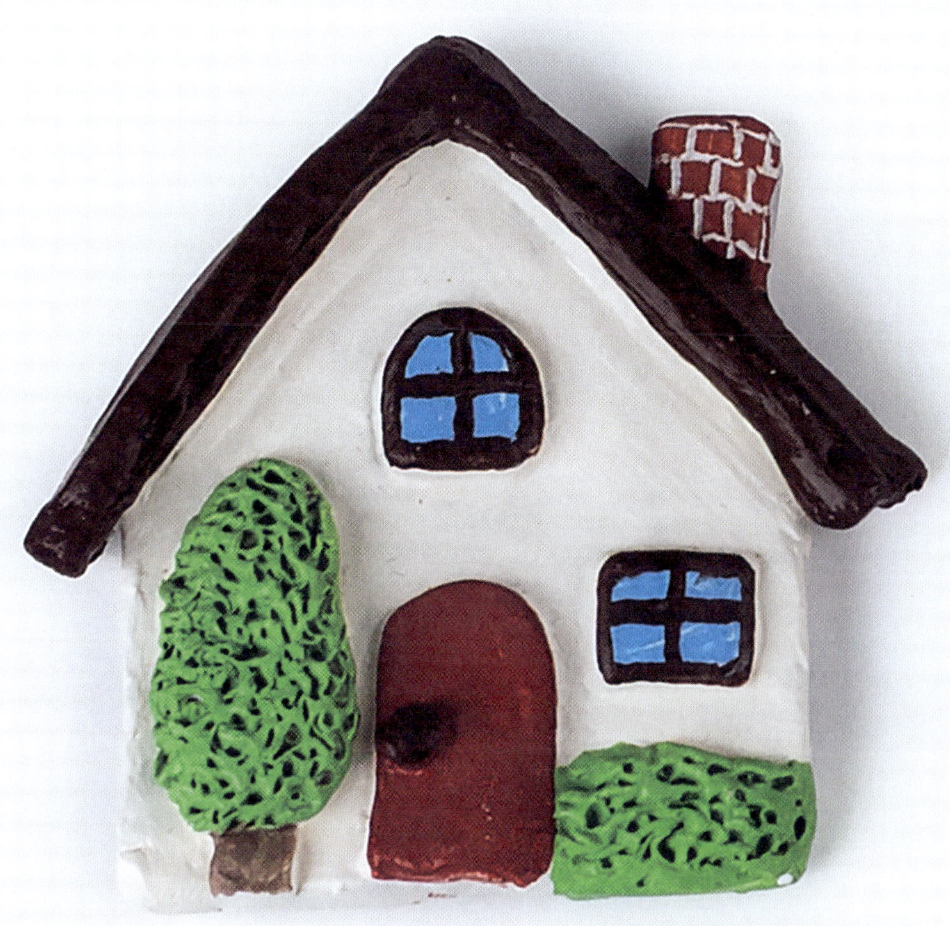

Index by Theme

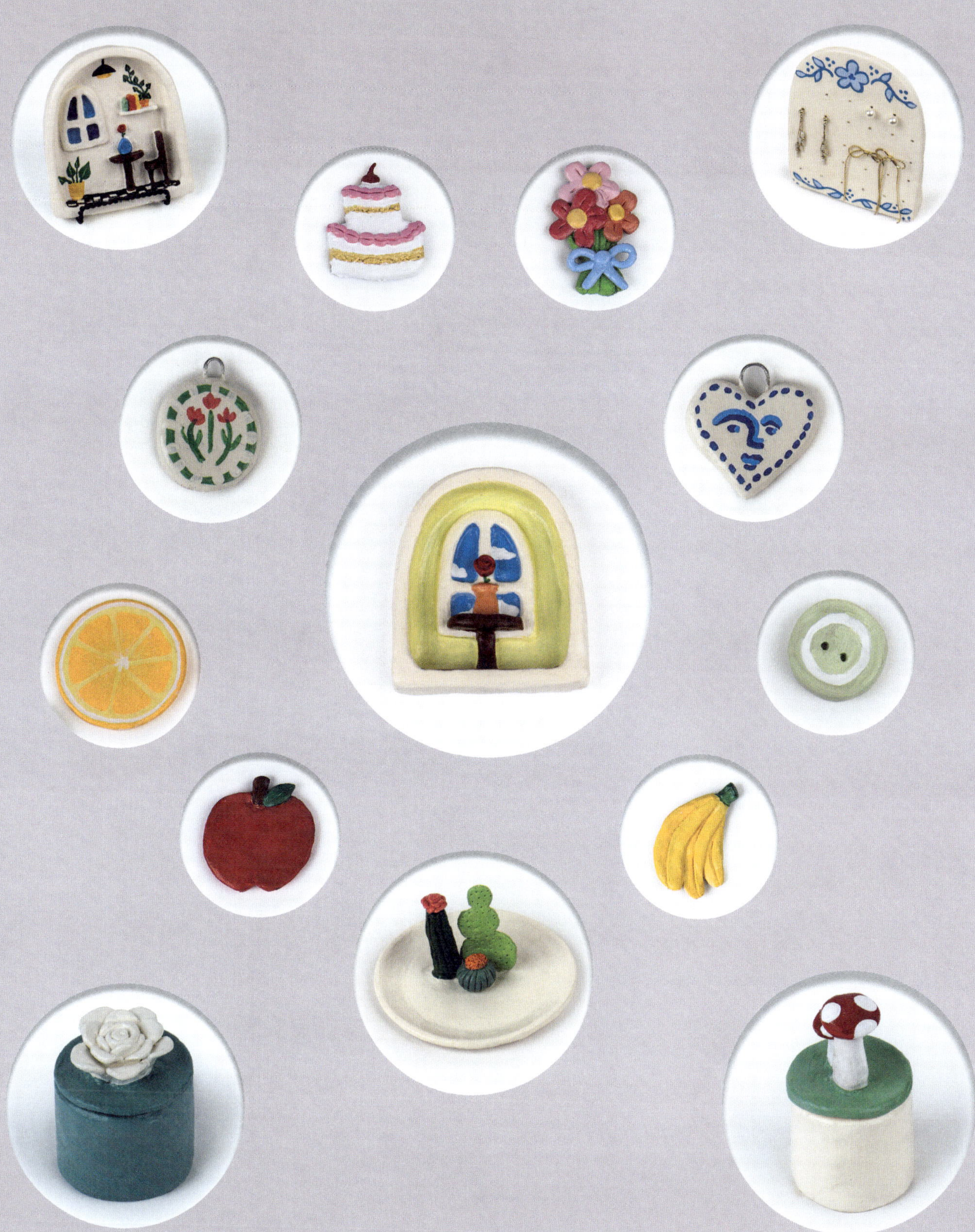

Index by Use

Bowls and Dishes

Crafts and Games

Decorations

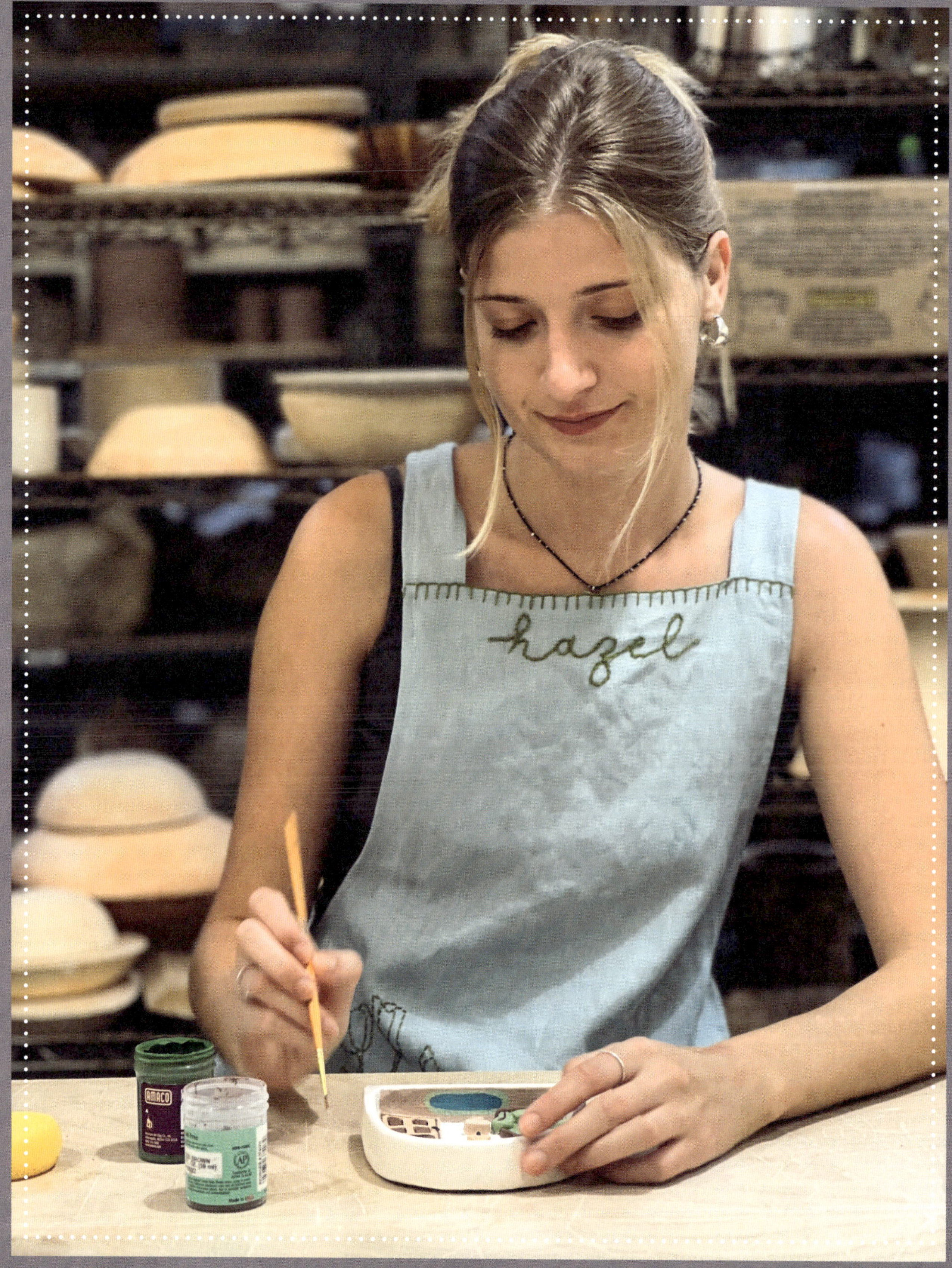
hazel
AMACO

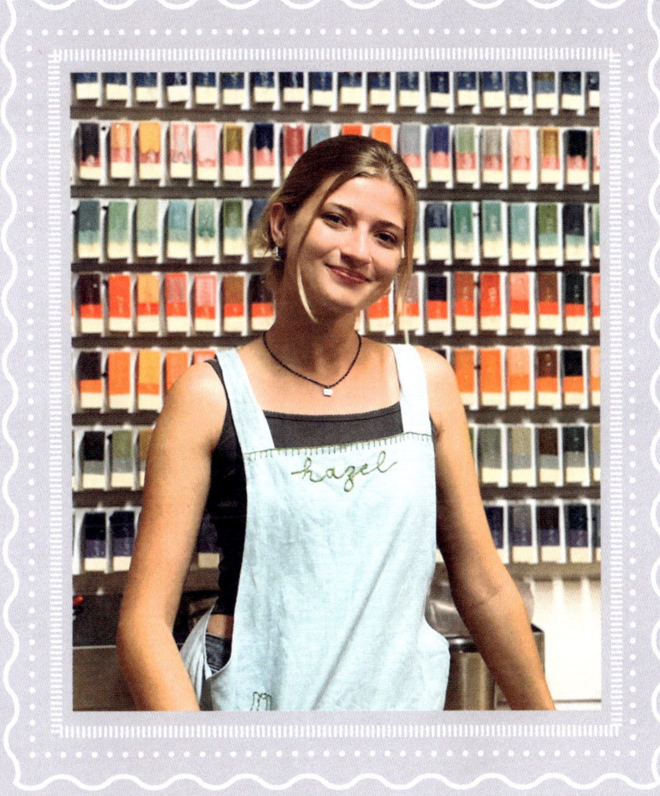

ABOUT THE AUTHOR

Hazel Brady is a ceramicist and artist based in Los Angeles, California. She specializes in framed cozy home sculpture scenes as well as trinket dishes for jewelry, which she sells through her Etsy business, Hazelbean Ceramics.

Find her online on Instagram
@hazelbean_ceramics
or on TikTok
@hazelbeanceramics1.

First published in 2026 by Rock Point,
an imprint of The Quarto Group,
135 West 36th Street, 13th Floor,
New York, NY 10018, USA
(212) 779-4972
www.Quarto.com

EEA Representation, WTS Tax d.o.o.,
Žanova ulica 3, 4000 Kranj, Slovenia.
www.wts-tax.si

Rock Point titles are also available at discount for retail, wholesale, promotional, and bulk purchase. For details, contact the Special Sales Manager by email at specialsales@quarto.com or by mail at The Quarto Group, Attn: Special Sales Manager, 100 Cummings Center Suite 265D, Beverly, MA 01915 USA.

10 9 8 7 6 5 4 3 2 1

ISBN: 978-1-57715-811-0

Digital edition published in 2026
eISBN: 978-1-57715-812-7

Library of Congress Cataloging-in-Publication Data

Names: Brady, Hazel author
Title: Air-dry masterpieces : over 50 creative projects for everyday spaces / Hazel Brady, owner of Hazelbean Ceramics.
Description: New York, NY : Rock Point, an imprint of The Quarto Group, 2026. | Includes index. | Summary: "Air-Dry Masterpieces features the latest crafting addiction, air-dry clay, while offering an accessible creative guide for anyone from beginner to seasoned crafter"-- Provided by publisher.
Identifiers: LCCN 2025050326 (print) | LCCN 2025050327 (ebook) | ISBN 9781577158110 paperback | ISBN 9781577158127 ebook
Subjects: LCSH: Pottery craft | Modeling
Classification: LCC TT920 .B693 2026 (print) | LCC TT920 (ebook)
LC record available at https://lccn.loc.gov/2025050326
LC ebook record available at https://lccn.loc.gov/2025050327

Group Publisher: Rage Kindelsperger
Creative Director: Laura Drew
Managing Editor: Cara Donaldson
Acquiring Editor: Sarah O'Connor
Editor: Flannery Wiest
Photography: Gina Cinardo
Back Cover Photo: Hazel Brady
Cover and Interior Design: Maeve Bargman

Printed in Huizhou City, Guangdong, China TT032026